Empowered by Design

Empowered by Design

*Decentralization and
the Gender Policy Trifecta*

MEG RINCKER

TEMPLE UNIVERSITY PRESS
Philadelphia • Rome • Tokyo

Meg Rincker is an Associate Professor of Political Science at Purdue University Northwest.

TEMPLE UNIVERSITY PRESS
Philadelphia, Pennsylvania 19122
www.temple.edu/tempress

Library of Congress Cataloging-in-Publication Data

Names: Rincker, Margaret Eileen, 1977– author.
Title: Empowered by design : decentralization and the gender policy trifecta /
  Meg Rincker.
Description: Philadelphia : Temple University Press, 2017. | Includes bibliographical
  references and index.
Identifiers: LCCN 2016042636| ISBN 9781439913963 (hardback) | ISBN 9781439913970
  (paper)
Subjects: LCSH: Gender mainstreaming. | Decentralization in government. | Women—
  Government policy. | BISAC: POLITICAL SCIENCE / Government / Comparative. |
  SOCIAL SCIENCE / Women's Studies.
Classification: LCC HQ1233 .R56 2017 | DDC 305.42—dc23 LC record available at https://
  lccn.loc.gov/2016042636

Printed in the United States of America

9 8 7 6 5 4 3 2 1

To my parents, Angela and James Bergin

Contents

Figures and Tables

FIGURES

TABLES

Acknowledgments

There are many different gifts, but always the same spirit.

—I CORINTHIANS 12

There are so many people to thank for their help in the preparation of this book. Each person mentioned here has unique talents, but all share the same spirit of generosity that must be recognized. First and foremost, I thank many teachers who taught me so much along the way. In sophomore chemistry, Mr. Gore told our class that many of us someday would write books, and the idea completely shocked me. I guess he was correct!

Many high school, college, and graduate school teachers and professors played important roles. Mrs. Bryant and Dr. Rye helped me through orchestra to perform and work past shyness, which was key in presenting this work and doing the fieldwork abroad necessary to collect original data. Mrs. Gore's passion for French language and culture was contagious and made me curious about life in other countries. Mr. Walk's geography class and exhortation to ask "why/where questions"—why are things located where they are—fed into this examination of women's interests in different regions of the same country and across countries.

At Illinois Wesleyan University (IWU), my undergraduate institution and also where I taught from 2006 to 2008, I received enormous encouragement for this project and the chance to present my book to campus in fall 2014. There are many inspirational and brilliant professors at IWU. I especially thank Kathleen Montgomery for mentoring me in the field of political science, for suggesting the United Kingdom case at a critical juncture in the book's development, and for her unending support of the book throughout the publication process. Many thanks go to Frank Boyd, William Munro, Tari Renner, Greg Shaw, and Jim Simeone for their insights and collegiality during my first two years of teaching. IWU was a fantastic place to work when I had my daughter Mary, and I thank all the professors, staff, and students for the insights they shared and kindness they showed me.

At Washington University in Saint Louis, I am very thankful for Lisa Baldez, who mentored me further in the subfield of gender and politics and who has supported my vision for the book throughout its gestation. I am indebted to Roger Peterson, who encouraged me in his seminal comparative politics seminar and convinced me that I belonged at Washington University when I was unsure myself. Olga Shvetsova helped me gain my sea legs in the field of Central and Eastern Europe. Lester Spence has encouraged me by always telling everyone I was his favorite grad student at Washington University. Randy Calvert and Gary Miller were fantastic teachers who expanded my knowledge of institutions, policy preferences, and bureaucracy. Their vocal support of me as a grad student, a mom of two, and a person who needed a place to pump milk was amazing. Bill Lowry's public policy course was the first place I encountered the Tiebout model, and I vividly remember discussions with Bill about testing whether in fact local politicians have better information than national ones—another key political science finding in this book. Itai Sened and Douglass North's Center for New Institutional Social Sciences (CNISS) supported my graduate certificate in institutional social sciences and, along with the Eisenhower Institute, supported my fieldwork in Poland. John Carey and Sunita Parikh were excellent dissertation chairs, and they prodded me through the publication of my first article, based on dissertation research on the unequal status of women in new Polish meso-level legislatures. Mona Lena Krook was a fabulous reader on my dissertation committee, and her influential work on gender and candidate selection appears throughout this book. Andy Mertha and Gautam Yadama were great supports and helped me flesh out some of the decentralization arguments in the opening chapters.

Fellow graduate students at Washington University were welcoming to and excellent mentors in the political science Ph.D. program, including Chris Hasselman, Scott McClurg, Michael Popovic, Jen Seeley, Nadeem Siddiqi, and Jen Nicoll Victor. Nadeem brought back a vase from Pakistan for me that sparked my tangible interest in the situation of women in Pakistan. Celeste Montoya not only was a great mentor to me while we were grad students in gender and politics and in teaching and research but also read many early drafts of this book and provided crucial encouragement that the country chapters were on track. Thanks also go to Juan Gabriel Gomez Albarello, Ingrid Dargin Anderson, Ann Collins, Tobias Gibson, Frances Henderson, Scott Hendrickson, Michael Lynch, Tony Madonna, Stephanie Milton,

Tasina Nitschke, Ryan Owens, Gina Yannitell Reinhardt, Jason Roberts, Erica Townsend-Bell, and Ryan Vander Wielen. I couldn't have had a better group to travel through grad school with. They made the graduate school process so worthwhile and endearing. René Lindstäedt, Chad Haddal, and my coauthor on a journal article about public opinion on decentralization, Martin Battle, remain some of my favorite Europeanists and karaoke performers to date. Martin in particular read many drafts of the manuscript. Jeff Staton provided critical advice on the publishing of this book. Mariana Medina, Diana O'Brien, Yael Shomer, and colleagues who came after me continue to shine and impress me with their work, and I greatly value their scholarship and friendship. Candice Ortbals has been a great coauthor on projects before this book and was instrumental in getting support for this project from the American Political Science Association Fund for the Study of Women and Politics, the Rita May Kelly Award, and the Carrie Chapman Catt Prize.

Beyond my teachers and professors, I have had the incredible fortune to work with friends abroad whose generosity of spirit indelibly shaped me and this work. I thank all of the women from organizations in Poland, Pakistan, and the United Kingdom who took the time to fill out my lengthy surveys and describe their workings with government officials at all levels of governance. They patiently explained to me past and current debates about gender in their societies and the up- and downsides of various reforms, validating and questioning this book's focus and forcing me to refine it. In Poland, I particularly thank Monika Ksieniewicz and Father Jarek Nowak and his family. Father Nowak's family warmly welcomed me and helped me on each and every research trip to Poland. I cannot thank them enough for their hospitality at their home and for helping me navigate the Polish language and train system! In addition, I thank Katarzyna Klukowska at *Gazeta Wyborcza*. Thanks also go to Conrad, Julian, Kinga, and Peter for research assistance while I was in Poland. Just as critical, consummate editor Brian Noggle edited many previous drafts of my manuscript. In the United Kingdom, I was very pleased to work with my former student Sneh Rajbhandari as we visited many women's organizations across the United Kingdom during winter 2011. Her ingenuity, hard work, and brilliance helped us win many of the interviews that feed into this book's analysis. In Pakistan, I give special thanks to Firdous Rani and Aqeel Ahmed for research assistance. I am grateful to Rukhsana Hassan for coordinating a wonderful conference at Fatima Jinnah Women's University in Rawalpindi in 2013. I learned so much about the entrepreneurial and hospitable spirit of the Pakistani people from the impressive scholars and students at this conference, and I received helpful and encouraging responses from the audience about my findings on women and decentralization politics in Pakistan. I thank Naheed Zia Khan, Omar

Malik, Adeela Rehman, and Muhammad Yusuf for their collegiality on my trip to Pakistan. Thanks also go to Mahwash Shazadi for taking me on my first trip to the market in Rawalpindi, Pakistan, and secretly buying me a hair clip to take home as a souvenir. My unending admiration goes to Tahira Abdullah for her generosity in helping me interpret current events, the movement toward decentralization, and democratization through the movement to restore judicial independence in Pakistan in 2007–2009. I also thank my Pakistani coauthors and friends, Ghazia Aslam and Mujtaba Isani. On many occasions they took time to help me develop case-specific knowledge about Pakistani politics and to challenge my biases in my interpretation of events. Sincere and heartfelt thanks go to Farida Jalalzai for her leadership and mentorship in reviewing my work on Pakistani politics and gender and politics and for her own influential work, which deeply influenced this book. In the subfield politics and gender, I especially thank Lee Ann Banaszak, Karen Beckwith, Amy Mazur, and Laurel Weldon for their support of my research and for reading and providing critical feedback on earlier versions of the manuscript. I thank my editor, Aaron Javsicas, as well as Gary Kramer, Nikki Miller, and Dave Wilson, at Temple University Press, and project manager Rebecca Logan at Newgen for their invaluable assistance and advice on the project. I am also grateful to the reviewers, whose comments improved the book considerably.

Closer to home, I thank colleagues and friends at the Department of Political Science, Economics, and World Languages and Cultures at Purdue University Northwest, especially April Clark, Ron Corthell, Rick Costello, Tom Keon, Paul McGrath, Ralph Mueller, Richard Rupp, Rachel Clapp Smith, Tanya Stabler, Jon Swarts, and Kathy Tobin. Frank Colucci provided helpful insights on the publication process on many occasions. Thanks go to Susan Schulze for doing the legwork on acquiring copyright permissions for images used in this book. I thank Karen Bishop-Morris, Joy Colwell, Lori Feldman, Lisa Goodnight, and Becky Stankowski for their mentorship. Undergraduate students provided excellent research assistance and copyedited previous versions of the manuscript, including Daniel Delgado, Marisa Henderson, Nela Taskovska, Michael Thomas, and Renato Vidigal. In and around Frankfort, Illinois, I am so lucky to have my Nevada Street neighbors and to be part of the grand Gould, Bergin, and Rincker clans. I thank my dear family for many meals and help with my kids! Scout Gibson, Peggy Kaufman, Theresa Pohlmann, Maria Seidelmann, and Sandi and Hank Tumborello provided invaluable child care to my kids, who were growing throughout this book process.

What gave me endurance for this project was undoubtedly the prayers of my family, the friendship of Jackie Hood, Zumba with Katie Brown and my friends at Gilda's Club at Advocate Christ Medical Center, going on training runs and eating brunch at the teahouse with Katie Schroeder, and countless chats with my college roommate Lisa Leali. Special thanks go to Irfan Nooruddin, who took more time than anyone else thinking about, reading through, and strategizing this book with me. He is a true mentor.

At home, I thank my grandmother lovingly known as Bomma; grandma Treva Watson; my mom and dad, Angela and James Bergin; my mother- and father-in-law, Joanne and Lee Rincker; and Rebecca and Tom Davidsmeier. In addition to many aunts, uncles, and cousins, including Sheila Bergin, who gave critical feedback on the book cover design, I thank my outstanding family in religion: Sister Charlotte Gould, Sister Janet Welsh, Sister Lynn Welsh, and Father Michael Gould. I also thank my brothers and sisters: Tim (and Kate), David (and Anne), Mary (and Michael), Patrick, Anne (and Steve), Kate, Molly (and Peter), and Michael. They were my first and best teachers. Nieces and nephews are a very great joy in my life and the source of each year's awesome calendar photos. My Bergin nieces and nephews include Paddy G., Brendan, Leah, Connor, Hannah, Christian, Paddy B., Celia, William, and Johnny. On the Rincker side, my nieces and nephews include Hannah, Myra, Sarah, Rachel, Joseph, Peter, Ezekiel, and Nineveh. I also send love to my god-daughter, Ava. In my immediate family, I thank Dominic, Theresa, and Mary for their patience with me and for keeping me distracted with their many gifts, including trumpet playing, hockey, figure skating, cross-country, and musicals. It is such a blessing to be their mom, and I love them dearly. The most thanks and love go to Brian, who supported my academic career and family goals—from the first semester I took women and politics courses at Illinois Wesleyan up through his editing of maps for me for this book the week I submitted the manuscript.

Part I

1

Three Guiding Questions about Decentralization and Women's Empowerment

Since the 1980s, politicians, scholars, and policy makers from the United Nations, the World Bank, the European Union, and the Asian Development Bank have heralded the benefits of decentralization. *Decentralization* is "a process of state reform composed by a set of public policies that transfer responsibilities, resources, or authority from higher to lower levels of government in the context of a specific type of state" (Falleti 2005, 328). Decentralization advocates argue that when decisions are made at a subnational level, all citizens will believe they can make a difference and will participate, thus injecting new blood into the political process (Blair 2000; Brady, Schlozman, and Verba 1999; Putnam 1993). By "subnational," I mean all levels of government below the national level. Most countries in the world can be considered to have three main levels of government: national, meso, and local.[1] Consequently, international organizations argue that decentralization of politics brings about more efficient, responsive public

---

1. For example, in the United States, national government offices are primarily located in Washington, D.C.; meso-level offices in the fifty state capitals; and local offices in cities, towns, and counties. Meso units go by different names in different countries: in the United States, meso units are states; in China, they are provinces; and in Switzerland, they are cantons. Because this book evaluates decentralization trends across many countries, I employ the term "meso" as most generalizable for governmental units situated one level below the national level of government (see Vengroff, Nyiri, and Fugeiro 2003). I use the term "local" to refer to units of government that are at neither the national nor the meso level, such as counties, municipalities, townships, villages, and hamlets (Darcy, Welch, and Clark 1994). When the causal logic of my argument applies to both meso and local levels of government, I use the umbrella term "subnational."

policies (Eaton and Schroeder 2010; Montinola, Qian, and Weingast 1995; Oates 1972; Rondinelli, Nellis, and Cheema 1983; Tiebout 1956; Treisman 2007) made by a more diverse set of local citizens than rarified policies made by elite politicians in a nation's capital (World Bank 2004).

Public officials have largely responded to these appeals to decentralize governance, but they have done so without questioning whether decentralization benefits women and men equally. My central aim in this book is to explain *under what conditions decentralization will lead to women's empowerment in countries around the globe.* As of 2010, at least 80 percent of countries had a meso tier of government between the national government and local municipalities.[2] Moreover, these meso-level governments accounted for 65 percent of government spending (Falleti 2005).

In her seminal discussion of decentralization, Tulia Falleti (2005, 2010) describes three relevant sectors of decentralization: political, administrative, and fiscal. Briefly, these sectors correspond to the power to choose meso-level or local officials, the power to spend at the meso or local level, and the power to tax at the meso or local level. More specifically, *political decentralization* refers to creating, moving, or reinvigorating subnational political spaces. Falleti states, "Examples of this type of reform are the popular election of mayors and governors who in previous constitutional periods were appointed, the creation of sub-national legislative assemblies, or constitutional reforms that strengthen the political autonomy of sub-national governments" (2005, 329). *Administrative decentralization* refers to the "administration and delivery of social services such as education, health, social welfare, or housing to subnational governments" (329). Falleti stresses that administrative decentralization might or might not entail authority over these policies and that they can be funded (by the national government) or unfunded (as the responsibility of the subnational unit, with its own preexisting revenues). *Fiscal decentralization* refers to measures to "increase the revenues or fiscal autonomy of subnational governments . . . such as an increase of transfers from the central government, the creation of new sub-national taxes, or the delegation of tax authority that was previously national" (329).

It is important to note that decentralization reforms arise in context-specific ways. In a given country, decentralization reforms might apply to some policy areas and not others. Countries can enact weak decentralization in a set of parliamentary laws that politicians can easily change after an election, or countries can enshrine rigid decentralization as a constitutional reform that protects the status of subnational units. Decentralization

---

2. Eighty percent is a conservative estimate. For example, Daniel Treisman (2002) collected data on tiers of government in 154 countries and found that all but Singapore had more than one tier of government.

as a reform of the 1980s onward occurs as an overlying reform, potentially affected by variables that preceded it. For example, countries adopt decentralization at different levels of development (high, middle, or lesser), and countries possess a preexisting constitutional structure (unitary, federal, or hybrid) and political party structures that themselves are centralized or decentralized in how they choose candidates (Hinojosa 2012). However, any package of decentralization reforms affects one or more of the political, administrative, or fiscal sectors.

The main argument I make in this book is that all three sectors of decentralization must be "engendered," or made inclusive of women, to achieve women's empowerment and gender equality. Engendering occurs only when what I term the *gender policy trifecta* is present. The gender policy trifecta consists of three nodes, all of which I argue are necessary and sufficient for women's empowerment in decentralized states around the globe (see Figure 1.1). I construct the gender policy trifecta in terms general enough to be useful in examining women's empowerment at any level of governance, but since the focus in this book is on decentralized politics, I examine countries in terms of whether this trifecta applies at the subnational level of governance.

The first node of the gender policy trifecta refers to legislative gender quotas, which enforce that legislative seats are open to women at the subnational level to engender political decentralization. The second node is gender mainstreaming, or consideration of policy implications on women and men, enforced by subnational women's policy agencies, to engender administrative decentralization. The third node is gender-responsive budgeting at the

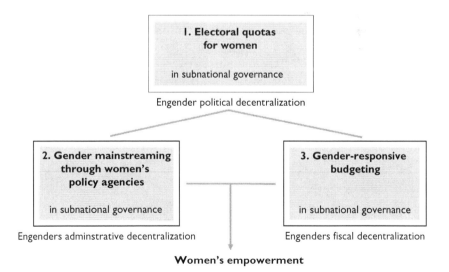

Figure 1.1 The gender policy trifecta in decentralization

subnational level, enforced to include women's organizations in civil society and engender fiscal decentralization. The United Nations defines gender-responsive budgeting as "government planning, programming and budgeting that contributes to the advancement of gender equality and the fulfillment of women's rights. It entails identifying and reflecting needed interventions to address gender gaps in government policies, plans and budgets" (United Nations Development Fund for Women, n.d.).

Decentralization entails the distribution of a set of complex political institutions that may affect men and women differently in terms of political power and decision making. While mainstream research on decentralization has not examined its gendered implications, international organizations have assumed it leads to only positive outcomes for women. Karen Beckwith (2005) notes gender can operate as both a category[3] and a process.[4] For example, the category of gender may help us explain why female meso-level legislators are more likely than male meso-level legislators to support government spending on shelters for battered women. The process of gender refers to the possible differential effects of the apparently gender-neutral policy of decentralization on women and men. If power is pushed from a diverse national government to local tribes to make policy more responsive to local needs, and through closer analysis we find that female politicians make up 20 percent of the national government but only 2 percent of tribal authorities, then the apparently gender-neutral institution of decentralization is not gender neutral at all. This second step of analyzing the process of gender has been lacking in the literature on decentralization. For example, Daniel Treisman's (2007) *The Architecture of Government* uses formal modeling and examples to test the outcomes of decentralization. He lists seven outcomes, ranging from efficiency to policy innovation. His elegant and nuanced analysis shows support mainly for the veto player hypothesis (the expectation that decentralization creates more policy players, leading to fewer policy changes) and mixed or no support for other outcomes, but his analysis does not address gendered implications of decentralization.

---

3. "By gender as category, I mean the multidimensional mapping of socially constructed, fluid, politically relevant identities, values, conventions, and practices conceived of as masculine and/or feminine, with the recognition that masculinity and femininity correspond only fleetingly and roughly to 'male' and 'female.' Using gender as a category permits us to delineate specific contexts in which feminine and masculine behaviors, actions, attitudes, and preferences, for example, result in particular outcomes, such as military intervention, social movement success, and electoral choice, among others" (Beckwith 2000, 131).

4. "By 'process,' I mean behaviors, conventions, practices, and dynamics engaged in by individuals, organizations, movements, institutions, and nations. . . . [G]ender as process is manifested as the differential effects of apparently gender-neutral structures and policies upon women and men, and upon masculine and/or feminine actors" (Beckwith 2000, 132).

In contrast, international organizations have largely assumed that decentralization leads to women's empowerment for three main reasons. First, some evidence suggests that subnational political offices are less competitive and more open to female candidates than sought-after, media-saturated national positions (Darcy, Welch, and Clark 1994; Lovenduski 1986; Randall 1987; Thomas and Wilcox 2005; Vengroff, Nyiri, and Fugiero 2003). Second, subnational governments tend to focus more heavily on policy areas like education, health, and social welfare—issues about which many women care deeply and therefore in which they participate (Darcy, Welch, and Clark 1994). Third, in terms of time, as in scheduling and daily commute, meso-level politics could provide a much more feasible sphere of participation for women by allowing more room for family and home responsibilities (Chaney, Mackay, and McAllister 2007; Vengroff, Nyiri, and Fugiero 2003). While research shows that more women are in meso-level elected offices in liberal democracies (see Schedler 1998; Vengroff, Nyiri, and Fugiero 2003), international organizations do not test these assumptions in the electoral democracies where they bankroll decentralization.[5] International organizations report positive findings in the literature studying liberal democracies and report some negative outcomes for women in countries with decentralization reforms, but they do not follow up by proposing and testing specific policy reforms to improve future rounds of decentralization for women. Decentralization could lead to more opportunities for women—a true democratization of politics such that elected officials respond to women and men and feel pressured to represent all constituents. Conversely, decentralization could push political power into the hands of local traditional elites who are predominantly male or who deprioritize women's political involvement, leading to stagnant or retrograde policy outcomes (Beall 2005). In contrast to the expectation of international organizations, decentralization could be a façade, giving the mere appearance of democratization (Rodriguez 1997). Decentralization could push political

---

5. Andreas Schedler creates a typology ranging from authoritarian regime to electoral democracy to liberal democracy to advanced democracy. An authoritarian regime lacks competitive elections and civil liberties. An electoral democracy follows procedures for competitive elections but "fail[s] to uphold the political and civil freedoms essential for liberal democracy" (Schedler 1998, 93). A liberal democracy has both competitive elections and civil freedoms, and advanced democracies "possess some positive traits over and above the minimal defining criteria of liberal democracy, and therefore rank higher in terms of democratic quality than many new democracies" (93). Because international organizations fund decentralization in so many electoral democracies, it is critical to test decentralization's impact on women's empowerment among countries that include electoral democracies and liberal democracies. The countries I selected to study include an advanced democracy (the United Kingdom), a liberal democracy (Poland), and an electoral democracy (Pakistan). To those who argue that democracy precedes women's rights, I say that the direction of that relationship is the reverse; as women are empowered, democracy in that country is strengthened.

decision making to meso units, where women are not ready to run for office or are excluded from political life (Keefer, Narayan, and Vishwanath 2006) or where women's organizations are too few or fragmented to make an impact (Haussman 2005; Haussman, Sawer, and Vickers 2010; Siahaan 2004).

Measuring Women's Empowerment and the Three Guiding Questions

How can we find the conditions under which decentralization leads to women's empowerment? The United Nations defines women's empowerment as "women's sense of self-worth; their right to have and to determine choices; their right to have access to opportunities and resources; their right to have the power to control their own lives, both within and outside the home; and their ability to influence the direction of social change to create a more just social and economic order, nationally and internationally" (United Nations 2010). Women's empowerment consists of not just individual agency, decision-making power, and economic access but also the ability to influence social and political institutions (United Nations 2010). The United Nations' definition of women's empowerment suggests that women's voices in "social and political institutions" matter and should therefore be heard at all levels of governance. Women's empowerment thus means women articulating their priorities in public life and not needing males to do it instead of them or on their behalf. Men are key allies in bringing about women's empowerment, but women's empowerment cannot happen through men alone. So women themselves must play an active role in decentralized governance. But how will we know women's empowerment when we see it? The next section presents three guiding questions that frame the book's inquiry in ways that are meaningful to policy makers, scholars, activists, and those interested in women's rights around the world.

Women, Feminist Policy, and Representation

In any country, women are a diverse group of individuals, and "women's interests" are plural and contested rather than unified and essentialized (Verloo 2007). Women are diverse by virtue of their social class, age, race or ethnicity, religion, language, and sexual orientation. Other significant categories and identities intersect within an individual woman, shaping her views and policy preferences (Celis 2009; Celis et al. 2008; Hancock 2004; hooks 2000). It is also important to emphasize that either women or men may advocate feminist policies. According to Amy Mazur (2002, 30–31), legislation qualifies as feminist policy if it meets at least three of five components:

- making women's status equal to men's
- reducing or eliminating gender hierarchies or patriarchies
- focusing on both public and private spheres or an approach that avoids distinctions between the two
- attending to both men and women
- acknowledging ideas associated with a recognized feminist group, movement, or actor in context

While women might share core policy interests, such as eliminating violence against women, most scholars today recognize the diversity of women's policy preferences and employ research designs that let women identify their top political priorities. For example, Lisa Baldez (2011, 2014) argues that we can begin to measure women's interests by looking at the statements women's organizations make to international entities like the United Nations Commission on the Status of Women, which requires 187 state parties to report annually on progress implementing the Convention on the Elimination of All Forms of Discrimination against Women (CEDAW). The unprecedented CEDAW treaty codifies core issues that women around the world share. *Empowered by Design* looks at what women want both within and across countries. Therefore, the first guiding question is *do women have diverse policy priorities that vary as much within one country as they do across different countries?*

Rural women from different countries might have very similar policy priorities, but urban and rural women residing in the same country might disagree markedly on public policy priorities. The original data I collected for this book allow me to address this guiding question about political aggregation (for further discussion of political aggregation, see Carey 2000). Depending on the unit of geographic analysis, different policy priorities emerge. Previous studies examined whether decentralization increases representation for particular women's groups of interest, such as Dalit women, LGBT women, and First Nations women (see, for example, Devika and Thampi 2012; Haussman, Sawer, and Vickers 2010), and this is critical work that is being done in the field from an intersectional point of view. In my study, however, I systematically surveyed a wide range of leaders of women's organizations in three countries: Poland, Pakistan, and United Kingdom. I asked these leaders to rank their top four policy priorities and can therefore test whether women's priorities vary as much across countries as they do within countries. When women's policy priorities vary considerably within a country, I argue that this constitutes a new and important justification for decentralization: countries should decentralize because of the potential of government to more closely match the policy priorities of women, who have historically been marginalized from politics.

Women's Descriptive and Substantive Representation

Is women's political representation any different from men's political representation? How do we understand women's representation in the broader context of politics? Hannah Pitkin's (1967) work identifies four dimensions of representation, which act individually and in combination with one another. The first is *formal* representation, which involves the rules for elections and selection of representatives. The second is *symbolic* representation, or the social and political consequences of who represents us. The third is *descriptive* representation, or the physical, or identity, attributes we use to describe our representatives, including gender, race, and age. The fourth is *substantive* representation, which refers to the policies those representatives support and advance while in office. In this book, I focus on the third and fourth of Pitkin's dimensions of representation. Pitkin and many scholars since have identified the significance and interrelated nature of descriptive and symbolic dimensions of representation. A lot of research examines whether women's higher descriptive representation (percentage of women in office) leads to better women's substantive representation (policies likely to address issues of particular concern to female constituents) (see, for example, Mazur 2002; Phillips 1998; Schwindt-Bayer and Mishler 2005). While men can substantively represent the interests of female constituents, having women in elected office has intrinsic value, which is why descriptive and substantive representation are kept conceptually distinct.

Looking at data from 2015, men held 78 percent of seats in national-level parliaments and assemblies worldwide, women only 22 percent. One take on this data is that the gender of the parliamentarians (or women's descriptive representation) is not that consequential, particularly in comparison to other categories, like party affiliation. For example, in David Mayhew's (1975) *Congress: The Electoral Connection*, all members, regardless of gender, race, religion, or sexual orientation, engage in the same essential behaviors: position taking, credit claiming, and advertising. Similarly, Anthony Down's (1957) model of democracy suggests that each candidate running for Congress, regardless of the person's gender, tends to favor the views of the median voter in his or her district.

However, in the *Politics of Presence*, Anne Phillips (1998) challenges previous literature because it fails to take into account how gender affects the type or quality of political representation. Phillips develops four reasons to explain why gender is a category that matters in terms of a legislative body. First, increasing the number of women in elected office provides role models for other women in society (Barnes and Burchard 2013). Second, seats should be open to all groups in society, including women, who are a predominant group by numbers, and increasing the number of women establishes justice between the sexes because the offices themselves come with status and perks that should be distributed across key groups in society.[6] This second reason highlights for Phillips and other scholars that the descriptive representation of women, or the numbers of women in office, is a valuable end unto itself.[7] Third, the presence of women affects the type of legislation introduced and ultimately what is passed, linking the descriptive with the substantive representation of women in some cases. For example, Susan Thomas (1994) found that women consistently prioritized issues related to child care, women's health, and women in the workplace more than men did. Likewise, other studies have shown that women are more likely to support bills that reflect an ethic of care. For example, Lyn Kathlene (1995) found that female legislators supported a more rehabilitative criminal code. Fourth, the gender composition of the legislative body affects the style of deliberation and can improve overall political life. In her in-depth studies of the Colorado legislature, Kathlene (1994) found statistically significant differences in the behavior of female and male legislators. For example, female legislators consulted a greater range of experts in writing and assessing bills, had a more inclusive chairing style, and interrupted speakers less frequently. In addition, their bills were more heavily scrutinized than those of their male counterparts.

There are four schools of thought on how decentralization affects women's descriptive and substantive representation. First, decentralization may lead to greater women's descriptive representation and then to enhanced women's substantive representation. For example, Raghabendra Chattopadhyay and Esther Duflo (2004) suggest that decentralization can lead to greater women's descriptive representation, or more women in government, resulting in women's substantive representation and empowerment.

Second, decentralization could lead to greater women's empowerment, without increasing women's descriptive representation. Because decentralization creates new subnational units of government, subnational politicians have better information about what women and men want and can match their preferences more directly (Hayek 1945). If subnational politicians have the resources and capacity to implement the will of their provincial citizens, they can do so more effectively than national politicians. National politicians have to juggle national and international issues. National-level

---

6. In later writing, Phillips (2002) concludes that the inclusive aspect of the descriptive representation of women is quite important. Pitkin (1967) places emphasis on substantive representation, but Phillips believes that descriptive representation is important in terms of women having seats at the table.

7. An interest in and focus on the numbers of women in office should not be interpreted to be equivalent to the notion that any female political candidate is preferable to any male political candidate.

politicians at times have to change priorities on the basis of conditions elsewhere in the country and in the world.

A third possibility is that decentralization could bring about no net change in the substantive representation of women. In short, the subnational level could replicate politics at other levels, where women are excluded to a greater degree than men. Fourth, decentralization might strengthen patriarchal or nondemocratic actors who capture local-level politics, which could ultimately result in new restrictions on women's rights and opportunities. In this scenario, women's substantive representation does not merely stay at the same level but actually declines, as we see in Pakistan (Keefer, Narayan, and Vishwanath 2006). To summarize, these four schools of thought show that studies of decentralization and women's empowerment should include analysis of both the number of women in subnational office and the sorts of policies being passed at the subnational level.[8] Why is there a shortage of women in political office in so many countries?

Women and Political Recruitment

Pippa Norris and Joni Lovenduski's (1995) generalized model of political recruitment helps us understand how, across many societies, women opt out of running for political office (Matland and Montgomery 2003, 21). In this model, Norris and Lovenduski conceive of political recruitment as a funnel-like process in which individuals progress from the broadest possible situation of being in the general population of a given country to technically being an *eligible*, or able to run for office, to publicly voicing an interest in politics as a political *aspirant* to becoming a formal *candidate* on a ballot and finally to being selected by voters as an *elected official*. While in most countries women and men are all eligibles, participation drops off thereafter. At the aspirant stage, girls and women in some places might be already less likely than boys and men to express political interest or ambition, unless they are socialized by their families to talk about or demonstrate an interest in politics. Even then, a visible female candidate in some countries, like the United States, is necessary to inspire parents to discuss politics with their girls. What follows then is the requirement that young girls show signs of future political

---

8. I conducted analyses on the frequencies with which the meso units of my study show positive outcomes for women's empowerment. Across the subnational units, the outcomes for women's empowerment were as follows: 44 percent had increased descriptive and substantive representation, 9 percent had no change in descriptive but had increased substantive representation, 30 percent had no change in either descriptive or substantive representation, and 17 percent had decreased women's substantive representation.

ambition and that this gets reinforced in family discussions (Campbell and Wolbrecht 2006). Women's disproportionate responsibilities in the private sphere and frequent experience with employment discrimination result in women being less confident that they possess the necessary qualifications to be an aspirant (Conway, Steuernagel, and Ahern 2005; Sanbonmatsu 2006). Whereas having a family boosts men's confidence to run for office, having a family, and particularly school-age children, decreases women's political aspirations. At the candidate stage, party leaders act as the major gatekeepers whom aspirants must convince to win the party nomination. In addition, at this stage, majoritarian election rules tend to favor male candidates. Proportional election rules encourage party leaders to favor balancing tickets with women and other minority candidates (Matland and Montgomery 2003; Rule and Zimmerman 1992).

At the election stage of the generalized model of political recruitment, voters might winnow out female candidates on the basis of their gender, particularly in countries that report low levels of support for the idea that women are just as suitable for office as men (Inglehart and Norris 2003). Cross-national variation is significant in mean country responses to the World Values Survey item (1995 Wave 3) "Men do not make better political leaders than women." Countries range from a mean value of 1.5 in Jordan to roughly 3.2 in the United States and 3.5 in Germany (Norris and Inglehart 2005, 254). These findings suggest that in countries like Armenia, Egypt, Georgia, and Jordan activists should focus on changing the sexist views of male and female voters to get more women into elected office. In contrast, in other countries, voters are relatively unsexist about actual vote choice (even if campaigning is fraught with sexist double standards for female candidates), but it is a huge challenge getting women to run. When women run for congressional seats in the United States, voters are just as likely to support female as male candidates (Darcy, Welch, and Clark 1994; Fox and Lawless 2004; Lawless and Fox 2010). In countries like the United States, the most effective strategies for increasing women's representation might be programs offering political training to female eligibles, public discussions about how male and female candidates are treated by the media, and systematic organizing to make political meeting times and work environments more family friendly. Another strategy that can increase women's descriptive representation is the passage of electoral gender quotas.

Electoral Gender Quotas at the National and Subnational Levels

According to the Global Database of Quotas for Women, gender quotas are "mandatory or targeted percentages of women candidates for public elections" (Global Database of Quotas for Women, n.d.).[9] Gender quotas are an institutional tool that can help women gain descriptive representation in parliaments and legislatures, and they potentially enable women's substantive representation (Jones 1996; Krook 2009; Weldon 2002a, 1154). On average, gender quota laws result in a 10 percent increase in the number of women in office (Htun and Jones 2002). Results of gender quotas have been mixed. While they increase the number of women in office, sometimes the electorate and other legislators discount women elected under a quota. Beliefs emerge that quota women are less qualified despite having qualifications comparable to their male counterparts, as shown by studies providing data on such countries as Argentina, France, Morocco, and Uganda (Franceschet, Krook, and Piscopo 2012). Gender quotas can lead to women's substantive representation when there is underlying cultural support for quotas but not when they are hotly contested or party leaders greatly constrain member initiative (Franceschet, Krook, and Piscopo 2012).

Gender quotas can be devised along four key dimensions (source, penalties, stage of game, and winnability), all of which ultimately influence how many women get elected and how party leaders and voters balance an official's gender with other salient dimensions of representation. The source of gender quotas can be voluntary, pursued by individual parties at their own discretion, or they can be statutory—required by law or constitution and applying to all political parties in a system (Krook 2009). Quota provisions can have significant penalties for parties if they fail to field enough candidates of a given gender. If penalties are low, parties might flout quotas and just pay the associated penalties for noncompliance (see Murray 2004). Quotas can target the game at the candidate stage or the elected official stage. Gender candidate quotas are set by declaring a minimum percentage of candidates of one gender that must be nominated by a political party (in proportional systems) or by twinning (in majoritarian systems, in which parties select one man and one woman to stand for each constituency seat), but quotas might not control the actual percentage of women elected. In contrast, a reservation system sets aside a certain number of seats that elected officials of one gender will hold. The benefit of candidate quotas is that they give voters discretion over final outcomes and the ability to vote, for example, for a male candidate over a female candidate if factors other than gender are more salient to the

---

9. The Global Database of Quotas for Women goes on to state, "An electoral quota for women may be constitutional, legislative or be in the form of a political party quota. It may apply to the number of women candidates proposed by a party for election, or may take the form of reserved seats in the legislature. Quotas and other affirmative action strategies may apply to minorities based on regional, ethnic, linguistic or religious cleavages. However, this Database focuses on gender quotas, that is quotas that apply to women for elective office."

voter. The benefit of reserved seats is that they remove the possibility of voters discounting nominated women.

Finally, some provisions on winnability have been devised to make sure parties do not meet quota requirements through numerical targets, which merely shuffle women to unwinnable positions without substantially changing their access to politics. In proportional electoral systems, these provisions are sometimes called zipping or zebras, because they alternate by gender the order of party lists to make sure that women are in winnable positions. In majoritarian elections, quotas may have district targeting to make sure the party is not just nominating women but running them in winnable districts. But some factors can limit the ability of quotas to increase the percentage of women in elected office. As Baldez (2007) and Magda Hinojosa (2012) show, exclusive centralized nominations are most beneficial to women, inclusive decentralized are least beneficial, and exclusive decentralized or inclusive centralized have middling effects on women's candidacies. Centralized methods benefit women over decentralized methods of candidate selection because, at a centralized level, when party leaders specifically ask women to run they overcome the confidence gap that many women have, and centralized party nominations also circumvent local power monopolies to which women have limited access (Hinojosa 2012, 51).

At the national level, research shows that in some cases candidate gender quotas also enhance substantive representation. Newly elected women under quota systems can provide substantive representation, pursing policies related to improving women's status in the public arena (Krook 2009; Mazur 2002) and to women's issues, defined as those traditionally faced by women in the private sphere (such as reproduction, child care, gender violence, and work-life balance). Still, studies are mixed on whether quotas result in a sea change for women's status and influence in political institutions (Franceschet, Krook, and Piscopo 2012; Krook and O'Brien 2010). Gender quotas can be necessary, but not sufficient, to engender legislatures.

Cross-national research shows that in developed countries the percentage of women in meso-level legislative assemblies is higher than in national parliaments (Vengroff, Nyiri, and Fugiero 2003). However, in developing countries, the percentage of women in meso-level assemblies is lower than in national office. In other work, I argue that in developing countries with fewer job opportunities meso-level legislatures are high-status places to work and can be extremely competitive and masculinized environments (Rincker 2009; Rincker, Aslam, and Isani 2016). So we already have evidence that decentralization does not automatically lead to a boost for women in meso-level legislatures. Subnational gender quotas may be necessary to ensure the descriptive representation of women in decentralizing countries. Therefore, a second guiding question is *is women's descriptive representation higher in meso-level assemblies that have gender quotas than in those that do not?*

Research on Gender and Political Institutions

Research on gender and politics is growing in important and innovative ways that help us understand the conditions under which decentralization empowers women. This section reviews insights and findings from key subareas in the study of gender and politics, including the comparative politics of gender and institutions, cross-institutional work on gender, and information from the Research Network on Gender Politics and the State about state reconfiguration. I discuss each in turn, deriving the third and final guiding question. A comparative politics of gender and institutions helps us "gain a deeper understanding of the way that gender shapes political institutions and also, through interaction with social actors, including feminists, the way gender norms can be disrupted to open new spaces for these actors" (Chappell 2006, 223).[10] Research on the comparative politics of gender strongly argues for cross-systemic analysis, moving beyond research conducted only in Western Europe and among advanced industrial democracies (Beckwith 2006, 2010; Krook and Mackay 2010; Tripp 2006; Waylen 2010; Weldon 2006). A key insight from the comparative politics of gender is the need for consulting literature from a wide range of countries, including what Freedom House (2014) categorizes as free and partly free countries, to test and consolidate the theory on how decentralization and state reconfiguration affect women, and Chapter 2 is this literature review.

Research on gender and politics makes increasingly clear that women and feminists organize not just in legislatures but also in bureaucracies and civil society groups to achieve representation. To achieve feminist policies, the triangle model posits, feminists must participate in three avenues, or nodes: legislatures, bureaucracies, and civil society and social movements (McBride and Mazur 1995; Outshoorn and Kantola 2007). Studies of "strategic constellations," "women's advocacy coalitions," "velvet triangles," and the "triangle of women's empowerment" all agree that measuring women's representation and feminist policy in the legislative arena alone is insufficient (Holli 2008; Lycklama à Nijeholt, Vargas, and Wieringa 1998; McBride and Mazur 2010). For example, in their celebrated work on women in Canadian multilevel governance, Linda Trimble, Jane Arscott, and Manon Tremblay note that

---

10. For example, Jill Vickers's (2013) innovative work describes how states make gender and how gender makes states, noting that states enact reforms that reinforce gender norms but also that changing gender norms in society has the ability to affect and change the way the state operates.

future comparative work should "consider links among extra-parliamentary feminist interests, elected politicians, and bureaucratic units charged with gender quality responsibilities" (2013, xix).

Research projects, including the Research Network on Gender Politics and the State, have greatly contributed to our awareness that women's policy agencies (WPAs), or bureaucracies, charged with policies affecting women are critical sites for women's political representation. WPA leaders from the bureaucratic side of the triangle play critical roles and can "represent women by transforming the policy process to include women's interests" (Weldon 2002b, 158). Amy Mazur argues that "[WPAs] have the potential to be major conduits for women's descriptive and substantive representation in three ways" (2005, 3). They bring women's interests into public policy debates, help women's activists influence policy debates, and ensure that women fill the ranks of the bureaucracy as more women are appointed to posts in WPA offices. Hester Eisenstein (1996) shows the critical impact of femocrats (feminist bureaucrats) working within the Australian bureaucracy on behalf of women. Laurel Weldon (2002a) further argues that WPAs provide better representation than any individual female legislator because they can liaise across government ministries, pursue cross-sectoral gender goals, and network with a variety of women in society—by hosting public forums for women's organizations that pool their policy preferences, for example. In the United States, feminists inside the government expanded women's rights through bureaucratic rule making, even when the women's movement on the outside lagged and under conservative presidents (Banaszak 2010). Leftist governments often empower WPAs to build capacity in the women's movement. But under coalition governments, when rightist parties control the women's ministry portfolio, they can dismantle WPAs or reorient them toward family policy rather than toward women's empowerment. However, Louise Chappell and Kathleen Teghtsoonian (2008) show that rightist parties at times have also facilitated women's empowerment through WPAs.

The three institutional sites of women's empowerment correspond with the functions of legislators, who promote and pass legislation; bureaucrats, who implement laws as public policy; and civil society, which articulates policy desires. This model "articulates women's demands, translates them into policy issues, and struggles to widen support for their agenda. The dynamism created between these actors accounts for the relative effectiveness with which women's interests can be defended" (Lycklama à Nijeholt, Vargas, and Wieringa 1998, 3–4). In other words, Beatrice Halsaa writes, "coming from different institutional sectors with shared feminist goals, women's movement leaders can form 'strategic partnerships' or advocacy coalitions to articulate important policy priorities, and women's policy agency leaders can connect these women to female legislators who in turn write laws and craft policies to address issues of greatest concern to women" (1988, 183).

While the triangle of women's empowerment has been helpful in identifying that women's representation often occurs across political institutions, this model has been challenged by research finding that other actors can be pivotal and that the specified actors are not always necessary and sufficient to achieve feminist policy outcomes. For example, Anne Maria Holli advocates use of the alternative term "women's co-operative constellation" because this term acknowledges the contributions of feminists who emerge from seemingly other sectors, like academia and women's party sections (2008, 169). Joni Lovenduski and Marila Guadagnini (2010) reaffirm that while important collaboration does occur across the triangle, critical actors in just one node can achieve the substantive representation of women even after these coalitions fall apart. Research conducted by McBride and Mazur (2010) and Lovenduski and Guadagnini (2010) contributes greatly to the comparative politics of gender and to the established findings that critical actors for women are at least as important as having a critical mass, or a certain minimum number of female political actors in an institution.

This book builds on this model by moving the discussion from feminist actors to engendered processes, from feminist legislators, women's groups, and women's policy agencies to gender candidate quotas, gender mainstreaming, and gender-responsive budgeting. The gender policy trifecta encourages activists, policy makers, citizens, and politicians to put in place institutionalized engendered processes rather than hanging all hopes on a point-in-time presence of critical women actors. As new actors fill new political offices, it is essential that the processes are engendered to increase the number of women and the standing of feminist viewpoints in policy making and that institutions for gender equality are maintained following elections and other changes in a country's political landscape. It also builds on the work of scholars advancing the "conditional approach" (Vickers 2010, 419–420; Chappell 2002)—that is, the study of conditions under which federal institutions situated in a given time or place possess more accurate information about women's diverse policy priorities, increased women's representation, and feminist outcomes, which are constituents of women's empowerment. Thus, the third guiding question in this book is *are subnational women's policy agencies and organizations, in subnational contexts, important sites of representation of women's policy priorities in decentralizing countries?*

The intention of these guiding questions is to speak directly to readers outside academia and think tanks and to present a reminder of the gender and politics research that is most relevant to everyday life for men and women in countries around the world. In this book, I consider cross-national and country-specific data on decentralization and women's empowerment, about which readers can ask themselves: Are politicians better matching the diverse priorities of women across this country when decentralization reforms happen? Is decentralization leading to subnational gender quotas and more women in elected office than before? Is decentralization leading to women working together across legislatures, agencies, and civil society to respond to female as well as male citizens? If, within a given country, the answers to these three questions are yes, then decentralization is empowering women in that country. An additional benefit of the questions is that they are a prism that helps us understand women's status both globally and locally. Women in very different parts of the world are more alike than we may suppose, but within the same country, women are more different from one another than we may guess. This is why I return to the three guiding questions in Chapter 6, demonstrating that this book makes significant contributions to our knowledge, not just in terms of the gendered implications of decentralization but also in how representatives go about understanding and aggregating diverse policy preferences.

Why the Aim of This Book Matters

Decentralization's impact on women in politics is critical to understand. It is important to know how 50 percent of the population is being affected by reforms that geographically reposition power in more than 80 percent of the world's countries. This study contributes the empirical analysis of gender to an existing policy literature that has traditionally evaluated decentralization along other dimensions, such as according to its ability to achieve fiscally efficient policies or reduce ethnic tensions or corruption (Bardhan and Mookherjee 2005; Bird and Villancourt 1998; Brancati 2009; Putnam 1993; Rodden and Wibbels 2002).

Ignoring the gendered implications of decentralization is unacceptable to those who want to understand the spread of democracy, human rights, and fundamental freedoms around the world. We live in a world where women represent 50 percent of the global population but, despite significant advancements, 70 percent of the poor (Freeland 2015). Moreover, up to 70 percent of all women experience physical or sexual violence in their lifetimes (UNITE, n.d.). It is not surprising that gender inequalities in poverty and violence are reflected in the halls of political power (Duerst-Lahti 2005). Women are not represented in parliaments in proportion to their presence in society. Just 22 percent of parliamentary seats worldwide are held by women (Inter-Parliamentary Union 2016). If decentralization facilitates democracy, as its supporters claim, decentralization would increase the numbers of women in office and the responsiveness to their policy priorities, ultimately reducing gender inequalities.

Some readers may be concerned that my focus on women will lead to another extreme, in which men's rights are gravely compromised. But the opposite is true. Research on women's policy priorities in India shows that the quality of both men's and women's representation increases after gender quotas are passed. Why? When more women hold political office, they bring the issues most salient to them to the agenda. Sometimes these issues are different from those that men prioritize, but this enhances the responsiveness of government to its diverse citizenry. For example, Rohini Pande and Deanna Ford (2011) found that after local gender quotas were passed in India new female politicians prioritized water investments in Rajasthan and road improvements in West Bengal. Despite these particular female leaders being poorer and having less education and experience than their male counterparts, their attention to water resources was associated with more government funds being allocated to these initiatives, and women and men benefited from better access to clean water. Thus, gender quotas, which ensure that women hold an equitable number of seats at the bargaining table, result in better overall government responsiveness—not just to what men believe matters but also to what women believe matters most (Asian Development Bank, Department for International Development, and World Bank 2004, 28; Chattopadhyay and Duflo 2004).

As India demonstrates, with the adoption of local council gender quotas and election of female mayors, *countries around the world need to engage in "engendering," or passing concrete institutional rules to empower women by design.* Countries cannot afford to wait decades for women to overcome obstacles and slowly matriculate into office. In *Rising Tide*, Ronald Inglehart and Pippa Norris (2003) argue that if the current pace of women's advancement in parliaments worldwide continues, it will take generations for women's representation in parliaments to equal men's. As with any other goal, to reach a specific outcome by a reasonable deadline, specific rules and benchmarks are required to bring about equitable percentages of women and men in office. Some wonder whether gender candidate quotas are defensible only initially, until the number of women in elected office increases from about 10 to 20 percent, at which point the quotas would be retracted. In my opinion, having gender quotas to ensure minimum levels of women's representation is as important as the specific percentage specified. Implementing a constitutional or legislative quota protects gains made, which are often hard fought and can slip away in the absence of a legal document. Barring the occasional matriarchal society, like the Mosuo in China, the default image of a political leader in many countries around the world is of a man, and government institutions and priorities naturally reflect the interests of incumbent male officeholders, consciously or unconsciously. If the percentages of female and male members of Congress had been flipped (85 percent female to 15 percent male), would it have taken until 2011 for a women's bathroom (built by Speaker of the House John Boehner) to be accessible to the House floor? The persistent underrepresentation of women in national and subnational government means that countries have to engender their political process to even elicit what women specifically want out of public policy. In our current systems, in which women make up one in five members of parliament, women do not always mobilize as women (Baldez 2002). They do so under only some conditions, such as when parties realign and women themselves are critical to elections. In addition to having other dimensions of identity that may be more salient at times, women may not fully enunciate their policy priorities in public opinion surveys. Unless a survey is primed for hearing their priorities, women may not view their sincere priorities as achievable or likely to appear on the political agenda. Therefore, women's public opinion responses can often look similar to men's in a given country context.

Unless there is gender parity in political party leadership and legislative institutions, a researcher has to signal to female respondents that she wants to hear their gender-based priorities. I asked leaders of women's organizations to rank their top four policy priorities for women. These organizations can remain open and active only if they prove that the issues they address are worth presenting to the government and to the female constituents they seek to represent. The priorities of politicians responsible for women are often different from those expressed by the leaders of women's groups. In the twentieth century, women's movements around the world mobilized to persuade citizens that women should have voting rights equal to men. In the twenty-first century, women's movements around the world are mobilizing to persuade citizens that women should hold an equal number of political offices as men. In neither case does change mean disenfranchisement for men. In both cases it means greater democracy for all.

Studying Decentralization and Women's Empowerment

The study of how a complicated reform like decentralization affects women's representation is a challenging research question. It entails testing the effects of decentralization (a multisectoral, multi-institution, multilevel, and longitudinal entity) on the difficult and contested outcome of women's empowerment. On one hand, this question is exciting because decentralization often creates new institutional offices, and changes before and after decentralization are observable (see Treisman 2007). For example, when I took my survey to Poland in 2007, there were sixteen new provinces and provincial parliaments where forty-nine weak county administrations had existed before.

(An initial reform priority for Poland in 1998 was local government.) I interviewed men and women in the provincial parliaments to see whether they felt that women held equal status to men in the new parliaments. On average, they told me that women were not equal to men in the new provincial parliaments. It was exciting to interview politicians in these brand-new roles, but this research question is daunting. As Treisman (2007) recommends, the best way to evaluate decentralization is to ask whether people are better off now than they were before. However, when decentralization reforms occur, the resulting change in the units of analysis becomes a liability. After 1998, Polish data was collected by populations within the sixteen new provincial boundaries, no longer by the forty-nine obsolete county boundaries, so I could not straightforwardly compare subnational data on women's office holding, employment, or other indicators before and after decentralization. Moreover, any progress for women might have happened because of the passage of time and not decentralization.

Another challenge is drawing meaningful conclusions about decentralization's general policy outcomes for women when women's empowerment improves in some subnational units, remains the same in other units, and deteriorates in yet others. Inherent to decentralization is the proposition that subnational units should be able to make their own unique policy decisions. Tiebout's (1956) seminal research shows that people's preferences vary spatially, and local governments that allow citizen mobility can better match these preferences. Maybe women's preferences vary spatially, too, and local bodies with better information (Hayek 1945) and equitable numbers of men and women would be better suited to match women's diverse preferences. Subnational units likely do different things for women in different units, but how do I compare levels of success across subnational units?

I have tackled these challenges over the past decade in a series of publications that led to this book's research design. First, I published an article on whether women's status was equal to men's in newly decentralized institutions (Rincker 2009). A colleague and I followed that piece by identifying the conditions under which subnational women's agencies were able to enact policy change for women (Rincker and Ortbals 2009) and examined research methods for fieldwork abroad (Ortbals and Rincker 2009a, 2009b), and then my colleagues and I examined women's representation cross-institutionally (Ortbals, Rincker, and Montoya 2011). This book builds on that prior research. I came to realize that answering the question of how decentralization affects women's empowerment required coming at it from a different angle. I had to start with what women want in terms of their public policy priorities. If I collected detailed (new) unit-specific descriptive data on policy priorities and checked them against subnational and national politicians' views of what women want, it would indicate whether decentralized politicians were more knowledgeable about or responsive to women's concerns. I could see whether the presence of the gender policy trifecta at the subnational level affected policy development for women in a given country.

This research design strategy also helped me broaden my questions and the implications of the project. Having worked for years at the intersection of gender equality and decentralization, I know firsthand that not everyone interested in gender equality is also interested in decentralization, and vice versa. Therefore, I have sought to ensure that the chapters on women's empowerment in Poland (Chapter 3), Pakistan (Chapter 4), and the United Kingdom (Chapter 5) are engaging for an audience wider than decentralization scholars, policy makers, think tanks, and nongovernmental organizations. Still, the guiding questions provide connective tissue throughout the book, so that in the conclusion the reader can see how women's representation compares across, as well as within, the three countries.

The wider import of the book, beyond its analysis of decentralization, is in my collection of original and comparable data on what women from far-flung parts of the world really want. Through innovative empirical analysis, this book makes key theoretical contributions to the study of representation and democratization, as well as decentralization and women's empowerment. To collect the data I first surveyed women's organizations in the three countries, having the organizations rank their top four policy priorities. I then aggregated these priorities at meso and national levels to find what women want out of public policy in a given political territory. Second, I tracked the number of women in political office at meso and national levels to see how numerous and influential they are. Third, I used a *Newlywed Game*-style method to test the responsiveness of male and female meso-level and national politicians to women's organizations.

Readers may recall that *The Newlywed Game* was a 1970s television game show that tested how well spouses knew each other by asking one spouse to predict what the other's opinion or preference would be on a certain matter. The audience was highly entertained by seeing the second spouse's reaction to the first spouse's answer if it was incorrect. In a similar way, I asked meso-level and national leaders what they thought the top four policy priorities of women's organizations were in their constituencies. This method allowed me to test whether male and female politicians at the meso and national levels are equally responsive to the policy priorities of women's organizations (see Appendix 1). Finally, I demonstrate that female politicians at the meso and national levels are often reluctant to pass legislation to respond to women's priorities if the legislation could be deemed "feminist." Greater women's political participation, policy priority matching, and feminist policy outcomes, in turn, show the conditions under which decentralization increases political responsiveness to women and deepens a country's democratization.

Methodology

In this book, I use a mixed-method, feminist-integrated approach to examine what women want in terms of their public policy priorities and to determine whether decentralized local government as opposed to national government better meets those needs. In the manner of cutting-edge work on methodology by Evan Lieberman (2005), Cresswell (2007), and McBride and Mazur (2010), I sequentially employ quantitative and qualitative methods as the most persuasive means to examine this research question, using the results from one aspect of the study to inform the next question and the best-suited methods to answer that question (George and Bennett 2005; Gerring 2012; Schwartz-Shea and Yanow 2012). In Chapter 2, I review the literature from around the world about decentralization and gender inequality. I reveal that the gender policy trifecta is present across diverse examples of decentralization when women's empowerment is the outcome. However, I rigorously challenge my proposition that the gender policy trifecta explains cross-national variance when decentralization empowers women. I present in Chapter 2 cross-national quantitative indicators of decentralization and gender equality around the world. The purpose of these data is to test whether each decentralization reform, in and of itself, in the absence of any node of the gender policy trifecta, leads to gender equality. These cross-national data show that decentralization reforms by themselves are not consistently and significantly related to gender equality. Next, I test whether the three nodes of the trifecta are necessary and sufficient to bring about women's political empowerment in three specifically chosen countries.

Selection Criteria

Case studies can be an invaluable inferential tool for testing theory (Eckstein 1975). Four criteria guided my selection of cases that rigorously test my central proposition: that the gender policy trifecta explains variation in which country empowers women after decentralization.

1. International organizations bankroll decentralization around the world, arguing that wherever decentralization is implemented, it leads to improvements in women's empowerment. Therefore, a relevant, problem-oriented, full-bodied evaluation of decentralization's potential as a political reform cannot be based on

countries drawn from just one or two regions of the world. The United Nations (2014) recognizes five regional groups: Africa, Asian-Pacific, Eastern European, Latin American and Caribbean, and Western European and Others.

2. It makes sense to choose countries in which decentralization reforms started within two years of one another, so as not to hold one country to a standard it cannot achieve merely because of a time disadvantage.

3. A current analysis should examine countries that underwent decentralization reforms in the late 1990s, because there must be adequate data on women's descriptive and substantive representation for both before and after decentralization. Choosing countries in which decentralization reforms occurred earlier, in the 1960s, 1970s, or 1980s, yields insufficient comparable data on women's descriptive and substantive representation preceding decentralization, particularly given criterion 1. Choosing countries in which decentralization occurred after the late 1990s allows criticism that not enough time has passed for implementation of decentralization or response to women's policy priorities.

4. I wanted the countries to vary with respect to the number of gender policy trifecta nodes—one, two, or three—that they possess.

Poland (one node), Pakistan (two nodes), and the United Kingdom (three nodes) are the best fits for these case-selection criteria.

The country-based chapters (3, 4, and 5), use data I collected from Poland, Pakistan, and the United Kingdom in 112 hybrid survey-interviews with leaders of women's organizations and meso- and national-level gender equality policy makers (see Table 1.1).

For survey-interviews of women's organizations, I surveyed their leaders in three to four cities in different meso units in each of three countries: in Poland, ten leaders each in Poznań in Wielkopolskie Province, Gdańsk in Pomorskie Province, and the national capital Warsaw in Mazowieckie Province; in Pakistan, eight in each of the national capital Islamabad, Lahore in Punjab Province, and Peshawar in what is now known as Khyber Pakhtunkhwa Province; in the United Kingdom, six to eight leaders each in Belfast, Northern Ireland; Cardiff, Wales; Edinburgh, Scotland; and London, England. This data set allowed me to empirically test the utility of decentralization for women and address my research questions. Just as Richard Fenno, in *Homestyle* (1978), traveled around with members of the U.S. Congress to understand their motivations and strategies, I tracked 112 leaders of women's organizations and gender equality policy makers in three countries separated

Table 1.1 Numbers, types, and locations of women's leaders and ministers interviewed

Country	Type and level of leader	Number of leaders
Poland	National ministers of gender equality	2
	Meso-level ministers of gender equality	16
	Women's organization leaders in Warsaw, Mazowieckie	10
	Women's organization leaders in Poznań, Wielkopolskie	10
	Women's organization leaders in Gdańsk, Pomorskie	10
Total		*48*
Pakistan	National minister of gender equality	1
	Meso-level ministers of gender equality	5
	Women's organization leaders in Islamabad	8
	Women's organization leaders in Peshawar, Khyber Pakhtunkhwa	8
	Women's organization leaders in Lahore, Punjab	8
Total		*30*
United Kingdom	National minister of gender equality	1
	Meso-level ministers of gender equality	3
	Women's organization leaders in London, England	8
	Women's organization leaders in Edinburgh, Scotland	8
	Women's organization leaders in Cardiff, Wales	6
	Women's organization leaders in Belfast, Northern Ireland	8
Total		*34*
Total (all countries)		112

Note: Interviews in Poland and Pakistan were conducted in spring 2007. Interviews in the United Kingdom were conducted in spring 2011.

from one another by thousands of miles, collecting systematic data on their policy priorities and how well various levels of government respond to these policy priorities (see Appendix 2).

Plan of the Book

Figure 1.2 shows the book's three distinct but interrelated parts. Part I consists of two chapters. This chapter lays out the central aim, approach, methodology, and plan of the book. In Chapter 2, I review the literature on decentralization and women's descriptive representation around the world, making the argument for the gender policy trifecta model. This model recognizes that new decentralized institutional reforms overlie existing gender inequalities and variance in women's opportunities across meso units. The model also presents for empirical testing the conditions under which decentralization leads to women's empowerment. I review international organizations' policy papers on decentralization, demonstrating that these entities

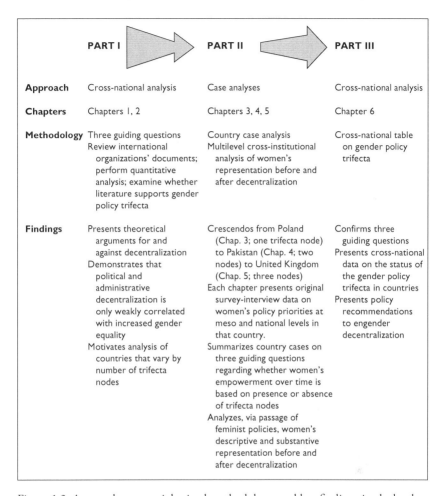

	PART I	PART II	PART III
Approach	Cross-national analysis	Case analyses	Cross-national analysis
Chapters	Chapters 1, 2	Chapters 3, 4, 5	Chapter 6
Methodology	Three guiding questions Review international organizations' documents; perform quantitative analysis; examine whether literature supports gender policy trifecta	Country case analysis Multilevel cross-institutional analysis of women's representation before and after decentralization	Cross-national table on gender policy trifecta
Findings	Presents theoretical arguments for and against decentralization Demonstrates that political and administrative decentralization is only weakly correlated with increased gender equality Motivates analysis of countries that vary by number of trifecta nodes	Crescendos from Poland (Chap. 3; one trifecta node) to Pakistan (Chap. 4; two nodes) to United Kingdom (Chap. 5; three nodes) Each chapter presents original survey-interview data on women's policy priorities at meso and national levels in that country. Summarizes country cases on three guiding questions regarding whether women's empowerment over time is based on presence or absence of trifecta nodes Analyzes, via passage of feminist policies, women's descriptive and substantive representation before and after decentralization	Confirms three guiding questions Presents cross-national data on the status of the gender policy trifecta in countries Presents policy recommendations to engender decentralization

Figure 1.2 Approach, sequential mixed methodology, and key findings in the book

largely support the argument that decentralization leads to women's empowerment even without election of more women subnationally, because making institutions more local means politicians have more accurate information and greater accountability. I present cross-national data on each country's level of political, administrative, and fiscal decentralization and its scores on gender equality. These data show that the presence of decentralization on its own is not strongly and significantly associated with gender equality in countries around the world. Therefore, rigorous in-depth case analyses are necessary to confirm mechanisms of the gender policy trifecta.

Part II consists of chapters that crescendo from one node (Poland, Chapter 3) to two nodes (Pakistan, Chapter 4) to three nodes (United Kingdom,

Chapter 5) of the gender policy trifecta. I structure each of the country chapters in a parallel format for maximum theoretical leverage. I begin each with an overview of the nodes of the triangle the country possesses and then provide the political context for women before decentralization and describe the actors pushing for decentralization. Next I show how women's descriptive representation changes after decentralization to see whether more women are elected at the subnational or national level (see also Appendix 3). I also describe how decentralization has affected women's organizations and policy agencies in each country. In the heart of each chapter, I report original interview data on what women want: the top policy priorities of the leaders of women's organizations at the meso level and then aggregated to the national level. To determine where in each country's public policy women's priorities are addressed, I use aggregate analysis of all legislation directly affecting women, advanced on the national and meso levels. Specifically, I check whether legislation in the fifteen-year span since decentralization responds to policy priorities of women's groups (both nonfeminist and feminist groups) or leads to feminist policy outcomes (See Appendixes 4–6). In the two countries that lack one or more of the nodes of the gender policy trifecta (Poland and Pakistan), I show that feminist policy making has not occurred, while the country with all three nodes (United Kingdom) does demonstrate both increased women's descriptive representation and feminist policy-making outcomes. Combining aggregate legislative analysis with quantitative data is an advantage of the mixed-method approach I use. The natural follow-up question from the Part II country analyses is, how prevalent are subnational gender policy trifectas outside the United Kingdom? The method best suited to answer this question is cross-national quantitative analysis.

In Part III, which contains Chapter 6, I demonstrate the larger significance of the book. I return to examine the three guiding questions, affirming that women's policy priorities differ as much within countries as they do across them, that subnational gender quotas are associated with higher numbers of women in government, and that multiple sites, or cross-institutional coordination, are key for women's representation. I then demonstrate that many countries do not yet have the gender policy trifecta at the level of governance to which they have been decentralized. Thus, my cross-national analysis identifies where reforms for gender equality are most needed in a way that speaks to activists as well as to policy makers. If states actively engender their decentralization processes, women's empowerment results. If they fail to engender decentralization, status quo or retrograde policies are the outcome for women.

The innovative sequencing strategy in *Empowered by Design* brings the best of quantitative and qualitative results into a dialogue with one another, demonstrating a plausibility and generalizability that support my theoretical innovations (Cresswell 2007; Lieberman 2005; McBride and Mazur 2010). I close Chapter 6 by applying the book's findings to the study of decentralization, comparative democratization, feminist comparative policy, representation, and quotas. I show that, overall, where gender policy trifectas are created, the highest levels of women's representation and feminist policy result.

2

Decentralization and Gender Inequality in the Absence of the Gender Policy Trifecta

In his foundational work, "A Pure Theory of Local Expenditures," Charles Tiebout (1956) argues that what citizens want out of government varies a lot across a given country. In Tiebout's view decentralization is a reform that leads to efficiency and responsiveness, because subnational governments become responsible for making policy. Subnational governments start to compete with one another as they respond to their current constituents' interests. If a subnational government does not do a good job responding to its residents, those residents will move to the jurisdiction of another, more responsive subnational government.[1] However, a shortcoming of the work is that Tiebout does not differentiate among citizens. Tiebout does not consider constituents' individual identities: they are of different races, ethnicities, and classes and have different gender characteristics. These identity characteristics can affect a constituent's ability to leave a subnational government. And if citizens cannot credibly threaten to exit, they cannot demand responsiveness from the subnational government. For example, female constituents are more likely than male constituents to be below the poverty line, earning less on average than their male counterparts, and they often do not work outside the home and are economically dependent on males. Women may have a lower ability to exit and thus a lower ability to demand governmental responsiveness.

---

1. As an example of subnational-unit competition for mobile citizens, a billboard on Interstate Highway 294 connecting Chicago to northwest Indiana reads, "Illinoyed by higher taxes? Come to Indiana—a state that works."

Government policies that engender male-dominated institutions may be necessary before subnational governments can respond to women.

In this chapter, I survey literature by international organizations (the United Nations, World Bank, European Union, and Asian Development Bank) that assumes decentralization by itself will lead to women's empowerment. I then put international organizations to the test. If decentralization on its own (without a gender policy trifecta) leads to gender equality, then cross-national indicators of decentralization on their own should be strongly and significantly associated with gender equality. However, through this analysis, I show that decentralization reforms on their own are not sufficient to bring about gender equality.[2] I next systematically evaluate studies of decentralization and gender from around the globe and look to insights from gender and politics literature to identify a model of the conditions under which we achieve women's empowerment. By marrying findings from the gender and politics literature with a broad examination of literature on gender and decentralization, I derive and present the key insight of this book: a gender policy trifecta at the subnational level of governance is necessary and sufficient to achieve the kind of decentralization that will empower women.

The key argument of this book is that for decentralization to empower women the gender policy trifecta must be put in place at a subnational level of governance. To respond to women's diverse policy priorities, there must be (1) subnational gender quotas ensuring that women hold seats in the meso-level legislatures, (2) subnational women's policy agencies ensuring gender mainstreaming across bureaucracies, and (3) subnational gender-responsive budgeting ensuring that women's organizations have access to meso-level government taxing and funding mechanisms. The gender policy trifecta engenders all three sectors of decentralization. My analysis in the country chapters (Part II) reveals that the gender policy trifecta is associated with measurable gains in women's representation and women's empowerment. I use cross-national data in Chapter 6 to show which nodes of the trifecta countries possess so that women can be empowered by design.

International Organizations: Decentralization Support, Scant Attention to Gender

Although international organizations spend extensively on decentralization and separately claim to also promote gender equality and women's empowerment, they have produced relatively little systematic research linking

---

2. The cross-national data in this chapter show that decentralization reforms (political, fiscal, and administrative) without attention to the gender policy trifecta are not associated with gender equality.

decentralization and gender equality (Agrawal, Yadama, et al. 2006; Pini and McDonald 2011). In this section, I critically examine published documents and policy statements from the United Nations, World Bank, European Union, and Asian Development Bank to see how well they engender decentralization programs that they bankroll. In other words, what budgetary commitment does each international organization put toward engendering decentralization programs? Has each specific international organization produced studies examining decentralization's gendered effects, and is there evidence of gendered policy-making feedback such that research findings on gender reshape the organization's subsequent decentralization programs or procedures? This section shows that international organizations largely assume that decentralization itself, without further engendering reforms, empowers women. With the exception of a recent United Nations conference and more programmatic action by the Asian Development Bank, international organizations rarely examine the gendered effects of decentralization. When they do, they often find negative outcomes for women, but these findings have yet to bring about changes in decentralization programs or evaluation tools.

Let us begin by looking at the United Nations and its documents regarding decentralization and gender equality. In February 2013, the United Nations hosted the Paris Local and Regional Governments' Global Agenda for Equality of Women and Men in Local Life. This important conference gathered local female politicians from around the globe to encourage, among other practices, the addition of gender quotas to the local level as a specific addition to Millennium Development Goal 3 Post-2015 (Global Conference of Local Elected Women 2013). The Millennium Development Goals for achieving human development represented eight (now seventeen) targets that countries agreed to during the UN Millennium Declaration of 2000 and that were to be assessed by 2015 (and are to be reviewed by 2030). Likewise, the United Nations has been critical in advancing key treaties on women, like the Convention on the Elimination of All Forms of Discrimination against Women (CEDAW), among others. Ostensibly, the Paris conference would not have been necessary if local- or meso-level elected posts had automatically been more open to women than nationally elected offices. Rather, at this set of meetings, organizers noted that women made up 5 percent of mayors and 20 percent of councilors worldwide and that "the participation of women in local decision making has stagnated since the late eighties when many affirmative mechanisms (such as quotas) were put in place around the planet" at the national level (United Cities and Local Governments 2013). While United Nations support of this conference to encourage women's descriptive representation in meso- and local-level government in decentralizing states is encouraging, it foreshadows that politics at all levels of governance require sustained engendering and that no level of governance is immune to gender-based inequalities.

As a key international organization working on decentralization, the World Bank has done little to study gendered effects of decentralization or to ameliorate gender-based inequalities in decentralization programs. The World Bank spends an increasing share of its budget on decentralization programs in developing and democratizing countries (Bird and Villancourt 1998; Litvack, Ahmad, and Bird 1998, 1). A World Bank report titled *Entering the 21st Century* exclaims that "the desire for self-determination and the devolution of power" is one of the main forces shaping "the world in which development policy will be defined and implemented" in the first decade of this century (1999, 31). In other reports, the World Bank purports to be the most advanced among development agencies in setting out a rigorous method of measuring women's empowerment (Malhotra, Schuler, and Boender 2002). Yet few World Bank studies on decentralization rigorously test whether decentralization leads to women's empowerment. Most World Bank publications on decentralization speak of nongendered citizens whose efficacy increases because of the reform. For example, George Matovu states, "The local government transformation and decentralization processes underway in sub-Saharan Africa have opened space for civil society empowerment, giving citizens opportunities to better participate in decision-making processes and administration" (2002, 24). Therefore, women and men are assumed to have similar rates of efficacy without further examination of the question. Generally, World Bank literature on decentralization focuses on issues of political economy, institutional capacity, local corruption, and subnational or class disparities in decentralization outcomes. Mention of the gendered effects of decentralization for half the population—women—is at the margin rather than the center of World Bank studies. A chapter on decentralization reforms briefly alludes to women not always winning after decentralization, stating:

> Greater participation . . . [after] decentralization through the empowerment . . . of marginalized groups may not always translate into more equitable resource allocations and more responsive service delivery. The opportunity of increased participation may initially raise expectations, but prove difficult to sustain over time especially because the opportunity costs are high and the apparent returns low. . . . [F]or these to be sustainable and produce tangible outcomes, arrangements . . . [such as] sufficient financing and staffing at the local and front-line levels, must be established. (Kaiser 2006, 334)

However, the World Bank does not follow up with studies or act on the point of view presented in its study, even though it counts women's empowerment as "one of the key constituent elements of poverty reduction, and as a primary development assistance goal" (Malhotra, Schuler, and Boender 2002). Other

World Bank studies that demonstrate gender-inequitable outcomes from decentralization stop short of criticizing decentralization policies for failing to address women's empowerment. For example, Rama Lakshminarayanan's (2003) analysis of health sector reforms shows that decentralization is guilty of unevenly providing for family planning services in heavily Catholic areas of the Philippines. He argues that the lack of women in local government offices (or low descriptive representation of women) contributes to less support for family planning services (substantive representation of women), although the word "women" is used in neither the title nor the abstract of the article. Arguably, using an explicitly gendered framework in decentralization analysis would demonstrate a substantial World Bank commitment to women's empowerment in its many development programs.

As another major international organization promoting decentralization, the European Union has done little to study or advance programs that address gender inequality in meso-level governance. The European Union itself was founded on the "subsidiarity" principle, which means that "decisions must be taken as closely as possible to the citizen" (Eurofound 2010). Also, it devotes more than one-third of its budget to regional policy that "aims to remove economic, social and territorial disparities across the EU" (Eurostat 2016). Supporters of the European Regional Development Fund, European Social Fund, and Cohesion Fund predict that decentralization will lead to more efficient policy making because state governments will compete for mobile voters. But key research examining decentralization's effects on women in Europe comes from academic rather than policy-making venues (see, for example, Celis and Woodward 2003; Mackay and Kenny 2011; Ortbals, Rincker, and Montoya 2011). While literature on gender mainstreaming (True 2003), gender budgeting, and state feminism has been developed through commissioned European Union projects, the extent to which these three engendered areas are implemented in member states is patchy. And efforts to engender subnational governments as part of the 2004 enlargement into ten Central and Eastern European countries is nonexistent.

Another major international organization promoting decentralization, the Asian Development Bank, is leading the way by paying attention to its gender implications. It notes that devolution has three aims: introduce new blood into a political system; provide positive measures for marginalized citizens—women, workers, peasants—to have access to politics; and create a stronger line of accountability between new politicians and a local electorate (Asian Development Bank, Department for International Development, and World Bank 2004, 1). The Asian Development Bank (2013) has been more proactive than other international organizations in incorporating gendered analysis into its decentralization programs. These programs, in place since

2008, have been implemented in countries like Nepal and Indonesia. So the Asian Development Bank appears to be leading other international organizations in just beginning to research and implement decentralization programs that pay attention to gendered outcomes. Thus, from policy-based research on decentralization, we have proponents and opponents of decentralization as a means to enhance democratic governance from nongendered perspectives. Systematic study of decentralization's gendered effects is necessary to know how this reform affects women—50 percent of the world's population.

I present for the first time cross-national correlations between individual sectors of decentralization and measurable indicators on gender equality as calculated by the global Gender Inequality Index (United Nations Development Programme, n.d.).[3] These data serve as a plausibility probe to test international organizations' claims that decentralization reforms in any sector (political, administrative, or fiscal) are associated with greater gender equality. The Gender Inequality Index is a way to quickly assess, across nations, women's descriptive and substantive representation, because it includes data on women in office and data on maternal mortality and access to education. I plot countries on their values on the political, administrative, and fiscal dimensions of decentralization to see whether higher values of these alone are associated with higher gender equality. If international organizations are correct, decentralization reforms on their own lead to greater information, accountability, and responsiveness to citizens (including women), so the correlations should be significant.

In stark contrast to international organizations' claims, the data in this chapter show only weak associations between two decentralization indicators and levels of gender equality. In essence, the cross-national data I present here refute the arguments of international organizations. Therefore, they push us to the next phase of the argument, that further reforms are needed to bring about women's empowerment. The data support the work of the UN Population Fund, which distinguishes between gender equality and women's empowerment: "Achieving gender equality requires women's empowerment to ensure that decision-making at private and public levels, and access to resources are no longer weighted in men's favour, so that both women and men can fully participate as equal partners in productive and reproductive life" (United Nations Population Fund 2005). The findings in this chapter also encourage us to proceed with the investigation of whether all three nodes of the gender policy trifecta are necessary and sufficient for decentralization to bring about women's empowerment.

---

3. Pippa Norris makes these data sets available online, at https://sites.google.com/site/pippanorris3/research/data#TOC-Democracy-Time-series-Data-Release-3.0-January-2009.

Measuring Gender Inequality

Many individuals, organizations, and entities have sought a way to quantify gender inequality that would allow us to understand it within one country over time and to compare levels of gender inequality in countries around the world. Such a measure would allow activists to pressure their governments to adopt new policies to advance the status of women. It would also help states and activists realize when they are making progress toward equality. The central indexes for gender equality that have been developed for cross-national comparison include the Gender Empowerment Measure, Gender-Related Development Index, Social Institutions and Gender Index, and Gender Inequality Index. To examine the relationships between the components of decentralization and gender inequality, I have chosen to use the Gender Inequality Index.

I ruled out the other measurements in the following way. The Gender Empowerment Measure includes women's economic and political resources. However, Mark McGillivray and J. Ram Pillarisetti (2006) argue that it is heavily determined by fertility rates and women's labor force participation rates and that it does not include women's suffrage. These authors also charge that it underestimates women's contributions to gross domestic product because it measures women's income in nonagricultural sectors in which the manufacturing segment is very small. The Gender-Related Development Index has been criticized for assuming women will live on average five years longer than men, which spreads women's contributions over a longer period and thus lowers their apparent inequality. More importantly, this index is based on the Human Development Index and is best conceived of as the loss of human development because of patriarchy. The Organisation for Economic Cooperation and Development's Social Institutions and Gender Index captures key rights for women but does not cover advanced Western democracies.

The Gender Inequality Index is preferable because it measures inequalities in reproductive health, access to education and politics, and labor force participation. The variable ranges between 0 and 1, where 0 represents full equality and 1 represents full inequality between women and men. Advocates of the measure note that it does not include income, a controversial component of both the Gender Empowerment Measure and the Gender-Related Development Index. I use the Gender Inequality Index because it measures women's autonomy in the private sphere, women's capacity in the workplace, and women's autonomy in politics, and because the measure is widely available for developing and developed countries.

In the figures that follow, I examine an indicator for each sector of decentralization: political, administrative, and fiscal. I display scatter plots showing how countries worldwide fare in terms of the sectors of decentralization and gender inequality. I describe the indicators for decentralization sectors as follows. For political decentralization, I use the work of Aaron Schneider (2003). He presents a factor analysis coefficient that loads both municipal and meso-level elections and is also used in Pippa Norris's *Driving Democracy* (2008).

For administrative decentralization, I use subnational expenditure as a percentage of total national expenditure. Tulia Falleti argues that subnational expenditure as a percentage of national expenditure is the correct proxy for administrative decentralization, because administrative decentralization is about control over expenditure at the subnational level. "Administrative decentralization comprises the set of policies that transfer the administration and delivery of social services such as education, health, social welfare, or housing to subnational governments" (2005, 329). She goes on to say, "Unlike other definitions of fiscal decentralization that collapse decentralization of revenues and expenditures, in this definition fiscal decentralization refers to revenues, whereas expenditures are part of administrative decentralization" (329).

For fiscal decentralization, I employ subnational revenue as a percentage of total revenue. (For further discussion of possible overestimation of the International Monetary Fund's Government Finance Statistics fiscal decentralization indicators, see Ebel and Yilmaz 2002, 7–10.) I justify the use of "subnational revenues as a percentage of all revenues" as a valid indicator of fiscal decentralization on the basis of Falleti's seminal work conceptualizing and measuring dimensions of decentralization. Falleti writes, "Fiscal decentralization refers to the set of policies designed to increase the revenues or fiscal autonomy of subnational governments" (2005, 329). When subnational revenue is a higher percentage of all revenue, fiscal decentralization is stronger.

Now let us examine globally *whether, as international organizations argue, political decentralization is associated with lower levels of gender inequality.* The *y*-axis variable is gender inequality, where 0 means complete equality and 1 means complete inequality. Therefore, the lower the value, the more gender equality. The *x*-axis variable is political decentralization, where a higher number indicates greater political decentralization. Therefore, we expect to see strong negative correlations, or a downward-sloping line in plots of gender inequality versus decentralization, if the proposition is true that political decentralization leads to gender equality. Figure 2.1 shows a weak, but statistically significant, relationship between gender inequality and political decentralization, with a correlation of $r = -.29$ significant at the .05 level. For a given level of political decentralization, there is a wide range of values in the dependent variable of gender inequality.

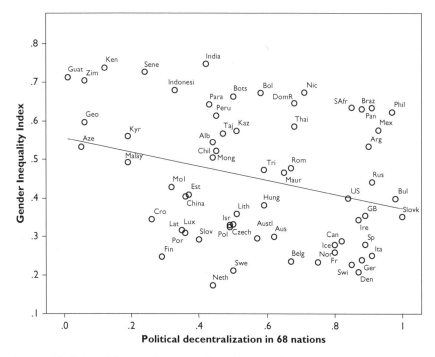

Figure 2.1 Political decentralization and gender inequality. $r = -.29$; $p = .05$.
(Sources: Schneider 2003; United Nations Development Programme, n.d.)

For example, the United States is above .8 on political decentralization because of strong local and state elections, but it ranks around .4 on gender inequality. It receives this relatively weak ranking because of restricted reproductive rights and a low percentage of women in Congress, but women's education and labor force participation mitigate inequality. Autocratic centralized states like Malaysia, Georgia, and Guatemala do not have local elections and also rank low on gender equality. Brazil and Russia score high on political decentralization but low on gender equality. Several smaller countries, primarily Scandinavian ones, rank low to middling on political decentralization but have very high levels of gender equality. Many Central and Eastern European countries have middling levels of political decentralization and gender equality. As Richard Vengroff, Zsolt Nyiri, and Melissa Fugiero (2003) demonstrate, subnationalization of politics benefits women in developed countries but has a negative influence on the number of women in office in developing countries. In these countries, with fewer job opportunities and where meso-level institutions are important fiscal actors, meso-level offices take on a very high status and are difficult for women to win. Reforms like gender quotas may be necessary for political decentralization to lead to gender equality.

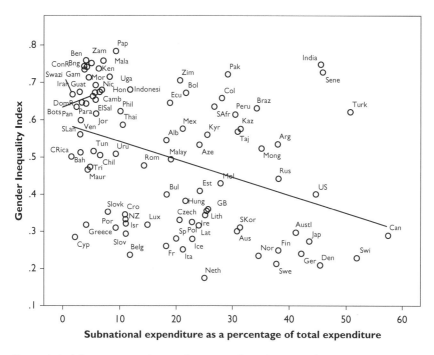

Figure 2.2 Administrative decentralization and gender inequality. $r = -.39$; $p = .01$. (Sources: 2002 data from the World Bank *Fiscal Decentralization Indicators* database, http://www1.worldbank.org/publicsector/decentralization/fiscalindicators .htm; United Nations Development Programme, n.d.)

Is administrative decentralization associated with lower levels of gender inequality? Figure 2.2 shows that subnational units with greater control over expenditures are weakly associated with decreased gender inequality ($r = -.39$; $p = .01$). Countries where subnational governments deliver most of the services, such as Canada, Sweden, and the United States, tend to have lower levels of gender inequality. Greater knowledge by meso-level politicians of women's policy priorities and the financial capacity to respond could explain this trend. Conversely, other cases from the figure show that authoritarian states, perhaps paranoid about local control, tend to severely curtail women's rights.[4] Countries in which local governments have almost no control over the delivery of services, such as Benin, Gambia, Democratic Republic of the Congo, Iran, and the Dominican Republic, tend to have high levels of gender inequality. However, it does not hold across the board that all decentralized countries have low levels of gender inequality. In addition, countries might need to establish subnational women's policy agencies

---

4. The data on India in this figure were collected before gender quota reform.

to implement gender mainstreaming or analysis of policy from a gendered perspective.

Is fiscal decentralization associated with lower levels of gender inequality? Figure 2.3 shows no discernable relationship between fiscal decentraliza- tion alone and the Gender Inequality Index. To some extent, the data might reflect that local governments in nondemocratic or emerging democracies are not effective tax collection agents. Most local officials prefer systems in which national government collects the taxes but local officials have spending power (Falleti 2005). Also, fiscal decentralization might matter, but only if in conjunction with reforms in at least one other sector. The lack of relation- ship between fiscal decentralization and gender equality is likely because economic decisions are primarily made by male politicians at varying levels of governance without gender-responsive budgeting directives. Some countries, like Bolivia and Brazil, have powerful subnational units in terms of tax- ing authority and also high levels of gender inequality, but other countries, like Belgium and the Netherlands, have low levels of gender inequality and little ability to collect taxes at the subnational level. Different still, Pakistan

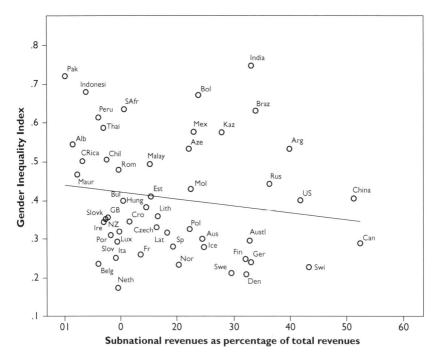

Figure 2.3 Fiscal decentralization and gender inequality. $r = -.16$; no significant relationship. (Sources: International Monetary Fund 1997; Norris 2008; United Nations Development Programme, n.d.)

exemplifies minimal subnational power to tax and high gender inequality. According to the gender policy trifecta, gender-responsive budgeting is necessary at all levels of governance responsible for equality policy to make fiscal decentralization reforms open to women citizens.

Summary

Cross-national plausibility probes show that political and administrative decentralization are weakly associated with lower levels of gender inequality and that fiscal decentralization is unrelated to gender inequality. Decentralization reforms on their own are not strongly and significantly correlated with gender equality as international organizations suggest. Scholarly and international organizations' exhortation for countries to adopt decentralization is insufficient to bring about women's empowerment and to enhance the democratic process for all citizens. Therefore, we need to look at the literature on women's empowerment and on previous research on gender and decentralization to identify factors explaining women's empowerment.

Innovative work on state architecture (Chaney, Mackay, and McAllister 2007; Chappell 2002; Chappell and Vickers 2011; Haussman and Sauer 2007; Haussman, Sawer, and Vickers 2010; Vickers 1994, 2010, 2011, 2013), state reconfiguration (Banaszak, Beckwith, and Rucht 2003) and multilevel governance (Celis and Woodward 2003; Outshoorn and Kantola 2007) identify and analyze state feminist structures emerging at local, meso, and national levels in states that were previously diverse federal, unitary, or hybrid systems. Key works by Louise Chappell, Jill Vickers, and others have shown how institutions can create opportunities for women's movements at various levels of governance. Chappell has argued that "the process of gender is complex, playing out differently in similar institutions in different polities and different institutions within the same polity" (2006, 232). Some might argue that the cases listed in Table 2.1 are too disparate to compare. Decentralization occurs in countries with a range of preexisting political structures, from two-hundred-year-old federations to unitary states with nondemocratic actors. Ronald Watts's (2008) categorization in Table 2.1 shows that countries vary in how they set up their governance structures. If the initial constitutional setup of a state was federal two hundred years ago and administrative decentralization occurs one hundred years later, it might affect women's participation in institutions differently than a unitary developing state that democratized in the 1980s that gets new meso-level legislatures in the 2000s. If the gender policy trifecta is shown to lead to feminist policy in spite of these regime differences, we have greater assurance of its causal importance.

At first glance, Table 2.1 shows disparate conclusions in recent years as to whether decentralization increases the number of women involved in

Table 2.1 Decentralization's effects on women's representation in recent years

	Australia	Brazil	Canada	India
Scholar(s)	Chappell (2002); Sawer (2003)	Macaulay (2006)	Chappell (2002); Haussman, Sawer, and Vickers (2010)	Chattopadhyay and Duflo (2004)
Watts's (2008) categorization	f	f	f	f
Assessment of decentralization for women	↑	↑	↓	↑
Main year(s) decentralized	1901	1983	1867, 1982	1992
Percentage of women in national/provincial assembly	27/31	9/12	22/22	11/33
National/subnational gender quotas (minimum percentage)	v40/v40	30/30	v25/none	none/33
Descriptive representation of women at subnational level	↑	—	—	↑
Gender-responsive budgeting	yes	yes	yes	yes
Effective MWPAs	yes	yes	no	yes
Women's substantive representation	↑	↑	mix	↑
Substantive representation of women	WPAs help women's organizations find best level of governance to voice their concerns	Leftist party works with women	Strong territoriality harms women	Women expand clean water access
Gender policy trifecta presence	yes	yes	no	yes

Sources: Araújo 2003; Center for Asia-Pacific Women in Politics, n.d., "State of Women"; Drabsch 2007; Global Database of Quotas for Women 2014, 2015a, 2015b, 2016a, 2016b; International Scientific Researchers 2012; Montoya 2009; Stotsky 2016; United Nations Development Programme 2010; "Women in the 40th Canadian Parliament" 2016.

Note: The list of scholars is not exhaustive. f − federal, u/d − unitary with decentralizing features, du − decentralized union, v − voluntary party quota, WPA = women's policy agency, MWPA = meso-level women's policy agency. Arrows indicate an improvement or decline in women's status, and dashes indicate no change. In the row on quotas, dashes indicate where data is unknown.

politics and improves their representation. These disparities result from five main causes. First, these studies tend to focus on one subset of women or one country case that contributes greatly to our knowledge of the process of decentralization but requires further theory-consolidating work. Second, research tends to evaluate only one dimension of representation, such as descriptive, which has been found to either increase or decrease depending on the country's level of development (Vengroff, Nyiri, and Fugiero 2003) and on the presence of meso-level gender candidate quotas. Third, the extant

Pakistan	South Africa	Spain	Switzerland	United States	Europe
Aslam and Yilmaz (2011); Reyes (2002)	Beall (2005)	Ortbals (2008)	Banaszak (1996)	Hancock (2004); Parry (2005)	Celis and Woodward (2003); Outshoorn and Kantola (2007)
f	f	f	f	f	mix
↓	↓	↑	↓	↓	mix
2000	1994	1978	1999	1789, 1994	1980–1990
20/17	41/32	36/41	28/26	17/25	mix
17/17	v50/50	40/50	v40/none	none/none	mix
↓	↓	↑	—	↑	mix
yes	no till 1998	yes	no	no	y
mix	no	yes	yes	no	n/a
n/a	↓	↑	—	mix	↑
Decentralization helps mostly male national elites buy off local elites and exclude women	Decentralization cuts social spending and helps mostly male national elites buy off local elites and exclude women	Meso-level gender quotas gain traction and spread up to national level	Pros and cons of federalism: progressive cantons pass progressive laws for women; conservative cantons pass retrograde laws for women	Decentralization means cuts in state welfare affect women, who are more likely to be poor	Officials are more focused on representation of citizens
no	no	yes	no	no	no

(continued)

literature tends to equate good women's substantive representation solely with exogenously given feminist policy outcomes rather than examining the policy priorities of feminist and nonfeminist actors at meso and national levels. If the substantive representation of women is diverse and contested, we should see agreement not on policy solutions but rather in articulation of the most pressing issues for women. Fourth, literature often examines decentralization in a limited time frame without variation on the party control of governments in meso units. Considerable literature (see, for example, Reynolds 1999) argues that leftist parties are associated with more robust welfare state conditions, labor market opportunities for women, and antidiscrimination laws. While important advances for women can and do happen under conservative or rightist party leadership (Chappell and Teghtsoonian

Table 2.1 continued

	Cuba	Uganda	Chile	Ghana
Scholar(s)	Luciak (2005)	Saito (2000)	Franceschet (2011, 2012); Franceschet, Krook, and Piscopo (2012); Macaulay (2006)	Crawford (2004)
Watts's (2008) categorization	u/d	u/d	du	du
Assessment of decentralization for women	↓	mix	↓	↓
Main year(s) decentralized	1992	1988	1983	1983
Percentage of women in national/provincial assembly	36/37	31/30	14/—	3/30
National/subnational gender quotas (minimum percentage)	none/none	1 per district/33	v20/none	30/none
Descriptive representation of women at subnational level	↓	↑	—	↓
Gender-responsive budgeting	no	no till 1999	no	no
Effective MWPAs	no	no	yes	no
Women's substantive representation	—	—	↓	↓
Substantive representation of women	Few women in high-status offices	Local politics not open to women	WPA not leftist party ally	Low status for women in decentralized institutions
Gender policy trifecta presence	no	no	no	no

2008), critics of decentralization argue that meso units, with their typically rural demographics, are more likely to be run by conservatives antithetical to women's participation (Siahaan 2004) and that feminists would bet on a leftist national government that protects women or a geographically distant rightist government that has lesser influence on women's local status and rights. In democracies, elections are going to happen and national and meso units will vary by party control. Institutionalizing women's participation across subnational channels of representation enables women to equally participate with men regardless of the political party in power at the national or subnational level.

The fifth and final reason for disparate evaluations of decentralization's effect on women is that scholars fail to emphasize the multisectoral reform of decentralization. A notable exception is the work of Lee Ann Banaszak, Karen Beckwith, and Dieter Rucht (2003), who simultaneously cover uploading to supranational organizations, downloading to meso-level or local institutions, offloading to nonstate actors, and lateral loading to nonelected state bodies

Indonesia	Italy	Poland	South Korea	United Kingdom	Cross-national
Siahaan (2004)	Montoya (2009); Ortbals, Rincker, and Montoya (2011)	Rincker (2009)	Chin (2004)	Chaney, Mackay, and McAllister, (2007)	Vengroff, Nyiri, and Fugiero (2003)
du ↓	du mix	du ↓	du ↓	du ↑	all mix
1999 19/13	1980 31/13	1998 24/24	1991 17/19	1998 22/31	mix mix
30/30	v50/mix	none/35	30/none	mix	n/a
↓	↓	—	↓	↑	yes
yes no ↓	no yes mix	no yes —	no no ↓	yes yes ↑	mix n/a n/a
Decentralization supports local patriarchy	Pros and cons for women	Meso level not more open to women	Women fare worse at the meso level, better at national level	Women want decentralization except in Northern Ireland	n/a
no	no	no	no	yes	n/a

and courts. The few studies that have directly or indirectly reported on the multisectoral nature of decentralization, describe women's descriptive and substantive representation, and measure women's policy priorities (feminist and nonfeminist) display regularity in the conditions under which decentralization increases the number of women in office, leads to policy responsiveness to women's policy priorities, and promotes feminist policy outcomes. As I present in more depth later in this chapter, the factor common to all studies that assess decentralization as positive for women is the presence of the gender policy trifecta: the subnational level of politics is engendered through subnational gender candidate quotas, subnational women's policy agencies, and subnational gender-responsive budgeting. Before laying out a research design to empirically test the gender policy trifecta, I note that this trifecta builds on important research conducted in countries around the globe.

For example, research on state governance architecture (Chappell 2002; Haussman and Sauer 2007; Haussman, Sawer, and Vickers 2010; Vickers, 2010, 2011, 2013) has made key contributions to our knowledge of how political institutions like state structure (federations, unitary states, and hybrids) and changes in multilevel governance create opportunities for feminists to find the level of politics most open to their claims (i.e., venue-shop). Much of the most important theorizing in this area has come from analysis of the long-standing federations of Canada, the United States, and Australia. More recently, it is being applied to other federations like India, Mexico, and Nigeria.[5] Even though decentralization occurs across many countries, those countries often begin with different structures. This body of research helps us specify a country's precise state architecture (Sawer and Vickers 2010).

Federations involve "a formal power-sharing agreement between a federal government and constituent units such as States or provinces, recorded in a written Constitution. An umpire is appointed—usually a superior court—to resolve conflicts" (Haussman, Sawer, and Vickers 2010, 4). Other key aspects of federations are that they often formed before women's political franchise and that the meso units' existence is protected by a rigid constitution. Meso units in federations might have power to tax, but this can lead to imbalances across units. Federations might have considerable intergovernmental policy-making powers (resembling a marble cake) or strict delineations of each level's function (as in a layer cake). Marian Sawer and Jill Vickers also argue that asymmetric relations between national and constituent levels matter, as "the more salient territory is, the harder it is to insert gender into federal political discourses as a political variable" (2010, 6). Sometimes women's rights are better protected when nationalized (Smith 2010); other times women with territorial identity want local feminist solutions (Rankin and Vickers 2010; Vickers 1991, 1994).

In long-standing federations, scholars have shown that state reconfiguration has conditional effects. Sometimes the configuration offers women's groups multiple sites for venue shopping, creating positive pressure for change. Other times the structure divides women's movements and diverts their resources unproductively (Banaszak, Beckwith, and Rucht 2003; Banaszak and Weldon 2011; Haussman, Sawer, and Vickers 2010). As Chappell argues:

> When certain institutional variables—in this case, bureaucracy, the party system, and federalism—are configured in a particular pattern

5. The analysis in this book is conducted in a comparative way as suggested by scholars seeking a comparative politics of gender (Beckwith 2010). For excellent examples, see Melissa Haussman, Marian Sawer, and Jill Vickers, *Federalism, Feminism, and Multilevel Governance* (2010), which includes cases of older federations in Europe and the newer federations of India, Mexico, and Nigeria, or the special edition of *Publius* on engendering federalism (Vickers, Chappell, Meier 2013), which includes cases like the Flanders region of Belgium, Scotland, Argentina, and Chile. However, these analyses focus primarily on feminist outcomes rather than nonfeminist groups of women.

at a certain point in time, they can help to bring about a positive political opportunity structure within a specific institutional realm. However, as the story of Canadian and Australian feminists' engagement has demonstrated, these intersections are neither certain nor stable. When one of the institutional variables "moves out of alignment" (e.g., when a conservative government is elected to office), openings can quickly be replaced by constraints. (Chappell 2002, 176)

For example, federalism in Canada can sometimes reduce the substantive representation of minority women (Haussman, Sawer, and Vickers 2010). In other cases, federalism can be a useful tool for women marginalized by territorial identity because the level that they see as legitimate to govern their territorial interests is the level at which they address issues they face as women (Rankin and Vickers 2001; Vickers 2010, 2011, 2013). Haussman (2005) argues that the federal structure has harmed feminist abortion activists in Canada and in the United States. Similarly, Miriam Smith (2010) argues that it is easier in the United States to launch campaigns to change state constitutions making same-sex marriage illegal and that LGBT rights and women's rights in the United States are state led. Research in state architecture tradition shows that the framework best suited to assessing how decentralization affects women's representation must do two things: allow for multiple types of political actors and recognize that women in any territorial unit are a diverse group that requires the ability to express its policy priorities.

I build on the conditional approach of examining the effects of state structures and conditions that lead to feminist policy outcomes. I describe and test state structures to identify mechanisms that assist or impede women's representation. However, my conceptualization of women's substantive representation differs from that commonly tested in state architecture literature. Whereas the state architecture literature focuses solely on feminist policy outcomes, I focus on women's substantive representation that includes responsiveness to the policy priorities defined by leaders of both feminist and nonfeminist women's groups and on feminist policy outcomes. I also test whether women's descriptive representation and this broader conceptualization of women's substantive representation are related. It is possible that state-reconfiguring reforms are less feminist but achieve greater substantive representation of women in terms of matching women's policy priorities. Further, while large-territory, long-standing federations compose an important share of the world's population, I argue that the democratizing forces that we really want to evaluate are occurring in the world's plurality of small unitary states going through decentralization. As of 2005, there were 144 unitary states, 22 hybrid states, and 25 federal states. Thus, as 75 percent of the world's countries, unitary states that are decentralizing should be an important focus in understanding current democratization trends. Smaller-territory states, like the United Kingdom, and democratizing states, both federal (Pakistan) and unitary (Poland), exemplify a change in global governance no less important than our understanding of women's mobilization in long-standing federations. The next section reviews and outlines key insights into how the preceding dynamics shape the descriptive and substantive representation of women.

The Gender Policy Trifecta

An examination of the broad comparative literature on how state reconfiguration and decentralization affect women's representation leads me to argue that the gender policy trifecta explains the conditions under which decentralization results in women's meso-level descriptive representation, responsiveness to women's policy priorities, and feminist policy outcomes. Specifically, I speak of the gender policy trifecta that at any level of governance is engendered through the following:

1. *Electoral gender quotas* bring about more equality in the number of women and men in elected office.
2. *Gender mainstreaming* through subnational women's policy agencies creates a bureaucratic home for gendered analysis of all public policy issues and engenders administrative decentralization.
3. *Gender-responsive budgeting* requires elected and appointed officials to analyze and adjust their taxing and spending patterns with women's and men's priorities in mind, providing a point of access for women's organization leaders.

I draw this definition of the gender policy trifecta broadly so that it can be applied at various levels of governance, although I focus primarily on the meso level in this book. I also note that countries can move into and out of a trifecta situation if they adopt subnational quotas and then parties backtrack on them or if countries establish meso-level women's policy agencies and then defund or close them. But when countries explicitly engender all sectors of decentralization (political, administrative, and fiscal) in their processes at a given level of politics (meso or municipal) and that level has power, women's empowerment will result.

Looking across nearly thirty scholarly books and articles on the subject in Table 2.1 covering countries from around the world, we see predominantly negative evaluations of decentralization's effect on women. Despite their diversity, five cases share important factors. In Australia, Brazil, India, the United Kingdom, and Spain, women's descriptive representation at the subnational level increased during the time of the relevant studies, and the study authors reported an overall positive evaluation of decentralization on women's substantive representation. Most importantly, all five cases display evidence of the gender policy trifecta. These five countries had increased descriptive representation of women in meso-level or local offices (depending on the level at which decentralization occurred) because of electoral gender quotas, they had active women's policy agencies at the level of decentralized governance, and they had gender-responsive budgeting measures at the time of the study. Chappell notes, "In Australia, feminists have been able to make gains through the bureaucracy and, at times, have been able to use federalism to good effect" (Chappell 2002, 172). Moreover, "feminist lobbyists have been able to take advantage of Australian federalism by shifting their focus between different levels of government, depending on where they can make the greatest inroads" (152). In Brazil, Fiona Macaulay (2006) writes, decentralization is one of the most prominent "new forms of popular democracy [that] can . . . bring about accountability and delivery of high quality, accessible social services." Raghabendra Chattopadhyay and Esther Duflo (2004) studied decentralization to local governments (panchayats) in India—half of which were randomly selected for gender quotas. The panchayats with gender quotas had less corruption and also greater allocation toward water resources, a policy priority for women. This important case of Indian decentralization evinces subnational gender quotas, subnational women's policy agencies, and gender-responsive budgeting. Likewise, in the United Kingdom, women's groups were pivotal in the fight for devolution of government and were instrumental in building the National Assembly for Wales, which achieved gender parity in descriptive representation. "There has been a significant and far-reaching conceptual shift in the approach to gender equality. . . . [Substantive representation of women] has been re-prioritized as a core political aim of the government in Wales" (Chaney, Mackay, and McAllister 2007, 184). Although Meryl Kenny (2014) shows that women's representation has stagnated in the Scottish and Welsh assemblies, I argue that the Scottish statutory gender equality duty has had path-dependent effects that are hard to erase even when women's representation declines in some election cycles. Because of this duty, all legislation is subject to scrutiny on the basis of gender equality. Because of women's activism, the assembly meets at family-friendly times, and a feminist definition of violence against women was codified by legislation in Scotland, where one did not exist previously. In Spain, "[each of the] triangle nodes provide[s] women with representation. Meso-level 'triangles' of empowerment have emerged as a result of meso-level gender quotas, and women's organizations and women's policy agencies collaborate and offer organizations subsidies and management training" (Ortbals, Rincker, and Montoya 2011, 17–18).

Listening to the Policy Literature

Analysis of statements by international organizations shows that they expect decentralization programs by themselves to lead to women's empowerment. Yet the cross-national statistical evidence shows that, except for subnational expenditure, decentralization is not strongly and significantly correlated with gender equality. Therefore, I examine recent studies of decentralization and women's representation using a cross-institutional lens. This yields a key insight: cases in which decentralization empowers women all share the gender policy trifecta. Further rigorous testing of the gender policy trifecta is needed, which I substantiate in the next section.

Measuring Women's Policy Priorities

The women's organizations I surveyed about their policy preferences, resources, allies, and opposition are peak organizations with some standing and longevity in the political system. These organizations included both feminist and traditional women's groups that I found in Internet searches for women's organizations in the country or in the *International Directory of Women's Organizations* (Asia Pacific InfoServ Party 2001). Asking women's organizations about their policy priorities and their perceptions of the priorities of politicians yields one answer to the fascinating question of how well interests are represented, but we must consider important counterarguments to the reasons that women's organizations give for selecting their top priorities. First, groups are likely to arise when there are needs in society. It is possible that groups arise in response to funding opportunities (Alvarez 1998), but they do not have capacity and are not sustained over the long term if they are not filling a real need in society. Second, groups asked for their top four policy priorities typically list other areas than the ones on which they directly focus. Many groups work in one or two primary areas and then three to five secondary areas. I believe their priority rankings reflect what they think are the most pressing areas in which the government needs to act, including areas outside their services but in areas that will advance their general goals for women's empowerment. I also asked national and subnational politicians to rank their policy priorities for women to examine how well the politicians' priorities matched those of women's groups within their constituencies.

In Part II, I use in-depth country analyses of decentralization in Poland (with one node of the gender policy trifecta; Chapter 3), Pakistan (with two nodes; Chapter 4), and the United Kingdom (with three nodes; Chapter 5). These case analyses are complex, multimethod analyses at multilevels using the country as the major unit of analysis. I present each analysis using the same structure to allow close comparison of the dynamics and outcomes across each country. In each chapter's introduction, I describe which nodes of the gender policy trifecta the country possesses. I report on women's status in that country and then the dynamics of decentralization reform. Next, I report on women's descriptive representation, examining whether women participate descriptively in greater numbers at the meso level of politics than the national level, and the strength of women's organizations and women's policy agencies at the national and subnational level. On the basis of original data on women's policy priorities, I show that women's policy priorities are diverse in each country.

When we look across the cases we find that Poland displays just one node of the trifecta for the first fifteen years of decentralization, and women's descriptive and substantive representation actually decreases. But Poland experiences great improvement in women's descriptive representation and substantive representation after European Union pressure and domestic organizing, which led to the passage of a 2011 gender quota law applying to most elections in Poland. Pakistan displays two nodes of the gender policy trifecta—subnational quotas and subnational women's policy agencies. However, Pakistan displays another kink in the decentralization process. While engendering reforms passed in 2000 created gender-responsive budgeting and quotas at the municipal level, the Eighteenth Amendment to the Pakistani constitution gave the meso level, or provinces, purview over women's rights.[6] Via a shell game, Pakistani leaders give the appearance of significant progress on women's representation at the municipal level, which has 33 percent gender quotas, while shifting equality policy to the meso level, where quotas are just 17 percent. The United Kingdom displays all three nodes of the gender policy trifecta and therefore also shows strong increases in women's descriptive and substantive representation, but the trifecta needs maintenance.

Because Part II demonstrates that the gender policy trifecta leads to women's descriptive and substantive representation and feminist policy outcomes, it is natural that in Chapter 6, I present new cross-national data on the presence of the gender policy trifecta. These data can be a resource for policy makers, advocacy groups, and readers as a whole to show in specific countries what nodes of the trifecta are already present and which nodes activists must build up to achieve women's empowerment. I show that decentralization reforms alone are not sufficient to increase gender equality, as

---

6. See Constitution of the Islamic Republic of Pakistan, available at http://www.pakistani.org/pakistan/constitution.

many international organizations imply. New subnational institutions must themselves be engendered through the gender policy trifecta for women to participate with men as fully democratic citizens at all levels of governance and for policy to respond to the priorities of women, who themselves are a diverse group.

Part II

3

Poland

One Node of the Gender Policy Trifecta

n Poland, decentralization reforms occurred because of the specific political context of socialist countries at the end of the Cold War. From 1945 to 1989, the centralized one-party state prohibited the free expression of political views, traditional Catholic religious beliefs, and differences or inequalities between the sexes (Funk and Mueller 1993; Regulska 1992). Decentralization for Poland, as for many other countries in Central and Eastern Europe, was to be the natural antidote to fifty years of communist rule. However, new neoliberal pressures and a lack of established political parties crowded women out of national and local political life for the first twenty years of democratization (Fuszara 2000; Gal and Kligman 2000; Jaquette and Wolchik 1998; Matland and Montgomery 2003; Regulska 1998; Rueschemeyer 1998; Siemieńska 2003). Poland's entry into the European Union in the ten-country wave from Eastern Europe on May 1, 2004, placed strong external pressures on the country to expand women's economic and political opportunities (Montoya 2013).

Despite expectations, decentralization initially hindered women's political participation in Poland at the meso and local levels. From 1998 to 2011 it had just one node of the gender policy trifecta: meso-level women's policy agencies. European Union influence in Poland combined with the bottom-up activism of the Kongress Kobiet (Congress of Women) led to the passage of the 2011 gender quota law. This statute requires that no gender have fewer than 35 percent of all places on candidate lists submitted by political parties for national and meso-level political offices. On October 25, 2015, the two candidates competing for Poland's office of prime minister were female, the first such European parliamentary election since Norway's in 1993. Beata Szydło's rightist Prawo i Sprawiedliwość (Law and Justice) won, beating out Ewa Kopacz's centrist Platforma Obywatelska (Civic Platform), to form a majority government. The missing node in Poland's gender policy trifecta as of 2015 is meso-level gender-responsive budgeting. Gender-responsive budgeting has not been adopted on the national scale in the National Action Plan for Equal Treatment or in the country's sixteen meso-level units.[1] Without an active node for gender-responsive budgeting at the meso level in Poland, it is difficult for female meso-level legislators or women's policy agency (WPA) leaders to effectively insert issues of taxation and spending on the agenda.

When I speak of decentralization in Poland, I refer to the 1998 creation of sixteen provinces and related legislation specifying meso-level election processes, administrative powers, and revenue sources for the provinces (*województwa*). Polish women actively pushed for democracy on local, meso, and national levels, but also understanding supranational pressure is critical to the Polish case. As part of the accession process, the European Union could not force, but strongly encouraged, adoption of EU gender equality soft law (nonbinding guidelines on gender equality) at the same time that the Kongress Kobiet successfully lobbied the parliament for a new gender quota law.[2] On January 31, 2011, President Bronisław Komorowski signed legislation introducing 35 percent quotas for both genders on party electoral lists. Figure 3.1 shows President Komorowski signing the bill with Kongress Kobiet activist and economist Henryka Bochniarz present.

After intensive lobbying for a 50 percent gender quota on all party lists, legislators compromised on 35 percent. The law requires that the number of candidates of either gender on the electoral lists may not be lower than 35 percent of the overall number of candidates on this list, and for lists that include three candidates, there must be at least one candidate of each gender (Global Database of Quotas for Women 2016c). A second provision ensures that parties do not place women candidates on the bottom of the party list in unelectable positions. This law applies to municipal (*gmina*), county (*powiat*), meso-level, lower house of the national parliament (Sejm), and European Parliament elections. However, it does not apply to elections in municipalities with fewer than twenty thousand residents or to Poland's national upper

---

1. The Network of East-West Women piloted gender-responsive budgeting in the city of Gdańsk (Bałandynowicz 2005), and in 2012 the United Nations Development Programme, with support from the Office of the Government's Plenipotentiary for the Equal Status of Women and Men, supported four pilot municipalities with six months of UN training on gender-responsive budgeting.

2. The Kongress Kobiet was led by Magdalena Środa, former head of the Office of the Government's Plenipotentiary for the Equal Status of Women and Men; the actress Krystyna Janda; and notable Polish politicians, including First Lady Maria Kaczyński and Izabela Jaruga-Nowacka.

Figure 3.1 Polish president Bronisław Komorowski and economist Henryka Bochniarz, president of the Kongress Kobiet, at the signing of Poland's gender quota law on January 31, 2011. (Source: Polish Press Agency)

house of parliament (Senat), which beginning in 2011 elected its members by single-member district instead of party lists, as the Sejm does. Whereas in countries like Spain decentralization fomented women's activism at the meso level and trickled up to quota reforms at the national level (Ortbals 2008), achieving gender equality in Poland's meso-level assemblies required pressure from the European Union and national top-down measures resulting from women's mobilization across the country.

After extensive interviews with male and female politicians in Polish meso-level assemblies in 2004 and 2007, I concluded that female meso-level legislators were masculinized or marginalized. Polish women in meso-level and local politics could express themselves freely—provided they kept women's issues out of the debate (Rincker 2009). My findings confirm a fascinating trend identified by Joanna Regulska and Anne Graham (1997) in their study of women's political opportunities in three Polish communities. They found that men devalued women's participation and experiences in mixed-gender groups organizing in local communities, and consequently, these women backed out of local politics. A Polish interviewee said:

> There is no gender equality: women earn less money, they have the same or more responsibilities than men, they are discriminated

against in the workplace but also in social life. If a woman is active locally, men perceive her not as a leader but as a hardworking no-name. Women can also be viewed as a decoration. Any issue is more important to local authorities than women. If a woman is determined to make a career in public life, people laugh at her; she is always not enough of a woman—not a beauty or something. If she can do it, then she is only a woman. Gender equality—ha![3]

Examination of Poland demonstrates that political, administrative, and fiscal decentralization without related engendering of these reforms does not help women's representation and can even hinder it (Regulska and Graham 1997). In the next section I provide some context on the status of women and democracy in Poland and background on decentralization. Then I lay out my plan for evaluating the gender policy trifecta in Poland.

Status of Women and Democracy

In June 1989, Poland held its first semidemocratic elections in some forty-five years. From 1945 to 1989, Soviet communist ideology heavily shaped the People's Republic of Poland, with a command economy and one-party rule by the Polish United Workers' Party. The socialist worker state constitutionally guaranteed equality of women and men. This constitutional provision was designed to modernize women, moving away from the traditional Catholic Virgin Mary figure of the *matka polka* (Polish mother) to the tractor-riding woman in the fields and factories who could do everything men could do and also manage household affairs (see Figure 3.2). During the socialist period, women achieved parity with men in the powerless Senat but lamented the triple burden of work in the fields and factories; responsibility for cooking, cleaning, and children; and managing the continuous shortage of basic foodstuffs, consumer goods, and even tampons under a government-planned economy (Drakulic 1993; Einhorn 1998; Regulska 1992, 1998; Siemieńska 2003).

The 1978 election of Polish Pope John Paul II and intense economic pressure on the Polish economy wrought by an overgenerous welfare state led electrician Lech Wałęsa in 1980 to establish Solidarity, the first independent trade union in Central and Eastern Europe. General Wojciech Jaruzelski responded to this threat to his authority and fear of Soviet intervention by declaring martial law. During almost ten months of martial law, female leaders

---

3. Interview by the author, May 2007, Poznań, Wielkopolskie, Poland (trans. Monika Ksieniewicz). I argue that "not enough of a woman" indicates masculinization; the phrase "only a woman" indicates marginalization.

MŁODZIEŻY- NAPRZÓD DO WALKI
O SZCZĘŚLIWĄ, SOCJALISTYCZNĄ WIEŚ POLSKĄ

Figure 3.2   Polish poster depicting
changes in women's roles in
public life in Poland, 1940

of the Solidarity movement kept the organization alive while many male leaders wasted away in jail (Penn 2005). By 1989, even political repression could
not silence the growing number of Poles who supported Wałęsa's Solidarity
movement–turned–political party. In the June 1989 elections, Solidarity won
all but one seat that it was allowed to contest. The Polish United Worker's
Party maintained a razor-thin majority in parliament, but it lost all legitimacy as the governing voice of the Polish people (Garton Ash 2002).

   Although we might expect democracy and free elections to bring about
greater rights and participation of women in politics, just the opposite occurred in Poland and in many postcommunist countries transitioning to
democracy (Matland and Montgomery 2003; Denise Walsh 2010; Waylen
2007). Many Poles viewed communist-era enforced equality between the
sexes as unnatural and yearned to express gender difference and Catholic
values rather than follow party-imposed rules. In the transition, women lost
significant formal political power, dropping from 20 to 10 percent of seats in
the Sejm. Remasculinization of politics came about in the 1990s in part because of the country's return to its traditional Catholic roots (Watson 1993).
The primary issue, other than the direction of basic economic reforms, was
the recriminalization of abortion in a 1993 law (see Appendix 4) after forty-
five years of abortion access under the socialist state. The halls of parliament

had few remaining elected women to protect reproductive rights, and hundreds of women's organizations protested to no avail.

Many Polish women gladly gave up their socialist-era political duties as one less burden to shoulder. Increasingly, women were not seen as appropriate for political office, although women and children often bore the brunt of the transition to a competitive, open economy: four years of harsh economic shock therapy entailing high unemployment for women and reduced income support for single mothers (Einhorn 1998). As a male Polish politician told me during an interview in 2004:

> Women in Poland are responsible for the household and the children. Some men will tell you they do equal work in the home, but this is a lie. Maybe something they say on their honeymoons. When children are sick, women will need to be staying home taking care of them, and I am a nice man. I cannot tell them, no, you cannot do that, so I prefer not to hire them. Maybe you can call this a kind of discrimination.[4]

These comments suggest that many women face traditional gender norms when it comes to the division of labor in the household and are penalized for upholding an ethic of care when they apply for private or public sector jobs. If people in workplaces, including political institutions, do not reflect on their biases and adopt engendering reforms, they can effectively exclude women.

In this chapter, I first provide a gendered analysis of the decentralization reform process. Second, I examine descriptive representation, or the number of women's organizations, women in bureaucracies, and women in legislative office at the meso and national levels. I find that wealthier meso units have more women's organizations, although they have generally grown and dispersed across the country since decentralization. In the bureaucratic sector, meso-level women's policy agencies (MWPAs) are important for women's substantive representation in Poland. Although funding is precarious and they are threatened by rightist presidents, MWPAs have displayed much greater responsiveness than meso-level legislatures to women's issues. As of 2015 the average meso-level assembly is at least 25 percent female. Third, I analyze how decentralization has influenced women's substantive representation. On the basis of reports from women's organization leaders in provinces, I find greater responsiveness to women's policy priorities by meso-level officials than those in the Sejm or the national government. Fourth, I examine whether feminist policies are being legislated in Poland and whether passage is associated with the growing influence of women in meso-level and national

---

4. Interview by the author, May 2004, Warsaw, Poland (trans. Kinga Pietrzak).

governance. I conclude by reiterating that women have not been fully empowered by democratization because they do not have all three nodes of the
gender policy trifecta. I now move to provide context for the decentralization
reforms in Poland.

Gendered Analysis of Decentralization

As women and men in Poland adjusted to the new competitive global economy and to harsh public sector cutbacks between 1990 and 1995, the nation
also began rewriting its constitution and re-creating its political institutions.
These reforms included suggestions that decentralization would naturally
break down central communist authority in Warsaw by reinvigorating local
political units at the village or town, county, and meso levels. The forty-
nine provinces in Poland at the time were small and economically weak.
Local-government reformer Jerzy Regulski (2003) recounts extensive discussions and debates with politicians across Poland between 1989 and 2000 as
to the form decentralization would take. By the mid-1990s, the Solidarity
movement had splintered into many political parties, many of which favored
strong decentralization to a smaller number of provinces. On the other side,
the main communist successor party, the Democratic Left Alliance, favored
weaker decentralization to more provinces. Slowly, administrative spending
began shifting to local-level municipalities.

A new constitution was enacted in 1997. It contained only basic statements of gender equality and did not flesh out the decentralized structure
of the new Poland. As in the communist period, the constitution established
de jure gender equality. The 1997 Polish Constitution, chapter 2, article 33,
states:

1. Men and women shall have equal rights in family, political, social
   and economic life in the Republic of Poland.
2. Men and women shall have equal rights, in particular, regarding
   education, employment and promotion, and shall have the right
   to equal compensation for work of similar value, to social security,
   to hold offices, and to receive public honours and decorations.[5]

In 1998, the Sejm passed the 1998 Law on Local Government at the Voivode-
ship Level, which created sixteen meso-level legal units, each with its own
directly elected parliament. The role of these "little Sejms," or *sejmiki*, would
be to implement national legislation and to apply for and allocate European

---

5. See Constitution of the Republic of Poland, available at http://www.sejm.gov.pl/prawo/
konst/angielski/kon1.htm.

Union regional economic development funds. Initially, the *sejmiki* could not tax and spend as they chose. As of 2011, fiscal administrative decentralization in Poland was moderate, with subnational governments collecting 22.2 percent of all taxes. Women would see the least decentralization effects in their descriptive representation.

The new provinces created during 1998 decentralization were more powerful, overall, in their administrative than legislative roles. They held particular responsibility in public safety, education, and economic development. During the late 1990s, health sector reforms that created sixteen provincial Patient Funds, subsidized by an income tax, gave provinces for a time even more political weight. However, the reforms' unpopularity, partly because of underfunding, led to the recentralization of health care in 2002 (Rincker and Battle 2011).

Women's Descriptive Representation in the Sejm and Meso-level Assemblies

Before quotas and decentralization in Poland—that is, before 1997—women's representation in the Sejm was at 13 percent. It increased to almost 24 percent by 2011 after the passage of the quota law. In 1997, the percentage of women in meso-level assemblies ranged from 2 to 20 percent, averaging 11 percent. Thus, before quotas meso-level assemblies were not automatically easier for women to participate in than the national legislature. The movement for quotas arose at the national level rather than being tried out in a few provinces and growing from the bottom up. In 2011, Poland ranged from a low of 13 percent women in the Podlaskie Province assembly up to 44 percent in Łódzkie's. (See Table 3.1.)

Women's representation in meso units grew after the quota law. Interestingly, leftist meso units are not where we see the most women in politics; it is Małopolskie, a largely rural province with high levels of religiosity and whose capital is Kraków. The women come from the rightist parties Samoobrona (Self-Defense of the Republic of Poland), Wspólnota Małopolska (Community Małopolskie Party), and Civic Platform.

Is the concept of leftist ideology meaningful in a postcommunist system like Poland's? In postcommunist systems, leftist and rightist parties might have flipped (Tavits and Letki 2009). The true issue is clericalism, or whether parties support the role of the Catholic Church in political life. I measured leftism in Poland as the percentage of the meso-level vote for the Democratic Left Alliance in the 2001 parliamentary elections (see Public Opinion Research Center 2000). I purposely did not choose presidential elections because personality drives those elections more than party affiliation. Poland's semipresidential system gives more power to the premier anyway.

Table 3.1 Women in national and meso-level assemblies and women by party delegation in Poland, 1997–2011

	1997 % women	2001 % women	2005 % women	2011 % women (no. of women/no. of seats)	Number of women from each party delegation, 2011
National lower house (Sejm)	13.0	20.2	20.4	23.9 (110/460)	16 SLD; 39 PO; 20 PiS; 8 PSL; 13 RP; 13 SP
Average at meso level for Poland	10.4	14.2	16.9	25.3 (142/562)	
Dolnośląskie	7.0	16.7	16.7	33.3 (12/36)	2 SLD; 7 PO; 2 PiS; 1 RD
Kujawsko-Pomorskie	16.0	21.2	15.2	24.2 (8/33)	3 SLD; 4 PO; 1 PSL
Lubelskie	10.0	18.2	21.2	15.8 (6/38)	1 SLD; 3 PO; 2 PiS
Lubuskie	4.4	6.7	10.0	23.3 (7/30)	2 SLD; 3 PO; 1 PiS; 1 PSL
Łódzkie	14.5	22.2	16.7	44.4 (16/36)	3 SLD; 7 PO; 4 PiS; 1 PSL; 1 other
Małopolskie	10.0	17.9	28.2	17.9 (7/39)	3 PO; 3 PiS; 1 SP
Mazowieckie	16.3	17.6	23.5	39.2 (20/51)	1 SLD; 7 PO; 7 PiS; 5 PSL
Opolskie	13.3	20.0	13.3	16.7 (5/30)	2 PO; 1 PSL; 2 independent
Podkarpackie	6.0	6.1	12.1	15.2 (5/33)	1 SLD; 1 PO; 3 PiS
Podlaskie	4.4	10.0	3.3	13.3 (4/30)	2 PO; 2 PiS
Pomorskie	20.0	18.2	21.2	27.3 (9/33)	1 SLD; 7 PO/PSL; 1 PiS
Śląskie	16.0	14.6	10.4	31.3 (15/48)	3 SLD; 9 PO; 3 PiS
Świętokrzyskie	2.2	3.3	10.0	19.2 (5/26)	1 PO; 1 PiS; 3 PSL
Warmińsko-Mazurskie	6.7	6.7	23.3	23.3 (7/30)	4 PO; 3 PSL
Wielkopolskie	6.7	10.3	28.2	17.9 (7/39)	6 PO; 1 PiS
Zachodniopomorskie	13.3	16.7	16.7	30.0 (9/30)	3 SLD; 6 PO

Sources: Druciarek et al. 2012; Global Database of Quotas for Women 2016c; Hinojosa 2012; Inter-Parliamentary Union 2011; Siemienska 2008; author's calculations from provincial assembly websites.

Note: SLD = Sojusz Lewicy Demokratycznej (Democratic Left Alliance), PO = Platforma Obywatelska (Civic Platform), PiS = Prawo i Sprawiedliwość (Law and Justice), RD = Ruch Demokratyczno-Społeczny (Democratic-Social Movement), PSL = Polskie Stronnictwo Ludowe (Polish Peasants' Party; in some regions a German minority party), SP = Solidavna Polska (United Poland), RP = Ruch Palikota (Palikot Movement).

The 2001 parliamentary elections came three elections after the first fully democratic elections in 1991, and I wanted to use election data consistent with the two-turnover democratization test (Huntington 1991). Although this election occurred after the first meso-level elections of 1998, it better taps real left-right sentiment because the election was not one of simply throwing out the rascals but a truer measure of meso units' leftist sentiment that remained after the storm died down. Political party scholar Aleks Szczerbiak (2001) notes a left-right divide in Polish politics in which meso units of the west and north vote leftist, and southern and eastern ones vote for post-Solidarity parties.

In 2007, the writer Manuela Gretowska, who wrote a manifesto titled *Poland Is a Woman*, formed the Women's Party (Partia Kobiet). Though representatives of the Women's Party failed to win representation in 2007 in the Sejm or the European Parliament, the party still planned to contest local elections. In a poster declaring, "Everything for the future: nothing to hide," women of the Women's Party bared all, appearing naked with private parts strategically covered, to raise attention for their electoral campaign in 2007. This ad campaign merits discussion in its own right.

Bell hooks defines feminism as "the movement to end sexism, sexist exploitation, and oppression," and the image of female Polish political candidates baring all reinforces sexism and sexist exploitation rather than challenging it (hooks 2000, 1). Male politicians at times show themselves shirtless (as did Vladimir Putin) to emphasize their masculinity but not fully nude. This ad is designed to draw attention to female candidate's bodies, perhaps reducing them to only their physical selves. The text of the ad suggests Women's Party members are not corrupt, because the women pictured say they have "nothing to hide," but their "everything for the future" stance does not suggest any specific policy positions. Ostensibly the Women's Party created this ad to draw media attention, even if negative, to the Women's Party, but it proved difficult to move past the controversy of the ad content to the policy issues the Women's Party sought to advance. While I believe the Women's Party platform is feminist, this political advertisement is not feminist because it is not working to end the sexist exploitation of women but is capitalizing on bodies to get on the agenda.

The Women's Party platform includes establishing nurseries, fighting discrimination, reimbursing in vitro fertilization costs, legislating abortion rights, providing honest sex education in schools, separating church and state, supporting civil unions, and supporting elder care. This party's activism might have helped the move for the quota law, but its lack of electoral success shows the difficulty in organizing politically on gender in Poland, even though issues like reproductive rights and violence against women are critical.

Table 3.1 lists the number of women in each party delegation in the Sejm and the sixteen meso-level assemblies as of 2014. Because they performed well in subnational elections, we find women in office are from primarily centrist or center-right parties—Civic Platform or Law and Justice. Some of the Civic Platform leadership came from the Freedom Union, a party that voluntarily adopted quotas in the early 1990s but failed to make electoral thresholds by the mid-1990s. Civic Platform supports the 35 percent gender quota. The Polish case shows again that meso-level quotas are needed to increase women's presence in decentralized institutions, affirmatively answering the second guiding question. Still, the Polish system reminds us that although in many countries leftist parties are better allies for women at large and women's representation, this is not true in all systems and at all times.

Capacity and Presence of Women's Organizations and Women's Policy Agencies

Women's groups in Poland have expanded and dispersed since decentralization. The 2002 directory of women's organizations in Poland, maintained by Poland's Center for the Advancement of Women, lists 383 women's organizations, including branches of the same organization in multiple locations (Centrum Promocji Kobiet 2002). Counting the groups and associated branches across the country by province reveals that groups are particularly concentrated in the province of Mazowieckie, with ninety women's groups and the national capital of Warsaw. At the low end, Opolskie reported just four women's groups. In 1997, there were eighty women's groups (not counting branches of the same group), and 60 percent of them were based outside Warsaw. The number grew to 64 percent by 2002. Women's groups such as Europa Donna and the Amazons have formed branches in most provinces, and antiviolence organizations have grown from one in the mid-1990s to thirty-three in 2011, with at least one in each province by 2008 (Ortbals, Rincker, and Montoya 2011).

Active feminists like Izabela Jaruga-Nowacka, Magdalena Środa, and Joanna Kluzik-Rostkowska have ably led the national WPA, which has gone by different names under different governments. Under the leftist Democratic Left Alliance government of Premier Leszek Miller between 2001 and 2004, the key agency for women was the standalone cabinet post of the Office of the Government's Plenipotentiary for the Equal Status of Women and Men, led by Minister Jaruga-Nowacka.[6] While this national ministry had no legislative proposal power, it had a separate budget, a place in cabinet-level discussions, and a ministry title that reflected a feminist agenda.

In 2001, Premier Miller created meso-level ombudspersons for gender equality. Jaruga-Nowacka spearheaded these reforms with the help of women's groups. These meso-level agencies were weakened under center-right coalitions led by Premier Jarosław Kaczyński in 2006 and Premier Donald Tusk in 2008. Women's groups had an ally in the new MWPAs.

---

6. Jaruga-Nowacka, Polish president Lech Kaczyński, First Lady Maria Kaczyński, and 129 other prominent Polish officials died in a TU-154 plane crash in Katyń, Poland, on April 10, 2010. They were on their way to mark the seventieth anniversary of the Katyń massacre, where, in 1940, Russian secret police killed an estimated 22,000 Polish officers, prisoners, and intellectuals. These parallel tragedies are of great significance to Polish citizens because in the same place, on two occasions, Poles lost many of their best and brightest leaders. Russia formally admitted responsibility for the Katyń massacre in 1990. Jaruga-Nowacka's face is the inspiration for the woman pictured in red on the cover of this book.

Gender equality bureaucracies at the national and meso levels have at times been controversial. I asked WPA leaders whether some people opposed the creation of their offices. One subnational ombudsperson said, "It is hard to point to one group against the ombudsperson, maybe because in the beginning it was not very visible. But it is important to underline that in the very beginning a lot of people not involved in gender and politics questioned their function."[7] Another said that her biggest opponents were "men for lack of understanding. They laughed at my work, because they didn't understand what I was doing based on stereotypes rooted in culture."[8] Despite the evidence of these comments, many men and women across Poland brush aside the need for WPAs because they believe that women are already equal to men, that the agency is just a throwback to communist times, or that the possibility of changing treatment of men and women in society causes traditional men (and sometimes women) to sexually harass or otherwise try to put women in their place. Under these circumstances, it can be difficult but is essential for women to stand up to sexist comments from men or women. As one interviewee suggested, "Women don't want to be treated right, because it would mean that they would have to admit that they weren't treated right before."[9] However, it is possible that the presence of WPAs at national and meso levels gave legitimacy to women's inequality. These WPA leaders, not all radical feminists, used their position to promote awareness about equality for women and men and social realities that are not deterministic but are highly probabilistic for women. These realities include the reduced ability to determine how many children to have, a one in eight chance of male partner violence, and perception by society of work productivity that is about 75 percent that of a man. These social obstacles required positive action for women, and the Office of the Government's Plenipotentiary for the Equal Status of Women and Men paved the way for gender quotas passed in 2011 under a rightist president.

After the 2006 parliamentary elections, rightist premier Jarosław Kaczyński closed the Office of the Government's Plenipotentiary for the Equal Status of Women and Men and moved its tasks to the Ministry of Labor and Social Policy. The ministry created a Department for Women, Family, and Counteracting Violence, with Joanna Kluzik-Rostkowska as its leader and half the former office's staff. Because the European Union itself is best suited to addressing policies related to common labor markets, European Union directives

---

7. Interview by the author, May 2007, Warsaw, Poland (trans. Monika Ksieniewicz).

8. Interview by the author, May 2007, Olsztyn, Warminsko-Mazurskie (trans. Monika Ksieniewicz).

9. Interview by the author, May 2007, Gdańsk, Pomorskie, Poland (trans. Monika Ksieniewicz).

also focus on equality of women and men in the workforce (see Montoya 2009). The European Union social funds also target funding for labor-related equality, so moving the agency to the Ministry of Labor made sense.

The Department for Women, Family, and Counteracting Violence focused mostly on women as workers, women's equality in the labor market, and ways to make women's careers in the workplace possible along with meeting familial responsibilities. Its top four priorities deal with women in the workplace. Kluzik-Rostkowska reported to the United Nations Commission on the Status of Women in January 2007 that the highest priority was erasing discrimination in the workplace for women, particularly those forty-five years old and older. After the 2007 elections, when Premier Donald Tusk formed the rightist coalition of Civic Platform and Polish Peasants' Party, he established a position of Plenipotentiary for Equality, naming Elżbieta Radziszewska to the post. This office had fewer resources than its predecessor and was more oriented toward church-accepted goals. Tusk made a strong effort to appear responsive to women's concerns but he offered no substantial policies (see "Poland's Women" 2014). After Tusk stepped down to run for the presidency of the European Council and the election of the second female prime minister, Ewa Kopacz (also from Civic Platform) in 2014, Małgorzata Fuszara was named Plenipotentiary.

Comparing the top policy priorities that leaders of women's organizations reported (see Table 3.2) with those reported in interviews by the national office in 2007, we find only one priority overlap. Why is there is so little matching between women's needs articulated in societal groups and policies pursued on behalf of women within the state apparatus? The positioning of the WPA in the Ministry of Labor shades the mandate and the primary goals of the agency. Its four goals relate to women in the workplace: encouraging hiring of women, educating society and businesses that gender-based employment discrimination is unconstitutional, encouraging family-friendly policies, and promoting work-life balance. So there may be a disconnect between what women's groups want in terms of public policy and the lead agency's

Table 3.2 What women want in Poland, 2007

Policy priorities of women's organizations, aggregated across the country	Policy priorities of national women's policy agency
1. Public awareness campaigns for women's equality (13)	1. Promoting women in the labor market
2. Elimination of violence against women (13)	2. Raising awareness about gender-based employment discrimination
3. Assisting women from rural areas (12)	3. Family-friendly policy
4. Raising awareness about gender-based employment discrimination (11)	4. Reconciliation of work and family life

Note: Numbers in parentheses are the number of leaders who listed the item as a top four priority.

reported priorities. Perhaps the Sejm is the most effective location to push for action on gender equality, particularly when the Sejm wants to signal the European Union that it is taking meaningful action on equality.

WPAs reported being under-resourced, particularly at the subnational level. For example,

> in 2004, the Ministry of Social Policy and Labor allocated 352,000 PLN (cca. 92,500 euros or about 7.6 percent) out of a total budget of 4,615,000 PLN (cca. 1,210,000 euros) for issues associated with violence in family, including centers of crisis intervention. The Ministry allocated 896,400 PLN (cca. 236,000 euros) for family counseling. Government programs to help women victimized by violence are financed by funds allocated to fight alcoholism, which further perpetuates stereotypes about violence against women. In 2004, the State Agency for Prevention of Alcohol Related Problems (PARPA) received state funding in the amount of 998,000 PLN (cca. 263,000 euros) for issues associated with violence in the family. (Open Society Institute 2006)

As of 2007, the national WPA had twelve full-time employees and about fifty part-time employees. In my survey, almost all MWPAs said they had no budget or that the budget was at the discretion of the meso-level-unit governor (*wojewoda*) or the director of the social services department. Zachodniopomorskie Province, the sole exception, had an annual budget of around 6,000 zlotys. None of the MWPAs mentioned having more than one employee. One MWPA director uses an alternative name to camouflage what she really works on. Thus, examining budgets for the ombudspersons is unlikely to yield comparative budgetary numbers when some provinces hide these funds and others simply give extra duties that promote gender equality to people already working in a social ministry.

Not all women's organizations were aware that there was an MWPA in their province, and therefore they did not collaborate. This may be because of the governor's power in appointing the ombudsperson and the relative importance the governor gives to the ombudsperson in terms of resources and other policy duties. One interviewee stated:

> I don't have an opinion about [MWPAs]. I never heard about such an office, and I don't have a clue if such a person works in my voivodeship. Gender equality in the voivodeship—the most glaring problem is gender pay gap. There is clear discrimination based on gender when it comes to higher positions in the private sector and among officials.

Women, if they are on the top ever, have huge achievements, like the vice-mayor of Gmina Nowe Skalmierzyce, Mrs. Bozena Budzik.[10]

From 2011 to 2014, Agnieszka Kozłowska-Rajewicz led the national WPA as a self-identified feminist. Kozłowska-Rajewicz supports gay rights and has partially fulfilled bell hooks's (2000) definition of a feminist as one who endeavors to end sexism, sexist exploitation, and oppression, but she has focused more on women's rights in the labor market. Prime Minister Tusk's subsequent appointment of Małgorzata Fuszara continued this feminist orientation at the national level, although the 2015 election of Prime Minister Szydło is anticipated to result in a more center-right appointment to the office. Most MWPAs are moderate in their rhetoric and implementation, but a few have been actively feminist. Still, many women's organizations view MWPAs as important allies in pushing for gender equality in Poland.

Women's Policy Priorities

With the increase in women's numbers in meso-level assemblies, are representatives addressing their priorities with policies? To determine women's groups' policy priorities, I selected ten women's organization leaders in each of three cities, for a total of thirty leaders, to participate in structured interviews in the summer of 2007. I chose the national capital of Warsaw, in Mazowieckie Province; Gdańsk, in left-leaning Pomorskie Province; and Poznań, in right-leaning Wielkopolskie Province. The latter two provinces have similar economic statuses. I first describe the highest, most frequently discussed policy priorities of women's organization leaders, and then I describe how women's organizations differ across provinces in their policy priorities (see Table 3.2 and Figure 3.3).

Interviews of women's organization leaders revealed they most frequently gave precedence to public awareness campaigns on women's equality. Almost half the organization leaders interviewed—thirteen of thirty—listed public awareness campaigns as one of their top four priorities. Thirteen of thirty leaders also had elimination of violence against women as their number-one priority. Twelve groups mentioned assisting women from rural areas as their key issue.

The first two policy priorities strike at the heart of a controversial campaign for women's equality pursued in the mid-1990s. The *bo zupa była za słona* (because the soup was too salty), public awareness campaign (see Figure 3.4) began in November 1997. It shows a woman whose partner physically

---

10. Interview by the author, May 2007, Poznań, Wielkopolskie, Poland (trans. Monika Ksieniewicz).

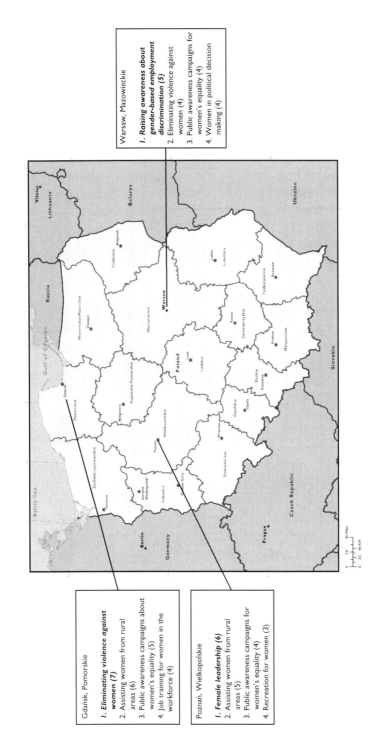

Warsaw, Mazowieckie

1. *Raising awareness about gender-based employment discrimination (5)*
2. Eliminating violence against women (4)
3. Public awareness campaigns for women's equality (4)
4. Women in political decision making (4)

Gdańsk, Pomorskie

1. *Eliminating violence against women (7)*
2. Assisting women from rural areas (6)
3. Public awareness campaigns about women's equality (5)
4. Job training for women in the workforce (4)

Poznań, Wielkopolskie

1. *Female leadership (6)*
2. Assisting women from rural areas (5)
3. Public awareness campaigns for women's equality (4)
4. Recreation for women (3)

Figure 3.3 Policy priorities of women's organizations in Poland, 2007. Numbers in parentheses are the number of leaders who listed the item as a top four priority.

Figure 3.4 Poland's 1997 public awareness campaign against domestic violence, "Because the soup was too salty." (Source: MullenLowe Warsaw; photo by Tomek Sikora)

abused her and justified the abuse by arguing that she had added too much salt to the soup.

Unfortunately, media pundits and comedians reframed the campaign, poking fun at the notion of the bad cook rather than focusing on the abuser's psychological tactic of blaming the victim. The response shows that testing, evaluation, and effective public relations of public awareness campaigns are critical in achieving the objective of changing hearts and minds on gender inequality issues.

The third most frequently mentioned policy priority was assisting women from rural areas. As one interviewee noted, "Women's [nongovernmental organizations] should take care of women from rural areas, but we don't have such opportunities. Nobody helps us. Nobody cares for women's issues. We are taking a step back to the Middle Ages."[11]

While women's organizations across the nation agreed that public awareness of women's equality, eliminating violence against women, assisting women from rural areas, and raising awareness about gender-based employment discrimination are of top importance, women's organizations in different provinces emphasized some distinct policy priorities. This evidence for provincial diversity in what women want is an important new justification for engendered decentralization.

In the northern province of Pomorskie, on the Baltic Sea, women were heavily involved in the shipyards and formation of the Solidarity movement in the 1970s and 1980s. Their history of political activism can be seen in

---

11. Interview by the author, May 2007, Gdańsk, Pomorskie, Poland.

relatively high levels of women's representation in *sejmik* elections in 1998, 2001, and 2005 (20.0, 18.2, and 21.2 percent, respectively). When interviewed, many members of women's groups described their first policy priority to be the elimination of violence against women. Their second priority was assisting women from rural areas, who are not included in wider social organizations that support women in the workplace, economic opportunity, and care for children or elders. The third priority women's organization leaders expressed was the need for public awareness campaigns on the equality of women. The fourth priority was job training, reflecting the downturn in demand from the shipyards in Gdańsk, Gdynia, and Sopot.

The western province of Wielkopolskie has a large number of women's organizations, thirty-two in 2002. Here, women's organization leaders emphasized the absolute need for female leadership across politics and business. Despite major gains in the percentage of women in the Wielkopolskie *sejmik* (6.7, 10.3, 28.2 percent, respectively), women's organization leaders did not think their viewpoints were important to meso-level politicians under the rightist Civic Platform. As one interviewee stated:

> In our voivodeship local authorities [of Civic Platform] don't take any actions for women. They don't even care about women's issues and the situation of women in the voivodeship. They don't respond to our invitations, and they don't even want to meet us.[12]

The second, third, and fourth policy priorities were assisting women from rural areas, the need for public awareness campaigns on women's equality with men, and recreation for women.

In Mazowieckie, women's organization leaders consistently described raising awareness about gender-based employment discrimination as the top priority issue. The capital city of Warsaw has many women's groups. Those surveyed ranged in membership from three members to five thousand, with an average of sixty-eight members. Mazowieckie, the largest province by population with over five million residents, boasts the highest gross domestic product per capita of all the provinces. Because it is a population and industry hub, it makes sense that women feel the gender pay gap most keenly here. The second priority was eliminating violence against women, and the third was the need for public awareness campaigns to raise awareness and educate the populace about gender inequality. Intimating the 2010 campaign for quotas, the fourth most often mentioned policy priority was women in political decision making.

---

12. Interview by the author, May 2007, Poznań, Wielkopolskie, Poland (trans. Monika Ksieniewicz).

While I could not survey women's organizations across all sixteen provinces, it is instructive that MWPAs in three provinces present a wide range of top policy priorities, including fourteen unique priorities MWPAs pursue that the national WPA does not. This reality suggests that the national WPA allows variation in what MWPAs pursue and that what women want differs significantly across meso units in Poland (see Table 3.3).

The reported policy priorities of MWPAs tend to match among themselves better than they do with the national WPA priorities. In Pomorskie,

Table 3.3 Differences in policy priorities between national and meso-level women's policy agencies (MWPAs) in Poland, 2007

Meso-level unit	Number of priority differences	MWPA priorities differing from the national WPA
Dolnośląskie	3	Advice for victims of mobbing Lectures about violence against women Lectures on EU law
Kujawsko-Pomorskie	3	Financial support of NGOs Grant assistance Legal assistance for abuse victims
Lubelskie	3	Foster care Eliminating violence against women Women's health
Łódzkie	3	Foster care Women's health Domestic violence
Mazowieckie	1	Public awareness of women's equality
Opolskie	3	Public awareness of women's equality Women in political decision making Food assistance
Pomorskie	4	Public awareness of women's equality Reproductive choice Gender budgeting Women in political decision making
Śląskie	3	Public awareness of women's equality Legal assistance Women as political leaders
Warmińsko-Mazurskie	2	Eliminating violence against women Foster care
Wielkopolskie	2	Public awareness of women's equality Legal assistance
Zachodniopomorskie	3	Foster care Eliminating violence against women Prenatal care
Total unique policy priority differences	14	

the reported policy priorities of the MWPA minister appointed under a left-ist governor were public awareness of equality, reproductive rights, gender budgeting, and women in political decision making. The Pomorskie WPA therefore matched one of the top four priorities of women's organizations in the meso-level unit, compared to the national WPA, which matched none. Interestingly, reproductive rights figured highly in the personal agenda of this minister. This interest is partly because of Pomorskie's location on the Baltic Sea. The Women on Waves movement helped ensure reproductive rights for women by shipping them outside the formal maritime Polish borders, to where they could lawfully have an abortion, recuperate, and return home. This minister might have perceived that her role in getting women from anywhere in Poland access to abortion was larger than that of most other MWPA ministers because only three other meso units have sea access. Her other priorities were increasing women's political presence and influence in decision making and changing views on women in society.

The subsequent Pomorskie omsbudperson, appointed under a conservative governor, expressed a very different set of policy priorities that were more in line with the national women's policy agency agenda. Her policy priorities included promoting family development and fighting exclusion, profamily policy, reconciliation of work and family life, and foster care. These priorities reflect a more conservative Catholic emphasis on the family rather than on the girl or woman as an individual and mesh with European Union priorities to improve women's access to the labor market. In Wielkopolskie, the MWPA reported that its policy priorities were public awareness of women's equality and counteracting discrimination, legal assistance for women, assistance for rural women, and reconciliation of work and family life, matching two of four women's organization priorities.

Assessment of Women's Descriptive and Substantive Representation

Since the passage of the 2011 quota law, women's descriptive representation has increased markedly. The percentage of women in meso-level office increased from 16.9 percent in 2005 to 25.3 percent in 2011, when the first regional elections after the quota law was passed were held. This 8 percent increase can be traced to the new quota law. While we see a few meso units actually drop in their percentage of women in office after the quota law (like Małopolskie, Lubelskie, and Wielkopolskie), this is more than offset by gains in other meso units, where a typical configuration is nine women and twenty-one men in a thirty-member assembly. In Śląskie, the percentage of women in office tripled in the first postquota election, to 31.3 percent. Measures to increase women's descriptive representation in Poland led to women increasing their presence by, on average, 4 percentage points every election before quotas, gaining more than 8 percent after the quota's institution.

In meso-level assemblies, gains in women's descriptive representation have not yet been matched by gains in women's substantive representation. The *sejmiki* thus far have not been sites of legislation on domestic violence, family-friendly policy, development of nurseries, or the other thirty policy areas affecting women and girls listed in my surveys. Decentralization has led to little in the way of substantive representation or responsiveness by meso-level legislatures to the top policy priorities of both traditional and feminist women's groups. For example, a women's group leader said:

> In my voivodeship there is no gender equality policy at all. Our local, small events have to be carried out in a subtle, delicate way, because this voivodeship is traditionally patriarchal. A family is a family, and maybe women themselves don't see the need for a change.[13]

Conclusion

In response to the survey in 2007, many women's organization leaders expressed disappointment in how Polish society and many elected officials were dealing with the issue of gender equality, often not taking it seriously. As Rosabeth Moss Kanter (1977) found in her seminal study of organizational behavior, a dominant group often belittles differences in a weaker group when they are pointed out, makes the group's issues humorous rather than taking them seriously, and points to token group members who have succeeded as proof that no discrimination exists, when these successful members of marginalized groups often face much more serious obstacles to that success. Most meso-level ombudspersons worked without a salary or resources, but through their commitment and sacrifice, they organized critical events to raise awareness about the frequency of violence against women, discrimination in the workplace, and the need for expanded child-care options and for fathers to serve equally as caregivers within the household. Still, Poland answers the second guiding question affirmatively, because more women were elected after passage of gender quotas. Before meso-level gender quotas, the percentage of women in meso-level assemblies lagged the percentage of women in the national parliament, growing only 4 percentage points each election. After quotas were passed in 2011, and first implemented in 2014, the number of women in meso-level office increased markedly. In 2018, during the second postquota round of meso-level elections in Poland, we will see whether women's descriptive representation has been affected by the 2011 quota law.

---

13. Interview by the author, May 2007, Gdańsk, Pomorskie, Poland.

Significant policy changes have occurred in Poland on the national and meso levels, including progress enshrined in the 2005 law on counteracting violence in the family, the 2011 child-care law, and the 2011 gender quota laws. While Poland's membership in the European Union has influenced these pieces of legislation, the debate and activism fomented on the meso level by the national WPA also influenced the 2010 Act for Equal Treatment, which sets out methods for counteracting violations of equal treatment. The Office of the Government's Plenipotentiary for the Equal Status of Women and Men and national and MWPA programs' goal of overcoming violence against women and unequal pay raised awareness of gender inequality. These government offices on gender equality inspired debate on these issues and the formation of the Kongress Kobiet, culminating in the first gender quotas in the postcommunist era. The passage of gender quotas in Poland was no small feat, especially in a country that had disdained quotas as a tool of the previous one-party socialist system.

On the basis of this research, my key policy recommendation is for Poland to pass gender-responsive budgeting at the national and meso levels, the only node of the gender policy trifecta that it lacks. Since 2011 Poland has had the other two nodes. (See Figure 3.5.)

Poland acted in 2011 to ensure women's participation in national and meso-level assemblies with a 35 percent candidate gender quota law. Poland already has active national and MWPAs on which to build. Gender-responsive

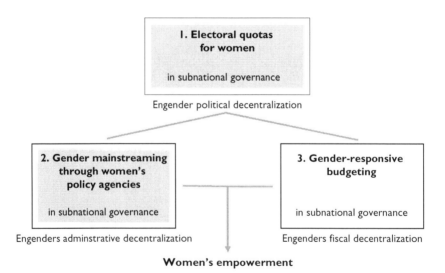

Figure 3.5 The gender policy trifecta in Poland. A shaded box means the node is present; an unshaded box means it is not. Poland had just one node of the trifecta (gender mainstreaming) until the gender quota law went into effect in 2011.

budgeting would encourage assembly members to seek input from women's organizations and would institutionalize women's policy priorities by requiring elected officials to justify that their expenses and revenues are taking into account the specific interests of women in their territorial units. If gender-responsive budgeting is adopted also in meso-level assemblies, I expect to see them acting to substantively represent women: working on job training programs for women in Pomorskie and advancing female leadership in industry and public life in Wielkopolskie. Women's organizations in these provinces mentioned these as top policy priorities. Affirmatively answering the first guiding question, women's policy priorities in Poland vary significantly within the country—as much as they do across Pakistan and the United Kingdom. Also, I found that MWPAs and women's organizations are extremely important for women's representation (answering the third guiding question), providing representation when meso-level legislatures were not open to gendered concerns. Adding the missing node of gender-responsive budgeting would increase budgetary support for the national WPA and MWPA leaders.

4

Pakistan

Two Nodes of the Gender Policy Trifecta

Why you are getting shattered and tired of every moment
Since your soul has been tolerating this enmity and aggression?
So now do not fear anything, as you are not less than anyone
There is life because of you, and there is brightness because of
    you
Your work is to delight everyone
Around you and along with the riverside, may all the waves get
    symmetry on your feet
So make your greatness and bravery part of yourself
And your tears will light up and glow the stars
There are some past few pictures left, and chains are being
    broken
The distance that is left is much less, and the destination is not
    that far

—Naveeda Sultan, "Kuch Sapanay Hain" (official song of
the Pakistani Ministry of Women's Development)[1]

In Pakistan, political leaders have established institutions like the Ministry of Women Development to increase women's status and political participation. Leaders have also enacted decentralization reforms under the guise of expanding freedom and democracy in the country. While women's participation in local government elections of 2000–2001 spurred their increased participation in the 2002 National Assembly elections (see Jamal 2013, 16), gender equality and decentralization reforms have not been aligned to fully empower women. Thus far, these reforms have been subjected to shell games, with shuffling and motion to look progressive but with limited improvements in democratization and gender equality. For example, decentralization in Pakistan appears to give locals power and stake in the system, but Pakistan's dictators have often designed decentralization to buy off a local cadre

---

1. The song, performed by Waqar Ali, is available at http://www.youtube.com/watch?v=NUmkvjdONnI.

who in turn elect an autocratic central president and then fail to allow local elections for decades at a time. Gender equality reforms appear to present all kinds of opportunities for women but too often benefit only female relatives of status quo, powerful male politicians. If Pakistani leaders had been sincere about legal and institutional reforms to engender governance, General Pervez Musharraf would have supported the fullest prosecution of the rapists in the 2002 Mukhtar Mai case (see below), rather than placing the victim under house arrest and preventing her from speaking abroad about her case and women's rights.[2] Likewise, Pakistani police officers would have stepped in to stop family members from the honor killing of pregnant twenty-five-year-old Farzana Iqbal on May 27, 2014, outside a Lahore court (see Raja and Houreld 2014). If Prime Minister Nawaz Sharif had been serious about women's legal equality in Pakistan, he would have advocated the extension of 33 percent gender quotas and the Gender Reform Action Plan to Pakistan's provinces, because the Pakistani constitution's Eighteenth Amendment provides that meso units have the right to make policies on women's rights and human rights.[3]

In this chapter, I examine how decentralization has affected women's political representation in Pakistan. Even though circumstances have improved since the 2007 state of emergency, pervasive challenges to democratization in Pakistan remain. For example, in spring 2014 journalist and Geo news anchor Hamid Mir was shot in the chest six times for speaking critically against the regime and Pakistani Taliban, the Karachi airport was attacked by the Pakistani Taliban and twenty-six killed, and the government shut down Geo media during the London trial of Altaf Hussain, leader of the Muttahida Quami Movement (a Pakistani political party) (see Khan 2014; Declan Walsh 2014; Walsh and Masood 2014).

Throughout this book, I have used Tulia Falleti's definition of decentralization as "a process of state reform composed by a set of public policies that transfer responsibilities, resources, or authority from higher to lower levels of government in the context of a specific type of state" (2005, 328). When I speak of decentralization in Pakistan, I refer to all the following: reforms in 2000 that transferred authority and some responsibilities to municipalities through the 2000 Local Government Ordinance, gender quota laws, the Gender Reform Action Plan affecting gender balance in municipal and meso-level bureaucracy, and the 2010 Eighteenth Amendment to the Pakistani constitution, which transferred authority to the meso level for policies

---

2. Ironically, Musharraf was put on Pakistan's exit control list and prevented from traveling abroad to escape murder charges and treason accusations for ordering the 2007 Emergency. See Agence France-Presse 2014.

3. See Constitution of the Islamic Republic of Pakistan, available at http://www.pakistani .org/pakistan/constitution.

on women's development and human rights.[4] While these decentralization policies appear to promote significant opportunities for women, in reality they have not led to a significant shift in the balance of power between men and women in Pakistani society. Most importantly, reforms for women have occurred only at the municipal level, while the Pakistani constitution states that provinces determine laws relating to the equal protection of women. This reality makes it extremely difficult for Pakistani women to form triangles of empowerment at any level of governance. Pakistan's dictators and generals have in the past touted decentralization reforms as expanding freedom in the country while apparently using them to garner municipal electoral support. Generally, local politicians help select, and therefore receive patronage from, provincial and national politicians. In Pakistan, provincial politicians include feudal landowners empowered under British colonial rule, and presidents often view them as rivals.

First, I provide some context on the status of women and democracy in Pakistan and then background on decentralization. Next, I lay out my plan for evaluating the gender policy trifecta in Pakistan.

Status of Women and Democracy

As in many countries, the status of women in Pakistan is a complicated issue with bright highs and dismal lows. Women are visible in high-profile political roles in Pakistan. For example, Figure 4.1 shows a member of the provincial assembly of Balochistan, Shama Parveen Magsi, discussing education policy with her former colleague Shafique Ahmed Khan. This photo shows the possibility of female political leadership in Pakistan, although in practice it is open only to women of the highest social class whose husbands have served in politics as well. Though more diverse women's participation in Pakistan is necessary, the photo nonetheless shows a bright high for the status of women in Pakistan.

On one hand, Pakistanis supported Benazir Bhutto's election to the high office of prime minister in 1988.[5] On the other hand, the 2012 Oscar-winning Pakistani film *Saving Face*, directed by Sharmeen Obaid-Chinoy, convinced many abroad that Pakistani women have no rights or privileges

---

4. These policies are summarized in Appendix 5 and are discussed at length later in the chapter.

5. Farida Jalalzai (2013) shows that Bhutto with her election cracked the glass ceiling in Pakistan, in contrast to other developing, nondemocratic countries where women have come to power because of familial ties to politics but were often undermined in their role. Bhutto was in office until 1990 and then again from 1993 to 1996. Her father, former Pakistani president and then prime minister Zulfikar Ali Bhutto, was removed from office by General Mohammad Zia-ul-Haq in a 1974 coup and executed.

Figure 4.1 Deliberations of members of provincial Pakistani parliaments, 2007. (Source: Courtesy of Irfan Mirza)

and that the women's movement in Pakistan is nonexistent. Admittedly, the number of Pakistani women professionals, the natural leaders of a women's movement, is fairly small. According to government statistics, about a quarter of women participate in the paid labor force. Yet women were very active in the 2007–2009 democratizing Lawyer's Movement in Pakistan, which used protests, demonstrations, and even two long marches to restore the independence of the Supreme Court (Rincker, Aslam, and Isani 2016). Moreover, women have been active in right-wing parties like Jamaat-e-Islami in articulating that, rather than seeking Western feminist ideas of autonomy and separation from their families, the state should uphold the ability of men of all classes to achieve *kafalat*. *Kafalat* is the "protection of women . . . necessary to maintain the gendered separation of responsibility and reduce social interaction between men and women . . . emphasized by Maulana Maududi [in 1939] as the cornerstone of an Islamic social system" (Jamal 2013, 187). However, women's contributions to the country's economy go underreported for religious and class-based reasons. For example, husbands in traditional households do not provide information to social scientists or surveyors about their wives or admit that their wives work. Women engage in many income-generating activities "at home, ranging from sewing and embroidery to small scale manufacturing, such as stringing garlands or gluing straps to shoes. However, all these income generating activities are not considered work either by them or the men in their families" (Ahmad and Khan 2010, 4). Despite women in Pakistan providing a huge resource of unpaid agricultural labor, they hardly ever hold title to the land and rarely inherit property. It is estimated that 73 percent of rural women work, but official government statistics of the past have noted just 193 women workers (Mumtaz and Shaheed 1988). But women's activism in Pakistan is greater than these facts and figures make it appear. Significant women's groups existed even before 1947, when women participated in public demonstrations and campaigns for education, the creation of a Pakistani homeland, and the caliphate movement (Javaid

2006). Women were an important constituency in the lead-up to independence, but women's issues fell to the wayside after 1947 as leaders dealt with the more pressing issues of refugees, war with India, and poverty. Pakistani women achieved the right to vote in all elections in 1956; before that only landed women (since 1935) or literate women could vote (1947).

From 2008 to 2013 Pakistan experienced its longest term of civilian rule. This was no small feat, as Pakistan had been dominated by military or communist-style dictatorships from the time of its formation (Rincker 2013). The founding of the Pakistani state came at the behest of Muhammad Ali Jinnah, "the great leader," or *quaid-i-azam*. After the subcontinent won its independence from Britain in 1947, Jinnah argued that Muslims would be marginalized or persecuted if they remained in the majority-Hindu India. Although Jinnah took power hoping to craft a secular state, Islam was the common thread uniting diverse ethnic peoples that included Pashtos, Punjabis, Balochis, Kashmiris, Sindhis, and Mohajirs (refugees). To some extent Islam even bound Shiite and Sunni sects (Sayeed 1997). Lawrence Ziring argues that Jinnah embraced the British "viceregal model," leading to a strong executive allied with the army and the feudal elite and a weak legislative and civil society (Ziring 1997, 149; McGrath 1996). Particularly during the first thirty years of its existence, Pakistan required a strong military state, as it unsuccessfully fought India to retain East Pakistan (Bangladesh) and Kashmir (Shafqat 1997). Pakistani elites therefore did not insist on democratic procedures and rule of law. In 1999, Musharraf deposed democratically elected Prime Minister Nawaz Sharif for alleged corruption. The Pakistani Supreme Court allowed Musharraf to seize power under the "doctrine of necessity" but ordered that elections be held within three years (Shah 2002, 67). Shortly after the September 11, 2001, attacks in the United States, President George W. Bush crafted a coalition to combat terrorism: in exchange for Pakistan's support, the United States gave aid to Pakistan and lifted economic and trade sanctions (Shah 2002).

Pakistan has a semipresidential system comprising a president and a prime minister. The Eighteenth Amendment to the Pakistani Constitution, passed in 2010, gave more power to the elected prime minister. An electoral college composed of members of the provincial legislatures and members of both houses of Parliament (Majlis-e-Shoora) select the president. The lower house of Parliament, the National Assembly, is the predominant decision-making body. Members are elected to the National Assembly by proportional representation. Although Pakistan's political party landscape is fluid, as of 2016, there are nine party groupings in Pakistan. These nine party groups draw on and cut across social cleavages in Pakistani society, including traditional army elites, agrarian interests, religious sectors, views on international relations, and ethnic groups. I organize my discussion of these nine parties into four party types: successor parties (PML-N and PML-Q), populist parties (PPP and PTI), religious parties (JI and JUI-F), and ethnically based parties (MQM, PMAP, and BNP).

Two political parties are successor parties that have roots in the Pakistan Muslim League social movement that was led by Mohammad Ali Jinnah. The first of these is the Pakistan Muslim League–Nawaz (PML-N), led by Nawaz Sharif; the second is the Pakistan Muslim League–Quaid-i-Azam (PML-Q), formed when Musharraf deposed Sharif in 1999, barred Sharif from subsequent elections, and exiled him. It was not until 2007 protests against Musharraf and the subsequent signing of the Legal Framework Order suspending court cases against Sharif and Benazir Bhutto for corruption that they were able to return to Pakistan from exile to contest in elections and oust Musharraf.

The two main populist parties are the Pakistan People's Party (PPP) and the Pakistan Tehreek-i-Insaf (PTI). The formerly leftist PPP emerged in 1967 after the civil war in which East Pakistan became the independent state of Bangladesh. Founded by Zulfikar Ali Bhutto, this party advocated a socialist platform and was elected to power in 1971 and 1977. However, after a controversial trial Bhutto was hanged. Bhutto's daughter Benazir served as prime minister between 1988 and 1990 and again between 1993 and 1996. Musharraf ceded control of the military in 2007, and Benazir returned from exile in December 2007 to compete in the January 2008 elections. A group allegedly linked to al-Qaeda assassinated Bhutto December 27, 2007, two weeks before the general election. In 2008, Bhutto's husband, Asif Ali Zardari, led the PPP and became president, and PPP member Yousaf Raza Gilani was elected premier of the National Assembly and minister of economic and social affairs. The second and more recently created populist party is the PTI, led by former cricketer Imran Khan. While it has a base among Pashtuns, this populist and youth-oriented party advocates social democracy and peace talks with the Pakistani Taliban. It has strengthened from 2007 onward but failed to perform in the 2013 elections, serving in opposition to the PML-N's Sharif. In 2012, Khan said that he supports women's rights but also supports modesty in clothing in traditional meso units (Mishra 2012).

Religion-based parties are also part of Pakistani politics, such as the now-disbanded Muttahida Majlis-e-Amal (MMA), which opposed Musharraf's coalition with the United States in the war on terrorism. As of 2016, the two main religion-based parties in Pakistan are the Jamaat-e-Islami (JI) and Jamiat Ulema-e-Islam (JUI-F, centered in southern Khyber Pakhtunkhwa and northern Balochistan). They stand for government policies that follow Islamic religious principles. Members of these parties often supported legal restrictions imposed by General Mohammad Zia-ul-Haq, such as the Hudood Ordinances (laws of evidence and punishment based on Sharia law) described in Appendix 5. A sizable section of urban middle-class Pakistani women who follow traditional norms of their religion and do not want to participate in public life, preferring *kafalat*, support and work with the Jamaat-e-Islami (Ahmad 2010; Iqtidar 2011; Jamal 2013).

Finally, three ethnically oriented parties sit in the National Assembly. The Muttahida Quami Movement (MQM), a party that emerged in 1978 to represent the interests of Muslim immigrants to Pakistan after the secession of Bangladesh from Pakistan in 1971. Mohajirs, or Urdu-speaking Muslim migrants, particularly resented quotas for Sindhis in Pakistani university slots and civil service. MQM party leader Altaf Hussain was arrested in London in 2014 for money laundering and is suspected of supporting violence against political opponents (see Reif 2009). Two smaller ethnically based parties are most active at the provincial level in Balochistan and Khyber Pakhtunkhwa: the Pakhtunkhwa Milli Awami Party (PMAP) and Balochistan National Party (BNP). Though they hold few seats in the National Assembly, I mention these smaller Pashtun and Balochi parties because they play a large role in the provincial assemblies of Khyber Pakhtunkhwa and Balochistan.

These nine party groups have held differing views on women's rights, but generally speaking, the former MMA and Jamaat-e-Islami have opposed laws to improve women's status in Pakistan. The PPP and PML-N have been somewhat supportive of women's rights but can be regarded as status quo parties, because their members tend to come from families with long political dynasties. Women in Pakistan face structural limitations because of their gender, but membership in a high social class lessens these limitations. For example, many PPP assembly members come from the rural gentry, sometimes called *vaderas*, or feudal-style landlords, who have resisted major social changes in landholding or agricultural work patterns. Critics called former PPP prime minister Benazir Bhutto a "feudal princess" who did not challenge the Hudood Ordinances (Darymple 2007). In short, urban upper-class women from the PML-N or rural *vadera*-class women from the PPP may enjoy rights and privileges greater than the vast population living under the poverty line. But choose one man and one woman from the same social class in Pakistan, and generally speaking the man will be accorded more worth, respect, and rights of movement, ownership, and bodily integrity.

Critics of Benazir Bhutto aside, many activists argue that Pakistani women held their highest status during the administration of PPP leader Zulfikar Ali Bhutto. During the 1970s, women achieved many notable firsts in highly prestigious and visible places in society. For example, women held the office of university chancellor, Speaker of the Parliament, and governor of Sindh Province (Javaid 2006, 43). Khawar Mumtaz and Farida Shaheed (1988) relate that a women's movement began to take shape in Pakistan only in the 1980s as a delayed reaction to the harsh policies against women instituted by Zia-ul-Haq. To provide some context, in 1977 Zulfikar Ali Bhutto's PPP was reelected in a landslide, but subsequently Bhutto faced charges of election-rigging and corruption. Zia-ul-Haq seized power and executed Bhutto and then sought to legitimize his authoritarian regime by drawing on traditional Muslim principles, including veiling for women.

How does the practice of veiling affect women's status in Pakistan? Leila Ahmed's brilliant work *Women and Gender in Islam* (1992) reminds us not to place too much attention on women's veiling as a marker of difference with nonveiling cultures or religions but to instead try to connect with and understand individual women as they practice Islam. As Pakistani girls grow into young women and prepare for marriage, family attitudes toward Islam, socioeconomic status, and levels of education all affect women's mobility and the extent to which they practice purdah, "the practice of modest behavior and seclusion from the view of men outside the family" (Halvorson 2005, 22). For example, wearing a hijab, head scarf, or burka, a full-length veil that covers even the eyes, separates women from nonfamilial men and shows purity and devotion to God. Yet there are strong debates among feminists about the role of purdah in women's subordination in Islamic culture (see, for example, Mernissi 1992; Scott 2010).

While women of any socioeconomic status might observe purdah by veiling, particularly for poorer women a burka functionally protects women from male strangers when they work outside the home (Bowen 2008; Mumtaz and Shaheed 1988). In short, the practice of purdah, through both veiling and the separation of male and female physical spaces, is nuanced and complex. For women, wearing a veil can be a sincere individual expression of religious values, a statement against the perceived empty values of Western society, a nonchoice for a woman enforced by family or larger community, a class marker, a dispensation from extra work, or any combination thereof. More than the choice of whether to wear a veil, the gendered nature of spaces in Pakistan, and the lack of enforceable rights for women who cross into these spaces, limits girls' and women's access to transportation services, health facilities, and work opportunities.[6]

Gendered Analysis of Decentralization

According to *Wikipedia*'s population clock, in 2016 Pakistan has the sixth-largest population in the world, with 194 million citizens ("List of Countries"

---

6. Halvorson notes, "A routine visit to the health center or school located in the middle of town requires crossing these invisible boundaries into the male domain" (2005, 30). Colloquially, girls' work is *chota kam*, or "small work" of household, child care, and fields. Boys' work is *bara kam*, or "big work" like chopping fuel, harvesting crops, and building irrigation systems (Halvorson 2005, 31).

2016). For most of its existence, military leaders have dominated Pakistan. Despite the 2008 parliamentary elections, Freedom House ranks Pakistan as a "partly free" country (Freedom House 2014). Corruption, underdevelopment, and poverty present major challenges to delivering the rule of law and a decent standard of living to the majority of the people. A quarter of Pakistan's population lives below the poverty line, and the literacy rate is under 50 percent. Pakistan has been central to U.S. foreign policy throughout the Cold War and particularly after the attacks of September 11, 2001, as it lies between Iran, Afghanistan, China, and India. Conflict continues between Pakistan and India related to historical disputes over Azad Jammu and Kashmir, India's assistance to Bangladesh in its breaking away from Pakistan, both countries' nuclear capabilities, and the alleged Pakistani identity of the 2008 Mumbai terrorists.

In theory, decentralization has been a key policy suggestion for making government more accessible to ordinary Pakistani citizens and thus more democratic. The 1956 constitution established Pakistan as a federal system consisting of the four provinces of Sindh, Punjab (home to half of Pakistan's population), Balochistan, and the North-West Frontier Province. In addition to the capital Islamabad, there are also the Federally Administered Tribal Areas, Azad Jammu and Kashmir, and Gilgit-Baltistan (formerly known as the Northern Areas). This gives Pakistan a total of eight subnational units.

The shell game strategy of decentralizing to look democratic while giving out patronage has an illustrious history in Pakistan. General Mohammad Ayub Khan created the "basic democracies," or local councils that seemed authentically democratic, but the "basic democrats" were his political allies and friends who could bypass the strength of provincial elites with ties to the British. The basic democrats conveniently received authority to serve as the electoral college to reelect Ayub Khan as president. To please the *vaderas*, national leaders like Zia-ul-Haq in 1971 and Musharraf in 2002 enforced decentralization of political power to the local notables to weaken potential provincial or midlevel elites who had been empowered under British colonial rule (Cheema, Khwaja, and Qadir 2006). Pakistan's history has primarily been as a nondemocratic state prone to military coups, and its leaders have promoted decentralization to seem democratic.

Musharraf used decentralization reforms and gender reforms to legitimize his authority to rule. He decentralized to the local level to bypass and counterweight the authority of provincial rivals. Musharraf's 2000 Decentralization of Power Program moved fiscal and political authority to the local or municipal level rather than the meso level. This was followed by the 2001 Local Government Ordinance (Aslam and Yilmaz 2011). Meso units, or provinces, are already quite strong and also have strong identities. Pakistan's fiscal decentralization is low, as provinces collect 0.45 percent of national revenues. Administrative decentralization accounts for 29.2 percent of government expenditures. The most robust facet is political decentralization, although strong connections to central politicians thwart this. Local governments receive revenue not as much from their own ability to tax as from provincial and national transfers. Trappings of local control, such as citizen community boards created to maintain accountability over local politicians and school management and water management committees, exist, but other avenues of decentralization have stalled. In Punjab, "political decentralization has superseded administrative and fiscal reforms" (World Bank 2009, vii). So spending authority has barely increased at the local level, and the ability to tax has not devolved significantly.

Also in 2000, Musharraf introduced the Gender Reform Action Plan (GRAP) to honor Pakistan's commitment to the United Nation's Convention on the Elimination of All Forms of Discrimination against Women (CEDAW) and other conventions and to present Pakistan as a modern, enlightened democracy where women are important political participants in the meso-level and local political systems. The GRAP establishes that effectively 29 percent of local-level elected councilors and bureaucrats will be women. While the GRAP appears to be a huge boost for women, in fact there are three key drawbacks. First, the GRAP increases women on councils but does not set a quota for leadership or mayoral positions. For example, a World Bank report notes, "the strongest figure in the Pakistan local government is that of district mayor [*nazim*] who heads both the council and the executive. He is indirectly elected by the council" (World Bank 2009, 14). Pakistani mayors tend to be male; this contrasts, for example, with the structure of Indian government and quotas that require that one-third of village councils, or panchayats, selected by lottery, have female mayors (Chattopadhyay and Duflo 2004). Further, social network analysis reveals that district mayors in Punjab are deeply embedded within informal networks of politicians connected to the central and provincial levels and therefore have an independent political standing (Aslam 2010). District mayors have first-degree familial links to the politicians that formally belong to a national political party, with the majority belonging to the ruling party at the center. Second, there are strong concerns that, in the early years of the GRAP, many illiterate women were being chosen by male *nazims* and other influential male politicians, limiting the power and autonomy of women in local office. Third, the structure of local elections in Pakistan does not facilitate the election of nonquota women. Local elections in Pakistan use the first-past-the-post method, which is not as representative of women as proportional representation. Also, as we see below, local governments are not the key political actors imbued with the rights to set policies to advance women's development or human rights. In short, the scope of government where women are most numerous is limited and male dominated despite the 29 percent GRAP quotas.

Despite Musharraf's decentralization and GRAP policies, women's status in Pakistan is gradually rising. Pakistan's gender empowerment ranking in 2007 was eighty-second out of ninety-three countries surveyed. Its low gender empowerment score contrasts with the United Kingdom, which has a high ranking of fourteen, and Poland, with a moderate ranking of thirty-nine.[7] Despite having 20 percent women in its National Assembly, Pakistan has a mere 2 percent of females in business leadership positions. Women hold about one-quarter of science and technical jobs but earn only 29 percent of what men do.

Across Pakistan, there is about a 10 percentage-point gender gap in participation by the voting-age population. Women turn out to vote at 44.4 percent; males vote at 55.6 percent. The meso units Lahore, Punjab; Islamabad; Quetta, Balochistan; and Karachi, Sindh, have comparable levels of female voter turnout. But still today, some very traditional villages fine women for voting or running for office or bar their participation altogether. For example, the percentage of women voting in the Federally Administered Tribal Areas is 25 percent, much lower than the national percentage (see Table 4.1). One scholar reports that "on election day the candidates/political parties usually strike a compromise deal wherein women are kept away from the political/electoral process" (Rauf 2005, 54).

The 2010 amendment to the constitution affects the presidential-parliamentary balance and the purview of provinces when it comes to gender equality policy. After a prolonged controversy involving his dismissal of Supreme Court Justice Iftikhar Chaudhry for rulings regarding the privatization of steel mills and the ability of Musharraf to run for president. Musharraf stepped down August 18, 2008. Also, on April 10, 2010, the Eighteenth Amendment to the Pakistani constitution was passed. This amendment moved Pakistan away from its tradition of dictatorial presidents by strengthening the office of prime minister (Aslam 2010). Among its many important reforms, four pertain to decentralization. First, the president could no longer unilaterally dissolve Parliament, which gave greater authority to the prime minister. As we have seen in Pakistan, traditionally the president has held dictatorial powers as leader of the army and has attained power through a military coup rather than a fair election. Second, provinces received more authority, including sole power to declare an emergency in their territory.

---

7. United Nations Development Programme 2007. In the 2013 Global Gender Gap Index, Pakistan ranked 135th out of 136 countries, with a score of 0.5128. Only Yemen was below Pakistan. See World Economic Forum 2013.

Table 4.1 Registered voters by province in Pakistan, 1997

Meso-level unit	Female percentage of total voters	Male percentage of total voters
Balochistan	45.2	54.7
Federally Administered Tribal Areas	25.2	74.8
Islamabad	45.4	54.6
Khyber Pakhtunkhwa	40.3	59.7
Punjab	46.2	53.8
Sindh	44.0	56.0

Source: Center for Asia-Pacific Women in Politics, n.d.

Third, the North-West Frontier Province's name changed from its British administrative moniker to Khyber Pakhtunkhwa, reflecting the dominant ethnic Pashtun group within its territory.

The fourth change empowered provinces "to legislate on issues related to women and human rights" (Imran 2011). But gender equality policy was sent to exactly the level of politics where there are the fewest women in office and where quotas or reservations for women are the lowest. As Mona Lena Krook (2009) shows, women's quotas in Pakistan are set at just 17.5 percent in national and provincial parliaments, contrasting with quotas from the GRAP of 29 percent in local units. As the Global Database of Quotas for Women describes, Pakistan has 60 reserved seats for women among the 342 seats in the National Assembly and 17 reserved seats out of 100 seats in the Senate (Global Database of Quotas for Women 2014). Women's representation overall is 22 percent, so a few additional women are winning elected office at the national level beyond quotas. The provincial level has 17.6 percent reservations, 128 seats held by women, short of the reservations primarily because of Khyber Pakhtunkhwa. The local level in descending order consists of districts, *tehsils*, and unions. Each level has a council with 33 percent reservations for women. There are two important caveats. First, the effective reservation level for women is 29 percent because women also occupy other reservations for peasants, workers, and minorities. Second, the union council is composed of directly elected officials, which in turn form electoral colleges for the *tehsil* and district levels. Therefore, local-level decentralization is not completely democratic in that those chosen through direct election select many other positions at the local level.

This means that key institutions in which women's rights are set, Pakistan's meso-level assemblies, have just 18 percent women, whereas women make up almost 30 percent of local political offices, which do not legislate their rights. Further, at the provincial level, internal party procedures choose the women who fill the reserved seats, and female members can at times be proxies for male family members. In Punjab Province, particularly, more numbers of women are elected than set by quotas, but that is rare. On the basis of the meso-level variance in women's voting participation in Pakistan in Table 4.1, and without all three nodes of the gender policy trifecta present at the municipal and meso levels, I argue that decentralization has led to differing standards across the provinces with regard to legislation affecting women.

I show that two nodes of the gender policy trifecta exist at the meso level (gender quotas and gender mainstreaming) and two at the municipal level (gender quotas and gender-responsive budgeting), but the most effective reform for women, if the least attainable, would be increasing meso quotas to 33 percent and adoption of gender-responsive budgeting in meso-level assemblies. Similar to India's regional outcomes, Pakistan is more likely to adopt gender-responsive budgeting at the municipal level than enact far-reaching outcomes in its meso-level assemblies. Because Pakistan is a federal country that used decentralization as a ruse to appear democratic while strengthening the center-local networks and bypassing powerful provinces, it has progressive municipalities with increased descriptive and substantive representation of women and rural communities with decreased descriptive and substantive representation of women.

Women's Descriptive Representation in the National Assembly and Meso-level Assemblies

Landed women on the Indian subcontinent became eligible to vote in various provincial elections in 1920 to 1929, but they have rarely run for political office (Praveen 2011). To this day women's participation is circumscribed in more traditional provinces of Pakistan and India. The Constituent Assembly of Pakistan governed the nation after independence until a constitution was adopted, and during this period two women served in the assembly.[8] Through much of the country's history, women's representation at the national level has remained between 5 and 10 percent. However, as the subsequent section explains, this dropped to zero when the system of reservations expired.

Table 4.2 shows three trends regarding women's descriptive representation in Pakistan. First, gender quotas, which in Pakistan's case are reserved seats for women in the National Assembly and provincial assemblies, are vital to ensuring the election of female politicians in Pakistan. At all tiers, few women are elected in Pakistan without quotas in the form of reserved seats. For example, in 1988, after reservations for women had expired, no

---

8. Jehanara Sha Nawaz and Shaista Iramullah, both activists in the Muslim League, fought in the Parliament for revisions to Sharia law to allow women to inherit land and property. They also fought unsuccessfully for 10 percent reserved seats for women in the National Assembly.

Table 4.2 Women in national and meso-level parliaments and women by party delegation in Pakistan, 1997–2013

	1997 % women	2002 % women	2008 % women	2013 % women (no. of women/no. of seats)	Number of women from each party
National Assembly	2.3	21.3	22.5	20.5 (70/342)	61 reserved seats, 9 general seats: 6 PTI; 13 PPP; 39 PML-N; 4 MQM; 4 JUI-F; 1 PML-F; 1 PMAP; 1 JI; 1 NPP
Average at meso level in Pakistan		16.0	17.2	19.4 (141/728)	
Balochistan	0	16.9	18.8	18.5 (12/65)	11 reserved seats, 1 general seat: 4 PML-N; 3 PMAP; 2 NP; 2 JUI-F; 1 PML-Q
Punjab	0	17.8	20.0	20.5 (76/371)	67 reserved seats, 9 general seats: 67 PML-N; 6 PTI; 1 PPP; 1 PML; 1 PML-Z
Sindh	0	17.3	17.3	18.5 (31/168)	29 reserved seats, 2 general seats: 18 PPP; 9 MQM; 2 PML-F; 1 PML-N; 1 PTI
Khyber Pakhtunkhwa	0	17.7	17.7	17.7 (22/124)	22 reserved seats: 10 PTI; 3 JUI; 3 PML-N; 6 other
Azad Jammu and Kashmir*	0	10.2	12.2	12.5 (6/48)	Party affiliation not reported

Sources: European Union Election Observation Mission 2008; Inter-Parliamentary Union 2011; Krook 2009; Zia 2013.

Note: PTI = Pakistan Tehreek i-Insaf, PPP = Pakistan People's Party, PML-N = Pakistan Muslim League–Nawaz, JI = Jamaat-e-Islami, MQM = Muttahida Quami Movement, PMAP = Pukhtunkhwa Milli Awami Party, JUI-F = Jamiat Ulema-e-Islam, PML-F = Pakistan Muslim League–Functional, PML-Z = Pakistan Muslim League–Zia-ul-Haq, NPP = National People's Party, NP = National Party, PML = Pakistan Muslim League.

* Azad Jammu and Kashmir contested with India; therefore, members are not included in the meso-level totals.

women served in meso-level assemblies, and the National Assembly had just 2.3 percent women from then until at least 1997. But when reservations were reintroduced in Pakistan in 2002, women's descriptive representation increased. Similarly, there were no women in provincial assemblies in the 1990s, an average of 2 percent in the early 2000s, but 17 percent when new quotas went into effect.

Second, percentages of women's descriptive representation in Pakistan decrease from the local level (29 percent) to the national level (20 percent) to the provincial level (18 percent). Since the 2000 GRAP, women are reserved 29 percent of local elected offices. In 2002 a reservation law was passed, guaranteeing a minimum of 17 percent to women in the National Assembly. In 2009, Pakistan had its first female Speaker of the National Assembly, Fahmida Mirza from the PPP. One women's organization leader in Punjab was hopeful, remarking, "Now, practically speaking, equality politics in Pakistan is possible with the appointment of a female Speaker of the National Assembly, and other females' participation."[9] Because of the new reservation law, reserved seats are "allocated to the political parties in proportion to the number of general seats obtained by these parties in each province." A similar practice holds at the provincial level, where four main provinces reserve seats for women in provincial assemblies: Punjab (66 seats), Sindh (29 seats), Khyber Pakhtunkhwa (22 seats), and Balochistan (11 seats) (Global Database of Quotas for Women 2014). This reservation system of gender quotas added additional seats in the legislature just for women, and political party leaders choose women to fill these seats on a basis of parties' proportional strength after local, provincial, and national elections (Krook and Mackay 2010). Surprisingly, more women have served in the National Assembly than its provincial assemblies, contrary to what occurs in many Western advanced-industrial democracies. After the May 2013 elections in Pakistan, women held 70 seats, or 20.5 percent of the 342-seat National Assembly, but only 18 percent of provincial assembly members and 17 percent of members of the upper house of Parliament (the Senate) were women.

Third, women are sometimes elected in numbers above reservation numbers. For example, in the 2013 elections to the National Assembly, seven women won nonreserved seats, three from the PPP and four from the PML-N. In the Khyber-Pakhtunkhwa meso-level assembly in 2014, no women won seats beyond the twenty-two reserved for them. But one female member in Balochistan (PML-N) and one female member in Sindh (PPP) were elected above the reservations. Ten more women were elected above reservation system numbers in Punjab Province; nine from the PML-N and one from the Tehreek-i-Insaf. Thus, women have relatively more access to the political system in the National Assembly and in Punjab.

The analysis of women's descriptive representation in the decentralized system of Poland in Chapter 3 found considerable variance in the percentage of women in meso-level office. While the Pakistan findings support the second guiding question, that women's descriptive representation is higher where there are gender quotas than where there are not, there is regional and institutional variance in women's representation beyond quotas. In the National Assembly and Punjab provincial assembly, there are higher women's descriptive representation and more opportunities for women in politics. In the next section, I analyze women's import in national and provincial politics to ascertain whether decentralization is increasing women's substantive representation.

---

9. Interview by the author, August 2007, Lahore, Punjab (trans. Firdous Rani).

Capacity and Presence of Women's Organizations and Women's Policy Agencies

Islamabad has an estimated twenty women's groups. Compared to Poland, Pakistan has a moderate women's civil society sector, weak women's national policy agency, and moderate women's legislative representation. The ministry and the GRAP have sought to build capacity of women's nongovernmental organizations (NGOs).

The Pakistani national ministry for women, while rhetorically feminist, has been occupied by women who do not describe themselves as feminist but rather take up social welfare issues and include women secondarily. In 1979, Zia-ul-Haq established the Women's Division in the Cabinet Secretariat and appointed another commission on the status of women (Asian Development Bank 2000, 22). In 2005 Musharraf revamped it into the national Ministry of Women Development (MOWD). When I surveyed the MOWD in 2007, the PML-Q held power in Parliament. MOWD staff reported that gender equality powers differed moderately from one meso unit to another. The ministry's development budget, provided by the federal government, was 163 million Pakistani rupees in 2005–2006. International organizations like the Aurat Foundation and UNICEF helped fund independent projects. The MOWD had 156 full-time employees. In a structured interview, a national MOWD spokesperson rated its communication with provincial offices as "very infrequent," and it contacts provincial women's development departments in Punjab and Sindh most because their larger populations mean their projects are larger.[10] The people at the MOWD rated themselves as having "moderate experience in women's organizations." With regard to questions on political party support, survey respondents indicated that they "don't know," but many did mention that the president strongly supported the agency by ensuring funding, backing programs, attending events, and forming policy. The MOWD claimed "frequent" communication with women's organizations despite not registering them. MOWD staff reported connecting women's organizations to financial support, staying in touch by mail with women's organizations, and meeting with representatives from women's organizations visiting ministry headquarters, but they did not otherwise indicate that they brought women's organizations together in any forums.

Musharraf's PML-Q party's national program for the development and empowerment of women created provincial women's policy agencies (WPAs) in Punjab and Sindh between 2003 and 2005.[11] Provincial women's

---

10. Interview by the author, 2007, Islamabad (trans. Firdous Rani).
11. Azad Jammu and Kashmir reported establishing a similar agency in 1992 and Balochistan in 1998.

development departments received staff, budget, and office space from the national ministry. The extent of their institutional capacity varies from one meso unit to another. Though funding comes from provincial assemblies, the ultimate source of monetary support for gender programs is the Asian Development Bank, World Bank, and other international lenders (see Asian Development Bank, Department for International Development, and World Bank 2004). As economic development, gender empowerment, and decentralization were part of a full package pushed by Musharraf and his PML-Q, the national and provincial levels focused on women's economic empowerment.

Contrasting with the national respondents, the staff in the provincial WPAs often reported "limited experience working with women's organizations." Pakistan's meso-level women's policy agencies (MWPAs) have low to moderate levels of institutional capacity. The MOWD is an autonomous office, and provincial legislatures have passed their own enabling orders. Budgetary evidence indicates that Pakistan's MWPAs have modest budgets and in some cases prodigious staff, but those staffers have more experience in social welfare provision than in women's organizations, and MWPAs tend to serve the interests of provincial feudal lords. Likewise, more traditional and rural meso units face uphill battles in truly changing policies on violence against women.

The political impetus for WPAs at the provincial level comes from provincial politicians rather than from national politicians or from women's groups. This reflects the dominance of rural gentry at the provincial level. However, all the WPAs I surveyed noted that quotas for women in local and provincial office are a sea change. Even though reservations for women and minorities began in 1952, their effects have been delayed, and the magnitude of the quotas and increasing abilities of women in office should make big differences in decades to come. Pakistan's top-down dynamics of decentralization have created MWPAs that have similar functions, even if their form differs. The elimination of the national WPA, the circumscribed extent of truly feminist perspectives of MWPA leaders, and in some meso units, the resistance of populations to those perspectives might limit abilities for widespread policy outcomes, but some evidence indicates that MWPA leaders, with the resources they have, are beginning to target the needs of women in their jurisdictions.

Women's Policy Priorities

Is decentralization leading to policies that reflect what women want in provinces of Pakistan? This section presents what women's organizations in various parts of the country identified as their top priorities. Pakistani women's organizations have a base made up of political parties and unions, because they emerged from concerned individuals and activists, male and female alike. As mentioned before, the number of women's groups is small for such a large national population, but the movement and particular groups are gaining influence in politics. Mumtaz and Shaheed report that "in 1979, despite the existence of feminist groups and individuals, the Hudood Ordinance was passed without a murmur of protest. . . . Today the level of consciousness is such that a similar move on the part of the government would elicit an immediate response, not only from [the Women's Action Forum NGO] . . . but from a host of other women's organizations and . . . from other sectors of society as well. . . . Pakistan is witnessing the slow growth of a women's movement, which at the moment is still in its infancy" (1988, 124). Therefore, I summarize the women's movement in Pakistan as weak and autonomous but growing in influence.

What women say they want out of politics depends on where they live. Their policy priorities depend on whether they live in Islamabad, Punjab, or Khyber Pakhtunkhwa (Figure 4.2). I find that WPAs have limited influence in meso units where a political party does not support but does control their activities. In Punjab and Sindh, MWPAs are more active. Even in provinces where traditional cultural roles challenge MWPAs, such as Khyber Pakhtunkhwa and Balochistan, these offices established partnerships in assemblies and with women's groups internationally and are making headway for women. In short, many more women participate in politics now than did before the 2002 decentralization and quotas because of openings in local politics, but low levels of women's literacy and political skills challenge women's involvement in politics close to home. As one interviewee noted, "[Gender equality] is often well reflected in government documents, but when is the time for actual implementation? Certain forces operate to determine this concept, and those forces include formal and informal structures."[12]

The top policy priorities of women's organization leaders across all Pakistan are as follows. The first policy priority is eliminating violence against women. This comes as no surprise with the incidence of honor killings, acid burnings, and the physical, emotional, and sexual abuse of women in Pakistan. The second is increasing public awareness of women's equality with men. The third is improving the literacy of school-age girls, a key concern in a country with vastly disparate literacy levels across provinces but also across gender. The fourth is increasing numbers of women in positions of political decision making. Seeing more women in political life is a key concern for women's organization leaders in Pakistan.

In Table 4.3 I compare women's policy priorities in Pakistan with those of the national MOWD. I coded each of the top four policy priorities, looked at how many listed a given priority as their first priority, and totaled those. Then

12. Interview by the author, August 2007, Punjab, Pakistan (trans. Firdous Rani).

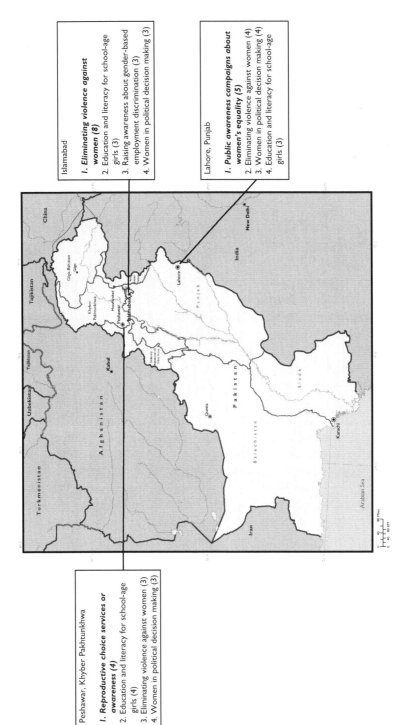

Islamabad

I. Eliminating violence against women (8)

2. Education and literacy for school-age girls (3)
3. Raising awareness about gender-based employment discrimination (3)
4. Women in political decision making (3)

Lahore, Punjab

I. Public awareness campaigns about women's equality (5)

2. Eliminating violence against women (4)
3. Women in political decision making (4)
4. Education and literacy for school-age girls (3)

Peshawar, Khyber Pakhtunkhwa

I. Reproductive choice services or awareness (4)

2. Education and literacy for school-age girls (4)
3. Eliminating violence against women (3)
4. Women in political decision making (3)

Figure 4.2 Policy priorities of women's organizations in Pakistan, 2007. Numbers in parentheses are the number of leaders who listed the item as a top priority.

Table 4.3 What women want in Pakistan, 2007

Policy priorities of women's organizations, aggregated across the country	Policy priorities of national women's policy agency
1. Elimination of violence against women (15)	1. Women's entrepreneurship and micro-credits for women
2. Public awareness campaigns about women's equality (10)	2. Education and literacy for school-age girls
3. Education and literacy for school-age girls (10)	3. Food assistance for girls and women
4. Women in political decision making (10)	4. Women in political decision making

Note: Numbers in parentheses are the number of leaders who listed the item as a top four priority.

I totaled all who listed that priority as their second and repeated this for third and fourth priorities. I summed for each priority the total number of groups that had identified it as one of their top four. I compared the frequencies of a policy priority being in the top four with the priority's distribution across the top four slots (for example, to see if a priority was mentioned often but always as a third or fourth priority). There were not inconsistencies in the sense that the priorities most frequently mentioned were clustered as first or second priorities. The only close call might be between political decision making, which four groups ranked as first, seventh, and fourth, and education, which nine groups ranked as second.

The MOWD listed as its top priorities women's entrepreneurship and microcredit, education and literacy for school-age girls, food assistance for girls and women, and women in decision making. Microcredit can help women entrepreneurs, but its increased priority for the MOWD, relative to women's organizations, might represent the ministry's international-facing role or microcredit's current popularity as a development trend. Only three of the women's organizations surveyed had microcredit as a top policy priority. Literacy for school-age girls was the third-highest priority for women's groups, so that reflects MOWD responsiveness. Food assistance is not necessarily a gendered policy area and is, in practice, often combined with the Islamic tradition of *zakat*, or charity to the poor. This explains why many provincial departments of women's development are named first as departments of social welfare, with "women development" tacked on to the end of their name—and to the end of the policy agenda. Provincial governments have combined departments this way to avoid controversy and save money, but in other countries this practice shuffles women's specific needs to the bottom of the deck. It is promising to see women in political decision making as one of the MOWD's top priorities.

My finding that microcredit is a top priority of the MOWD but not for women's groups comports with some feminist critiques of microcredit, such as that microcredit's heavy emphasis on development supports "glass walls," or women not being hired by larger employers (Naples and Desai 2007). Another feminist criticism of microcredit is that it might not change the status of women within their families and not reduce male violence against women, as male-run businesses also receive microcredit. Again, the MOWD might be seeking international funding, which supports microcredit, and promoting microcredit to boost Pakistan's reputation abroad. After the earthquake in 2005 and the popularity of microcredit internationally, the MOWD may be responding to pressures to work specifically on these issues. Disaster relief is also an issue in which money is arguably coordinated best at the national level.

The MOWD is working on two key issues expressed by Pakistani women's groups: literacy for school-age girls and women in political decision making. Globally there is a lot of support for universal children's education, such as the World Bank's Education for All and the UN's Sustainable Development Goal 4: quality education. Moreover, in Muslim societies like Afghanistan and Pakistan, there is a strong desire to maintain separate educational facilities for boys and girls, but fewer resources should not mean that girls just get left behind on education. That said, there is much work to be done to expand educational capacity in rural areas throughout Pakistan, especially in Khyber Pakhtunkhwa and Balochistan. The other key priority the MOWD is pursuing is women in political decision making. While the largest gender reservations operate at the municipal level, illiteracy might impede women from participating fully in local politics and pushing for policies. Some limited political schools and workshops are being held to train women on political skills like speechmaking and community organizing, but increasing the literacy of women serving on district and *tehsil* councils gives them a chance for wider representation and less chance of remaining silent or acting as pure proxies for powerful male relatives.

However, the MOWD did not report as priorities two issues that women's groups view as central: eliminating violence against women and public awareness campaigns about women's equality. One might argue that the MOWD video of a performance of the song in the chapter's epigraph is precisely a public awareness campaign. But Internet usage rates are low in the country, particularly in many rural areas. As of 2012, overall Internet usage in Pakistan was estimated at just 10 percent of the population compared to 80 percent of Americans (World Bank 2012). To work effectively on public awareness campaigns, the MOWD should promote street plays, television ads, newspaper ads, or billboards that highlight women's equality or question traditional beliefs that women are unacceptable in public life. Likewise, one might counter that the MOWD represented women in its support for the 2006 Women's Protection Act, which allows authorities to bring rape charges without requiring four adult male witnesses and with no automatic fornication charge under Sharia law. Is this not precisely the government action that women were looking for?

However, Pakistani women's groups said the Women's Protection Act did not go far enough. They argued that the act should have included provision for awareness campaigns of the problem of violence against women, showing that this problem is endemic to societies around the world, and legally defining violence against women and referencing its many manifestations, including sexual violence, sexual harassment, and sex trafficking. For example, the Women's Protection Act does not recognize marital rape, which the United Nations Declaration on the Elimination of Violence against Women established as a human rights violation. In Pakistan, the assumption remains that a woman must provide sex, or "conjugal right," to her husband. The presence of civil courts for trying rape does not mean that police officers have been adequately trained to deal with charges of sexual violence or are required to investigate all charges of rape (Montoya 2013). In the 2002 Mukhtar Mai case, a widely reported gang rape, the panchayat sanctioned the rapists for "adultery," but five of the six were acquitted, and the sixth's death sentence was commuted to a life sentence. Mukhtar Mai herself was tried under the Hudood Ordinances, which place adultery in the category of *zina*, or fornication. According to the laws of punishment, or *hadd*, an adult of sound mind committing *zina* should be sentenced to one hundred lashes or death by stoning. After the 2006 Protection of Women Act, civil courts, not Sharia courts, try cases of rape (Weaver 2007).

Perhaps provincial ministries or the legislative arena match the policy priorities of women's groups better. This section explores what women's organizations want in three parts of Pakistan: the Islamabad Capital Territory; Peshawar, Khyber Pakhtunkhwa (still called North-West Frontier Province at the time of my 2007 interviews); and Lahore, Punjab. Interviews revealed how well provincial versus national government agencies matched the priorities of women's groups. After discussing context-specific policy desires of women in each part, I discuss whether their subnational WPAs and legislatures are meeting those priorities.

Women's organization leaders in Islamabad viewed eliminating violence against women as the number-one issue. Islamabad itself has a population of 805,235. The literacy rate is 72 percent, and inhabitants speak mainly Urdu and English. Some have described Islamabad as a city of transplants and government bureaucrats. Women's organizations in Islamabad ranked education and literacy for school-age girls as their second priority, raising awareness about gender-based employment discrimination third, and women in political decision making fourth. Women's policy priorities in Islamabad and across the country reflect that the government is not adequately challenging violence against women. High-profile assassinations of, for example, former prime minister Benazir Bhutto and Punjab Minister of Social Affairs Zilla Huma Usman for not wearing a head scarf and for advocating women's equality have made many women rightfully afraid for their physical safety if they push traditional boundaries. The lack of rule of law in Pakistan heightens this fear (see "The War" 2013). About one-fourth of the surveyed Islamabad women's groups ranked the MOWD's actions "very successful." One women's group echoed the sentiment that Pakistan talks the talk on gender equality but fails to walk the walk. While the MOWD might espouse strong goals for equality of women and men in society, according to one interviewee, "NGOs are doing equality work, not the government."[13] Also, women's groups in Islamabad mentioned some unique policy priorities that did not emerge elsewhere in Pakistan, including campaigns against dowry, health issues, and advocacy on AIDS for sex workers.

As in other national capitals, women's groups in Islamabad express more concern about gender-based employment discrimination. How has the national parliament addressed what women want in Islamabad? Appendix 5 describes policies and events directly affecting women in Pakistan since 1973. No major pieces of legislation have established or enforce women's equality in the workplace. This comes as little surprise; maintaining gendered but equal physical spaces is tricky. This might explain the MOWD's emphasis on microcredit, to help women work for themselves and the benefit of their families. Appendix 5 also shows no public awareness initiatives about hiring women or expanding the female workforce in the private sector (the GRAP addresses government jobs).

I next move to the priorities of women's organization leaders in Lahore. Punjab Province has a population of 81 million, half the nation's population. Lahore is the provincial capital, and inhabitants speak Punjabi and Urdu. The literacy rate in Punjab is 60 percent. Lahore is a modern city and an Internet technology hub for South Asia. Women's organizations in Lahore named as their first priority public awareness campaigns about women's equality. This was followed closely by eliminating violence against women, increasing numbers of women in political decision making, and educating school-age girls. It is important to note that other policy priorities not mentioned elsewhere in Pakistan emerged in Punjab. For example, training female police officers to handle cases of violence against women, protecting minority rights, and achieving peace between India and Pakistan. Lahore women's groups had memberships ranging from 15 to 1,550 members. Women's groups felt that the MWPAs emphasized the same issues but gave literacy more prominence. One interviewee said, "For gender equality to occur, other strategies to reduce gender bias need to evolve. Quotas for females are not up to the challenge. There is a great need to change textbooks to improve the gender equality situation in Pakistan."[14]

---

13. Interview by the author, March 2007, Islamabad, Pakistan.
14. Interview by the author, March 2007, Punjab, Pakistan.

However, it appears the MWPA in Punjab was more representative of Punjabi women's groups than the MOWD. Punjab's MWPA's second priority, public awareness about women's equality, was a low-level issue for the MOWD. Tellingly, when I asked women's organizations in Punjab which level of government they worked with most, they answered the MWPA, but they also said they worked with local and national councilors instead of members of the provincial assembly. On the legislative front, the main change that has occurred for women in the Punjab assembly is the creation of a cross-party women's caucus. This is no small feat in a country where political parties are extremely polarized and walkouts and altercations are frequent in the political process. In 2012 the provincial assembly created a board to address needs of acid burn survivors and put forth policy for home-based workers and job training centers. However, more significant legislation in policy areas such as public awareness campaigns about women's equality and education and literacy for girls has not passed in this assembly. Thus, the MWPA has advocated more strongly for what women in Punjab want than has the assembly.

Next, I discuss women's organizations policy priorities in North-West Frontier Province (now Khyber Pakhtunkhwa Province). A mountainous and isolated province of Pakistan, Khyber Pakhtunkhwa has a population of 20 million people, the majority Pashtuns, an ethnic group spanning Afghanistan and Pakistan, and, therefore, it has a large population of Afghan refugees. The provincial capital is Peshawar. As of 1995, only 12 percent of rural women in this province were literate (Asian Development Bank 2000, 2–3).

Women's groups in Khyber Pakhtunkhwa place reproductive choice services and awareness as being of paramount importance in their province, followed by education and literacy for school-age girls. Third on their priority list is eliminating violence against women, and fourth is women in political decision making. A prominent trend among women's groups is many more "don't know" responses regarding MWPAs and the MOWD. This reflects the historical and current challenges of the government in extending its reach to Khyber Pakhtunkhwa. At the provincial and national levels, recruiting women in political decision making positions is a top priority. There is interaction with local government and foreign donors, but little with the Pakistani national government, reflecting a hollowing out of the state. Partisan politics reflects this as well, as the PML-Q was in power in 2007, but the Muttahida Majlis-e-Amal dominated Khyber Pakhtunkhwa politics. Five of the eight women's groups I surveyed consider the PML-Q to be the most helpful, and three consider the PPP to be the least helpful. Seven groups mentioned contacting local councilors. Most women's groups contact only the United Nations, donors, or other NGOs. Only one group mentioned the provincial women's development department.

Some groups in Khyber Pakhtunkhwa were very positive about the MWPA. One group leader said, "The local government system is very successful here. They are raising awareness for women's rights in different forums. Projects are in progress here on the political equality of women."[15] Another respondent seemed to support the central government, saying, "In the Musharraf government, female participation in Parliament was 33 percent. Females should be participating in every field at least 33 percent."[16] A third respondent was much more positive about NGO representation for women than governmental representation, stating, "NGOs are trying their best. Let's see what happens."[17]

How is the Khyber Pakhtunkhwa assembly doing with regard to the substantive representation of women? The primary legislative action in the Khyber Pakhtunkhwa assembly of direct concern to women's status deals with proposed changes to the marriage law to make it more equitable for women. These changes have come from the All Pakistan Women's Association, headed by Zari Sarfaraz, who served on the Commission for Status of Women; Rahat Agha; and Kalsoom Saifullah. This suggests that women who have served in all three nodes of the gender policy trifecta are best situated to challenge gender norms.

Thus, women's policy priorities vary markedly across the country by meso unit. Table 4.4 supports the argument that MWPAs provide bureaucrats who take separate tailored actions to meet the distinct needs of women in their constituencies. Across all MWPAs, they report eight unique policy areas that they address that the MOWD did not report addressing.

Assessment of Women's Descriptive and Substantive Representation

Because most women in Pakistani politics gain their seats through reservations—the specific seats voted on by women, for women—female politicians have less bargaining power in political life. For example, Nasreen Akhtar (2006) reports that even though women's representation is up to 20 percent in the National Assembly, their influence is not that great. Male politicians who did not meet education requirements to serve merely fielded their wives and daughters with college degrees in competitive elections:

As for women reserved seats, the incumbents are mostly the women who are relatives of the selected politicians or beneficiaries who have

---

15. Interview by the author, July 2007, Peshawar, Pakistan (trans. Firdous Rani).
16. Interview by the author, July 2007, Peshawar, Pakistan (trans. Firdous Rani).
17. Interview by the author, July 2007, Peshawar, Pakistan (trans. Firdous Rani).

Table 4.4 Differences in policy priorities between national and meso-level women's policy agencies (MWPAs) in Pakistan, 2007

Meso unit	Number of policy differences	MWPA priorities differing from the national WPA
Azad Jammu and Kashmir	2	Reconstruction from earthquake Forest, greenery, and technical skills
Balochistan	3	Eliminating violence against women Promoting women in labor market Legal assistance for women
Khyber Pakhtunkhwa	2	Legal assistance for women Shelter for homeless women (*dar-ul-aman*)
Punjab	2	Economic empowerment Eliminating violence against women
Sindh	3	Legal assistance for women Shelter for homeless women (*dar-ul-aman*) Eliminating female trafficking
Total unique policy priorities	8	

knowledge of politics. Therefore, they are yet unable to raise even a single issue. They sit static in the session and leave the legislative sessions without uttering a word. There's a tendency, in the current assembly, that only those women speak who know English. (Akthar 2006, 73)

Provincial assemblies in Poland have not tended to respond to women's policy priorities directly, even as women's numbers have increased. In Pakistani provincial assemblies, there are mixed results in terms of responding to women's concerns as legislators and citizens. All parties except the Awami National Party have a women's wing, but it tends to be ghettoized from the rest of the party and mostly gets out the vote for women rather than serving the needs of women citizens (Rauf 2005). Women in the provincial assemblies are often less comfortable than their national counterparts in bringing up gender issues. Farah Aqil Shah, Awani National Party member of Khyber Pakhtunkhwa assembly, believes obstacles to the full participation of women in the assembly still exist. "[Shah] was unhappy over the non-utilization of development funds allocated to her constituency according to the needs of the people and according to her wish. The main reason: Khyber Pakhtunkhwa being a male-dominated society" (Rauf 2005, 5).

However, Shagufta Naz of the Muttahida Majlis-e-Amal expressed "pride in being part of the decision-making institutions" (Rauf 2005, 50). Those who have succeeded in Khyber Pakhtunkhwa politics have come from the elite, or feudal, class, though they sought to expand participation to women of all social classes. These women include "Begum Zari Sarfaraz,

Begum Rahat Agha, Begum Kalsoom Saifullah and Begum Masim Wali Khan" (54). In Sindh, female legislators have been crucial in introducing legislation to reduce violence against women and to establish women's complaint cells at police stations throughout Sindh. This meso unit has also proposed establishing women's courts to administer justice more fairly. In short, the provinces of Punjab and Sindh have greater women's literacy and labor force participation and have even fielded competitive women in nonreserved seats. However, movement is coming from Balochistan and Khyber Pakhtunkhwa to increase reserved seats in provincial assemblies to 33 percent, while in 2013 Sindh and Punjab moved to cap reserved seats for women in provincial assemblies at 22 percent and 10 percent, respectively (Global Database of Quotas for Women 2014).

Conclusion

Although Pakistan affirmatively answers guiding question 2 (women's descriptive representation is highest where there are quotas), decentralization has yet to produce full gains for women's empowerment in Pakistan, because the strongest reforms, the GRAP and the 33 percent gender quotas, constitute only two nodes of the gender policy trifecta at the municipal level. Political decentralization to provinces occurred in 2010, including the important Eighteenth Amendment to the Pakistani constitution, which in part specifies that women's policies and human rights are the purview of provinces. Decentralization to the meso level in Pakistan was not matched with GRAP provisions at the meso level or a boost in meso-level assembly quotas from 17.5 to 33 percent. I characterize decentralization and gender reforms as a shell game because they give the appearance of expanding rights and participation while serving very opposite ends. As Figure 4.3 shows, the municipal level of Pakistan has two nodes of the gender policy trifecta: subnational gender quotas (33 percent) and gender-responsive budgeting through the GRAP. However, Pakistani municipalities do not yet have WPAs; only meso units have these. Furthermore, Pakistani meso units lack gender-responsive budgeting. After European Union intervention, Poland (Chapter 3) has had two nodes of the trifecta: subnational gender quotas and gender mainstreaming WPAs at the meso level, but no gender-responsive budgeting. Examination of Pakistani municipalities shows that subnational quotas and gender-responsive budgeting by themselves are not enough to lead to women's descriptive and substantive representation: gender mainstreaming through WPAs is also necessary.

On the basis of this research, my policy recommendation for Pakistan is to extend the GRAP and 33 percent quotas to the provincial level. Because the Pakistani constitution specifies that provinces will make women's policies,

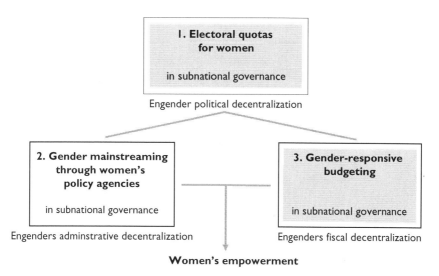

Figure 4.3 The gender policy trifecta in Pakistan at the municipal level of governance. A shaded box means the node is present; an unshaded box means it is not.

women need to occupy a larger proportion of the legislative assemblies and the offices of feminist bureaucracy. Even more important is expanding female literacy so that women who serve in provincial bureaucracy and legislatures can participate fully, not as proxies of powerful male relatives. MWPAs do reflect varied priorities for women, but the ability to translate this into policy and implementation depends on the ability to actually bring up such issues in provincial assemblies. The provincial assemblies are heavily occupied by the rural gentry class that hesitates to change gender norms or threaten land ownership patterns in Pakistan. It will take a larger percentage of women in office at the provincial level and adoption of principles of gender-responsive budgeting in Pakistan's meso-level assemblies to make real changes in policy for women.

5

The United Kingdom

Three Nodes of the Gender Policy Trifecta

By many indications, 1999 decentralization reforms in the United Kingdom have enhanced women's political representation in civil society, in meso-level women's policy agencies (MWPAs), and in meso-level (or devolved) assemblies in Scotland, Wales, and Northern Ireland. As Fiona Mackay, Fiona Myers, and Alice Brown aptly describe it:

> The process of devolution has resulted not only in the renegotiation of powers between the centre and the sub-state nation or region, but also in the redistribution of political power between the sexes. High levels of women's representation were not a "natural" or inevitable outcome of devolution, rather they were the result of sustained struggle by a pluralist coalition of women who seized the opportunities presented by constitutional change. (2003, 84)

Similarly, a Welsh women's group leader argued that many women's groups actively pushed for decentralization and worked to engender governance. "When the Welsh Assembly Government was established as part of UK devolution, there was a commitment to do things differently—to ensure that women's voices were heard and that the assembly members themselves were reflective of society. [Unlike the UK Parliament in Westminster,] the Welsh Assembly Government endeavors to be closer to the people, and it is relatively easy to make contact with these politicians."[1] Another important

---

1. Interview by the author, January 2011, Cardiff, Wales.

manifestation of "do[ing] things differently" was the UK gender equality duty, of the Equality Act of 2006, which entered into force in April 2007.[2] The act created the protected categories of age, disability, gender, gender reassignment, race, religion or belief, and sexual orientation. In 2010, an eighth category, pregnancy and maternity, was added to the Equality Act of 2010. The Equality Acts require the provision of goods and services throughout the United Kingdom regardless of an individual's sex or other protected categories. Loosely based on Westminster's legislation is the separate Equality Commission for Northern Ireland. The gender equality duty requires civil servants to incorporate gender into every area of public policy (see Htun and Weldon 2010) and to take positive actions to bring about equality. In addition to such areas as treating equally men and women when they seek government housing loans and girls and boys in British schools, policy makers and civil servants in the Housing Ministry and Education Ministry must implement plans to bring about equality between the sexes. The combination of gender quotas of leftist parties, MWPAs operating in the context of a gender equality duty, and gender-responsive budgeting has led to periods of all three nodes of the gender policy trifecta functioning in the United Kingdom. However, this trifecta requires maintenance, especially after the United Kingdom's June 2016 "Brexit" from the European Union and the subsequent election of conservative prime minister Theresa May.

For example, the same women's activist in Cardiff who spoke positively about decentralization expressed serious concerns about the Welsh government's ability to fulfill its equalities duty after the 2010 general election. She was concerned about the 19 percent, on average, government spending cuts announced by conservative British prime minister David Cameron (Lyall and Cowell 2010). The budget cuts were predicted to disproportionately affect women and the meso units of the United Kingdom (see Figure 5.1). For example, in October 2011, Cameron announced the closing of the Women's National Commission effective December 31, 2011. The commission was the preeminent organization in bringing together, since 1969, women's groups across England, Wales, Scotland, and Northern Ireland. The commission also had an international role as the liaison between the British government and the United Nations Convention on the Elimination of All Forms of Discrimination against Women (CEDAW) committee. However, because of fiscal centralization in the United Kingdom, female policy makers in 2011 had to work creatively around severe budget cuts made by Cameron's Conservative-Liberal Democrat coalition government. On August 1, 2010, the Fawcett Society, a women's organization named for the mother of the British women's

---

2. See Paul Chaney, Fiona Mackay, and Laura McAllister's (2007) pathbreaking account of constitutional change in Wales and throughout the UK system.

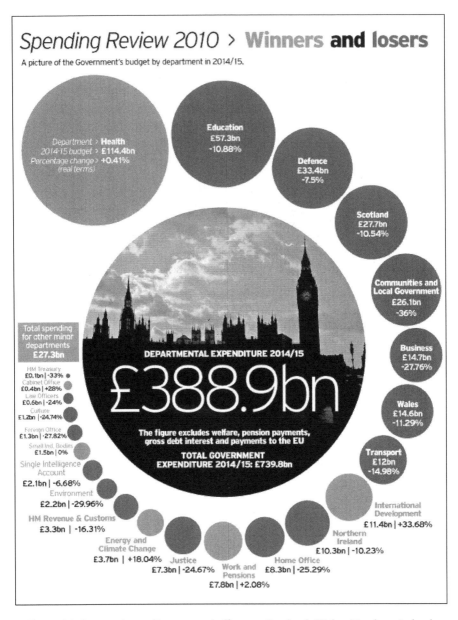

Figure 5.1 Proposed spending cuts and effects on Scotland, Wales, Northern Ireland, and local communities, 2010. (Source: "Spending Review" 2010)

suffrage movement, fronted a legal challenge to the government's austerity budget. As discussed later in this chapter, the British High Court denied the possibility of judicial review over the budget, but Cameron's government did agree to provide gender impact analysis with future budgets.

The case of the United Kingdom shows that even after a gender policy trifecta is in place in a country, political actors must continue working to maintain that trifecta. For example, Meryl Kenny and Fiona Mackay (2011b) argue that political parties' positions on gender quotas may change over time. Although the Scottish Labour Party was largely responsible for ushering in a 39.5 percent female Scottish Parliament in 2003 (Kenny and Mackay 2011b, 2012, 2013; Kenny and Verge 2013), the party has failed to achieve over 24 percent local women councilors (Kenny and Mackay 2013). In decentralized systems, weakening any node of the gender policy trifecta can adversely affect women's mobilization.[3] Women and men serving in UK meso-level elected office should cultivate the next generation of female politicians. Women's organization leaders and female bureaucrats in the United Kingdom need to work with female meso-level legislators to maintain support for gender quotas and gender-responsive policies when support for decentralization wanes.

Further, the 2010 and 2015 elections of Conservative-led governments, with concomitant policies of fiscal centralization, reversed some of the hard-won gender equality policy successes in the meso units. Even gains in female leadership in the United Kingdom are not without costs for women. Following David Cameron's July 13, 2016, formal resignation after 52 percent of Britons voted to leave the European Union (a move known as "Brexit"), former Equalities minister and Home secretary Theresa May won Conservative leadership elections to become the second female British prime minister in the country's history. Yet scholars recognizing Theresa May's extensive qualifications for prime minister still noted the "glass cliff"—the tendency of women to be recognized for their qualifications and gain executive power during crises instigated by previous (male) leaders that are unlikely to have a favorable settlement that voters will later reward (Bennhold 2016). Even when significant political decentralization occurs and new assemblies are created with gender equality principles in mind, national governments affect the resources and direction of policy at local levels, producing mixed results for women. Under decentralization and in the presence of a gender policy trifecta, women's organizations may need to plan for times when the national political landscape is conservative and to pursue private or international

---

3. Statutory quotas or centralized mechanisms ensuring baseline percentages of female candidates and penalties for parties that do not meet quota requirements may be necessary (see Kenny and Mackay 2012).

funding supplementation during these times. In systems with fiscal centralization, gains in women's substantive representation may be more easily reversed if meso units do not have the ability to raise revenues and have to cut expenditures. In the next section, I provide some context on the status of women and democracy in the United Kingdom. Then I lay out my plan for evaluating the gender policy trifecta and women's representation in the United Kingdom.

Status of Women and Democracy

Freedom House categorizes the United Kingdom as a "free" political system, and women have had formal rights and suffrage since 1928. A first-wave women's movement formed in the United Kingdom in 1897, when Millicent Fawcett unified groups of middle-class and working women into an organization called the National Union of Women's Suffrage Societies to demand that women have the right to vote. In 1903, the movement split. Emmeline Pankhurst's Women's Social Political Union opted for a more militant hunger-striking suffragette strategy, while other women supported a more traditional lobby campaign. Pankhurst's group increased visibility for the cause, and Parliament passed the 1913 Prisoners (Temporary Discharge for Illness) Act—more commonly known as the Cat and Mouse Act—which released hunger-striking suffragettes, although they had to return to prison when their health recovered. A pause in mobilization efforts occurred during World War I, but in 1928, women received full suffrage at age twenty-one for all elections. Women's activism surged a second time in the United Kingdom during the late 1960s with the Dagenham strike of 1968, leading to the Equal Pay Act in 1970 and the Sex Discrimination Act of 1975.

When the women's movement in the United Kingdom drew together again in 2010 because of new fiscal challenges, the Fawcett Society appealed to the High Court to review the June 2010 national budget announced by the Conservative-Liberal Democrat coalition government. In August, the Fawcett Society charged that the government did not undertake a required analysis of the effect of the budget cuts on protected groups as required by the Sex Discrimination Act of 1975. The Fawcett Society further argued that because of women's higher likelihood of being in poverty, "72 per cent of cuts will be met from women's income as opposed to 28 per cent from men's" (Conley 2012, 349). The Fawcett Society also pointed out that women make up 65 percent of government workers, so cuts to public sector employment were more likely to affect women. However, the High Court denied the Fawcett Society's request for judicial review, saying the society had delayed too long in bringing its request for judicial review before the court ("Fawcett Society Loses" 2010). Still, the suit led government officials to concede that in some areas women bear heavier burdens in budget cuts, such as public sector pay and benefits freezes. The coalition government committed to having all future budgets contain a gender impact assessment.

How have high levels of political and administrative decentralization but low levels of fiscal decentralization in the United Kingdom affected the participation of women in politics and the substantive output of legislative assemblies? Recall that the definition of decentralization employed here is "a process of state reform composed by a set of public policies that transfer responsibilities, resources, or authority from higher to lower levels of government in the context of a specific type of state" (Falleti 2005, 328). Changes in UK politics around 1999 resulted in the creation of legislative assemblies in Wales and Scotland, the reinvigoration of the Northern Ireland Assembly, and the granting of administrative powers to the Welsh government in Cardiff, the Scottish government in Edinburgh, and the Northern Ireland government in Belfast. These changes constitute decentralization for this study. Thus far, the ability of the meso units to raise or adjust tax rates is limited, highlighting the low levels of fiscal decentralization explored in this case.

I first provide a gendered analysis of UK decentralization. Second, I examine women's descriptive representation in the meso-level and national parliaments. In the bureaucratic sector, MWPAs are vibrant and occupied mostly by women who identify themselves as feminist in bell hooks's (2000) sense of aspiring to equality across all the dimensions protected under the 2006 and 2010 Equality Acts. After showing how women's policy priorities vary across the meso units, I demonstrate that the gender policy trifecta of gender quotas, women's policy machinery, and gender-responsive budgeting in meso units has at times operated in the United Kingdom.

Gendered Analysis of Decentralization

What powers did lower units gain after late-1990s devolution? In Wales, the 1998 Government of Wales Act initially gave limited powers to the directly elected National Assembly for Wales, including the ability to reform certain public bodies, like Welsh Health Authorities, and to make policies relating to sport, the Welsh language, and historic buildings.[4] The 2006 Government of Wales Act distributed the devolved powers between the Welsh Assembly Government and National Assembly for Wales. The assembly also may now enact measures that are functionally equivalent to acts of Parliament. In a March 2011 referendum the Welsh people confirmed the assembly's power to make measures in twenty-one policy areas, one of which (devolved taxes) was

---

4. The text of the legislation is available at http://www.legislation.gov.uk/ukpga/1998/38/contents.

added to the amended Schedule 5 list in 2014, after the 2011 referendum.[5] The assembly "can gain further legislative competence by the amendment to Schedule 5. There are two ways in which this can happen: either as a result of the clauses included in legislation passed by an Act of Parliament at Westminster, or by Legislative Competency Orders (LCOs) granted by Parliament in response to a request from the National Assembly itself" ("Government of Wales Act 2006" 2016).

The assembly emphasizes women's issues through voluntary cross-party groups that reflect policy concerns of members: black and minority ethnic issues, trafficking of women and children, women and democracy, and nursing and midwifery (see Chaney, Mackay, and McAllister 2007). These cross-party groups representing women's multiple identities, which were not formally represented in cross-party groups in Westminster, show clear evidence that when decentralization activates new subnational institutions, more women participate in politics. These women bring about a substantive change in the way women are represented politically. While the Welsh cross-party groups have no formal role in the policy process, they must include members from at least three different political parties. In interviews about cross-party groups, female assembly members noted that women's presence in high numbers and feminist beliefs led to more consensus-style rather than adversarial politics. Measurable effects of women's presence in the Welsh assembly include prioritization of children's issues and the 2001 creation of the office of Children's Commissioner for Wales, a model for other countries that have created a children's commissioner, including Scotland and Northern Ireland in 2003 and England in 2004 ("Women AMs" 2009).

In Scotland, the creation of the Scottish Parliament and subsequent boost in women's political presence in it led to significant focus on eliminating violence against women and, secondarily, on reducing occupational segregation between the sexes. The Scottish government recognized that violence against women is a form of gender inequality and also perpetuates gender inequality. In formulating policy, Scotland followed closely the definition of violence against women established in the United Nations Declaration on the Elimination of Violence against Women (1993). This statement defines violence against women as "any act of gender-based violence that results in, or is likely to result in, physical, sexual or psychological harm or suffering to women, including threats of such acts, coercion or arbitrary deprivation of liberty,

5. These twenty-one areas are agriculture, monuments, culture, economic development, education and training, environment, fire safety and rescue, food, health and health services, highways and transport, housing, local government, internal operations of the National Assembly for Wales, public administration, social welfare, sport, tourism, devolved taxes, town and country planning, water and flood defense, and Welsh language. National Assembly for Wales, n.d.; "Government of Wales Act 2006" 2016.

whether occurring in public or in private life." The Scottish Government notes that violence against women includes "domestic abuse, rape, incest and child sexual abuse; sexual harassment and intimidation at work and in the public sphere; commercial sexual exploitation including prostitution, pornography and trafficking; dowry related violence; forced and child marriages; [and] honour crimes" (Scottish Government 2016). The impetus to address these issues came from women in the Scottish Parliament and because Scotland had passed more significant legislation to prevent violence against women than Westminster.

Tellingly, women have a noticeable subnational identity in UK international reports only after decentralization took root. Specifically, the UK's 1995 "Third Periodic Report" to CEDAW mentions women from Scotland, Wales, and Northern Ireland only when breaking down statistics by subnational unit on crime and on women in public life and not in any other realms (United Nations CEDAW 1995). By 2007, in the heart of devolutionary times, Scotland, Wales, and Northern Ireland appear in their own sections at the front of the "Sixth Periodic Report" to CEDAW (United Nations CEDAW 2007) and in most of the specific CEDAW articles, including those on health, education, and public life. The standing of the political subunits of Scotland, Wales, and Northern Ireland and of women within them merited analysis at a decentralized level in presentation to the United Nations.

This system of asymmetric decentralization (referred to in the United Kingdom as asymmetric devolution) affected the levels and sequence of decentralization in the meso units. England is the only UK meso unit with no distinct political representation other than the assembly of the Greater London Authority. Wales, a lesser case of devolution, received the right to originate legislation in March 2011. Northern Ireland has stronger devolution by reason of nationalist conflict between Nationalists and Unionists. Scotland has the strongest devolution of all (David 2009).[6] Because fiscal powers have not been granted to the meso units of Scotland, Wales, and Northern

6. In Scotland, the Scotland Act created a transfer of powers, or political decentralization, especially in education and health. Administrative decentralization has occurred, but fiscal steps were pushed only in 2011. Within the Scottish Government, a motion was passed on December 6, 2007, by Labour to form the Commission on Scottish Devolution, also known as the Calman Commission. The Calman Commission met over two years and proposed changes between Westminster and the Scottish Parliament in 2009. Scotland technically can raise or lower tax rates but has not used that power, which would amount to meaningful fiscal decentralization. An interview with a high-level Scottish bureaucrat revealed that even Scottish officials supportive of greater autonomy from Westminster who sit on the Financial Issues Advisory Group did not challenge the overall block grant from the Treasury to Scotland (as well as Northern Ireland and Wales), known as the Barnett Formula. Interview by the author, January 2011, Edinburgh, Scotland.

Ireland, they remain dependent on Westminster and the government ministries in Whitehall.

Many women's organizations in Wales and Scotland support decentralization, but in Northern Ireland the left-right dimension of government intervention into the economy does not really apply. Decentralization is contested on the basis of religious identity. Catholicism or Protestantism and position on the Good Friday Agreements form the key cleavages in Northern Irish politics. Religious differences are more salient than economic ones, but the Social Democratic and Labour Party and Sinn Féin are the parties that most often speak up or advance policies to raise women's status (Galligan and Knight 2011, 589).

In contrast, in Scotland and Wales gender equality and women's issues seem to permeate more political parties and meso-level institutions as a whole. A Scottish member of Parliament in Edinburgh told me that "gender equality was really built into the bricks of the place."[7] In Wales, gender equality is one of the founding principles of the Welsh assembly. After the publication of the July 1997 "Devolution White Paper," Welsh groups formed to support devolution, including "Anglican ministers for devolution, women for devolution, farmers for devolution, poets for devolution and even quango [quasiautonomous nongovernmental organization] members for devolution" (Chaney, Mackay, and McAllister 2007). In contrast, Northern Ireland experienced Westminster flip-flopping between decentralization and centralization for a long time. During the Troubles, a period of sectarian violence between Nationalists (generally Roman Catholics) and Unionists (generally Protestants) in Northern Ireland, British Prime Minister Margaret Thatcher revoked home rule by the parliament in Belfast and asserted direct rule by Westminster. Generally, Catholics support decentralization in terms of allowing Northern Ireland autonomy from the Crown and potentially allowing Northern Ireland to realign with the Republic of Ireland, while many Protestants prefer the direct rule of Westminster.

I surveyed UK women in meso units and aggregated their top four policy priorities: eliminating violence against women, public awareness campaigns on women's equality, female leadership, and education and literacy for women (see Table 5.2, later in the chapter). In contrast to Poland and Pakistan, Scotland and Wales had *explicitly gendered movements advocating decentralization and local governance.* For example, women for devolution did not form movements during Poland's or Pakistan's decentralization. In Northern Ireland, women actively sought home rule in the Good Friday Agreements of 1998 and sought decentralization and self-government after sectarian violence.

---

7. Interview by the author, January 2011, Edinburgh, Scotland.

Thus, women in Northern Ireland and women in provinces of Pakistan might have in common wanting decentralization so as to stem conflict.

Between 1999 and 2006, distinct women's policy priorities were reflected in gender equality agencies operating in England, Scotland, Wales, and Northern Ireland. The Women's National Commission established branches in the meso-unit capitals for articulating and enforcing women's rights throughout the United Kingdom. Thus, through a gendered analysis of decentralization we can see that the process was generally embraced and advanced by women's groups across the meso units and that, as implied by work like Charles Tiebout's (1956), women began expressing different policy priorities across the units.

Women's Descriptive Representation in Parliament and the Devolved Assemblies

For many years, women's presence in Westminster lingered under 10 percent. With its innovative all-women shortlists, the British Labour Party set forth a policy that in half of all winnable districts only women would be on the shortlists for party nomination (Childs 2004; Lovenduski 1999; Squires 2005). Thus, Labour Party members decide who gets their nomination in the district, and the electorate decides across parties who represents the district. Thus, Labour advanced female candidates in equal proportion to male candidates in areas where the party could actually win rather than in a token way, by nominating women only where opposition parties had the race sewn up.

All-women shortlists are a type of gender quota policy that can be used in single-member districts that select winners according to the plurality of votes, the first-past-the-post (FPTP) electoral method. A quota for FPTP is harder to finagle than in a proportional representation system in which the party controls the nomination and often the ordering of the party list and can specify the percentage of women on the ballot and the proportions of men versus women in winnable spots (such as the practice of zipping, or gender alternating throughout the party list). The slots at the top of the ballot are guaranteed election and those at the bottom are guaranteed not to be elected. All-women shortlists were used by the Labour Party in the 2005 and 2010 elections and in the run-up to the 2015 general elections. Twinning, in which a party pairs constituency seats, often geographically close to one another and that the party is equally likely to win, and runs a male candidate in one constituency and a female candidate in the other, was used by the Scottish Labour Party in the run-up to the Scottish Parliament elections in 1999 and in the elections for the first National Assembly for Wales (see Lovenduski 2005; Squires 2005, 17). In response to a court challenge to the all-women shortlist policy, the Sex Discrimination (Election Candidates) Act of 2002 "allows political parties the freedom to introduce positive measures, such as quotas, when selecting candidates for [the UK] Parliament, local government and the devolved assembles, without risk of legal challenge The [act's] remit includes elections for Westminster, the European Parliament, the Scottish Parliament and National Assembly for Wales and local government elections, although it excludes election for the Mayor of London and other directly elected Mayors" (Squires 2005, 14).

At the meso level in the United Kingdom, gender equality in women's descriptive representation becomes more common. Before the first subnational elections, feminists feared that the newly elected assemblies would replicate the masculine domain of politics. However, in 2003, Wales had the first assembly in the world with gender parity in formal representation: the sixty-member body had thirty women and thirty men (Chaney, Mackay, and McAllister 2007). Around the same time, women's numbers in the Scottish Parliament were at 39.5 percent compared to 17.9 percent in Westminster. In Northern Ireland, however, women's descriptive representation was at 14 percent and has tended to lag behind the UK standard. See Table 5.1.

Table 5.1 Women in national and meso-level parliaments and women by party delegation in the United Kingdom, 1997–2014

	1997 % women	2001 % women	2005 % women	2014 % women (no. of women/ no. of seats)	Number of women from each party, 2014
House of Commons	18.2	17.9	19.8	22.0 (143/650)	81 British Labour; 7 Liberal Democratic; 49 Conservative; 6 other
Average at meso level for the United Kingdom	30.4	34.5	32.3	28.3 (84/297)	
Scotland	37.2	39.5	33.3	30.2 (39/129)	18 Scottish Labour; 17 Scottish National Party; 4 other
Wales	40.0	50.0	46.7	41.7 (25/60)	15 Welsh Labour; 4 Plaid Cyrmu; 2 Liberal Democratic; 4 Conservative
Northern Ireland	13.9	14.0	16.7	18.5 (20/108)	3 Social Democratic Labor Party; 8 Sinn Féin; 2 Alliance; 5 Democratic Unionist; 2 Ulster Union

Sources: Burness 2011; Childs and Webb 2012; Global Database of Quotas for Women 2013; Hinojosa 2012; McTavish 2016; North South Inter-Parliamentary Association 2015; Scottish Parliament Information Centre 2016; Squires 2005; UK Political Info, n.d.

Note: The United Kingdom has voluntary party quotas for women. The Labour Party requires all-women short lists for 50 percent of all vacant seats. The Liberal Democratic Party aims for a target of 40 percent women. The Conservative Party gives preferred consideration to women and black, Asian, and other ethnic minority candidates. Years are national election years; meso-level figures are from the election closest to the national election year. Election years for Scotland and Wales were 1999, 2003, 2007, and 2011. For Northern Ireland, they were 1998, 2003, 2007, and 2011.

Where leftist parties are strong in the United Kingdom, women are more numerous in political office. The largest party delegations of women hail from the Labour Party across the meso units of Scotland and Wales, from parts of England, and from the Sinn Féin in Northern Ireland. While the Liberal Democrats adopted only a 40 percent soft target for women's candidacies, the Labour Party's robust gender quota systems significantly boosted the numbers of women in office. Because the United Kingdom does not have statutory quotas to maintain the legislative node of the gender policy trifecta, it has room for improvement. While the Labour Party and leftist parties have provided the most access for women of any party in the UK system, the gender policy trifecta in the United Kingdom can arguably be best maintained through the adoption of statutory gender quotas, although cross-party agreement to increase equality in politics has put pressure on all parties to recruit and advance female candidates and make succession plans when female politicians near retirement.

Capacity and Presence of Women's Organizations and Women's Policy Agencies

In the United Kingdom, the key governmental body responsible for gender equality policy is the Government Equalities Office. Before its establishment, the relevant agency was the ministerial group on women's issues created in 1987. In 1992, the ministerial group became the Cabinet Sub-committee for Women's Issues, led by Secretary of State for Employment Gillian Sheppard (United Nations CEDAW 1995, 7). The Government Equalities Office was created in October 2007, five months into Prime Minister Gordon Brown's Labour government. According to Statutory Instrument 2007 (2914), the office performs functions formerly held by other equalities commissions on race and gender combined into a larger "equalities regime," or one commission with fewer resources ("The Transfer of Functions" 2007). One justification for the merger was to make it easier for other public agencies seeking advice and consent to address one equalities commission rather than multiple separate commissions. On the other hand, advocacy groups for individual causes—such as LGBT rights; black, Asian, or minority ethnic (BAME) rights; and women's rights—worried that combining these marginalized groups into an equalities unit would lead bureaucrats to prioritize some groups or identities over others. The potential permeability of local institutions to women's rights has been lost as women compete within an equality framework also responsible for the categories of age, disability, gender reassignment, marriage and civil partnership, pregnancy and maternity, race, religion or belief, and sexual orientation.

Also in October 2007, the Equality and Human Rights Commission was created as an arm's-length commission for England, Scotland, and Wales to inform people of their rights; work with employers, employees, and other organizations to implement statutes on equalities; and pursue limited judicial enforcement of those rights. Prime Minister David Cameron's government disbanded the Women's National Commission in October 2010. Without that commission, the Government Equalities Office and the Equality and Human Rights Commission become central to this story of devolution in the United Kingdom.

The structure of equalities policy making is somewhat centralized in the Government Equalities Office, and the 2010 government was a Conservative–Liberal Democrat coalition. This means the degree of leftism in the meso units might not be as well translated in the content of policies. For example, Wales, Scotland, and England have all had budget cuts, and Northern Ireland takes its cues from the UK Equality and Human Rights Commission. Under Cameron's government, the Government Equalities Office reduced the mandate and budget of the Equality and Human Rights Commission, eliminated the Women's National Commission, and announced that it would not require businesses to report their gender pay figures. In the eyes of some, these steps gutted the 2010 Equality Act.

In Wales and Scotland, the leadership of women's policy agencies identified as feminist, but this was not the case in the Government Equalities Office or the Equality Commission for Northern Ireland. The capacities of these offices range widely, too. Labour governments in Westminster and the devolved assemblies have passed important legislation for women since their creation in 1999, but the strength of the women's movement in UK meso units explains much of the remaining support for feminist policies.

Women's Policy Priorities

Drawing on structured interviews with women's groups across the United Kingdom, I now report women's policy priorities. After learning what policies women's groups find important and vital, I then ascertain which level of governance responds most closely to their policy priorities. First, I present the aggregate results on the top policy priorities across all women's groups I surveyed, and then I examine the more detailed results for women's groups in London, Cardiff, Edinburgh, and Belfast to see if there are subnational differences in the policy priorities of women. I test whether devolved or national gender equality bureaucrats better represent the policy priorities of women's groups in the meso unit. As described in Chapter 1, my conceptualization of representation of women's interests revolves around how closely elected or appointed officials' policy priorities match the policy priorities of women in

Table 5.2 What women want in the United Kingdom, 2011

Policy priorities of women's organizations, aggregated across the country	Policy priorities of national women's policy agency
1. Eliminating violence against women (16)	1. Promoting women in the labor market
2. Public awareness campaigns on women's equality (14)	2. Raising awareness about gender-based employment discrimination
3. Female leadership (7)	3. LGBT rights
4. Adult education and literacy for women (6)	4. Eliminating violence against women

Note: Numbers in parentheses are the number of leaders who listed the item as a top four priority.

their meso unit. Interviews with women's groups show that they prioritize four issues (see Table 5.2 and Figure 5.2). In the United Kingdom, I interviewed women's organization leaders in London, Cardiff, Edinburgh, and Belfast.

First, women's groups believe more must be done to eliminate violence against women. Second, women's groups want to see public awareness campaigns about women's equality. Third, women's groups desire expansion of female leadership. The fourth policy priority is adult education and literacy for women. We can look to two places to see how well women's policy priorities have been represented: Westminster's record (the legislative path) and the record of the Government Equalities Office (the bureaucratic path). Within Westminster itself, we see little action on women's top four priorities. Westminster created the environment and pressure to stop equality awareness campaigns as part of the 2011 budget cuts and gave no indication of when campaigns would restart. The 2004 Domestic Violence Act passed, but Scotland is ahead of this legislation by defining violence itself as coming from patriarchy. The greatest strides in increasing female leadership were made under the 1997 Labour Party's all-women shortlists (Childs 2004). The Conservative Party experimented with its own A-list for women and black and minority ethnic candidates (Childs and Webb 2012) but kept it more vague and adaptable, which the party believed would ensure the recruitment of women in future elections. The House of Lords is considering measures for greater gender balance in its unelected membership. Last, the Cameron government has not announced specific measures to encourage education and literacy for adult women. Parliament has not addressed migrant and BAME women's lack of "recourse to public funds" (i.e., they have a residence permit to live in the United Kingdom but cannot claim state benefits, tax credits, or housing assistance; see UK Visas and Immigration 2014). Therefore, the government has been responsive on two of the four issues during the leftist Labour government (1997–2010) but not during the rightist Conservative–Liberal Democrat coalition government (2010–2011).

The Government Equalities Office articulates and coordinates policies to advance equality between women and men, girls and boys. If it is representing

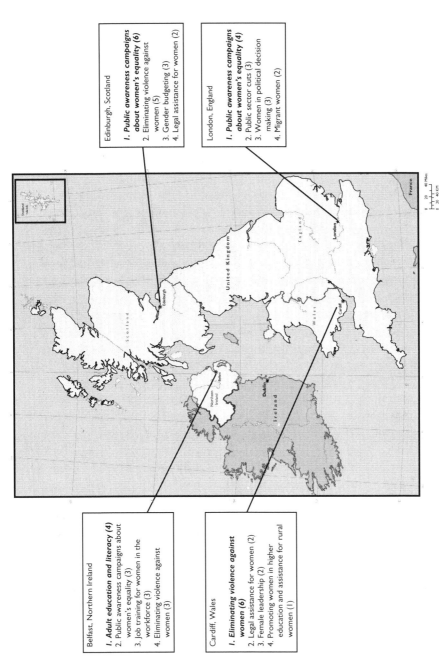

Edinburgh, Scotland

1. Public awareness campaigns about women's equality (6)
2. Eliminating violence against women (5)
3. Gender budgeting (3)
4. Legal assistance for women (2)

London, England

1. Public awareness campaigns about women's equality (4)
2. Public sector cuts (3)
3. Women in political decision making (3)
4. Migrant women (2)

Belfast, Northern Ireland

1. Adult education and literacy (4)
2. Public awareness campaigns about women's equality (3)
3. Job training for women in the workforce (3)
4. Eliminating violence against women (3)

Cardiff, Wales

1. Eliminating violence against women (6)
2. Legal assistance for women (2)
3. Female leadership (2)
4. Promoting women in higher education and assistance for rural women (1)

Figure 5.2 Policy priorities of women's organizations in the United Kingdom, 2011. Numbers in parentheses are the number of leaders who listed the item as a top priority.

women well, its priorities should closely match what women within its borders want. However, the office matches just one of these four priorities. First, it is striking that public awareness campaigns about women's equality are the number-one priority of women's organizations across the United Kingdom, but the office does not mention them as a policy priority. As in Poland and Pakistan, public awareness campaigns about women's equality are often needed to jumpstart a gender equality policy discussion. In the budget cuts of spring 2011, the office did not project spending any money to raise awareness and create an environment for cultural change. Fiscal conservatives could likely attack this sort of publicly financed advertisement about women's equality as an unnecessary expenditure during times of austerity and could argue that women's organizations or charities can perform this function if it is important to them. On the other hand, a state bureau's attention lends weight to an issue and can start a public discussion about gender equality, as media or conservative interests might marginalize feminist groups as being too extreme for sponsoring the same public awareness campaign.

What about other priorities of the Government Equalities Office? In response to my interview questions, officials said their focus has been on policies to enhance the status of women as individuals rather than collective actions to address women's inequality. Its top four policy priorities were promoting women in the labor market, raising awareness about gender-based employment discrimination, promoting LGBT rights, and eliminating violence against women.

While the office wanted to promote women in the labor market, its then minister, Theresa May, did not fight fellow cabinet ministers on the 2010 public sector cutbacks affecting women's employment. Instead she focused on encouraging private businesses to include women on their boards of directors. The Government Equalities Office does not prioritize fighting for cross-party gender quotas to expand women's political decision-making power, as quotas are seen as restricting individual liberty to run for election. Gender-based employment discrimination via the gender pay gap remains a concern of the office, but May announced that she would not enforce the Equality Act of 2010 with respect to requiring businesses to report on salaries; May's predecessor, Harriet Harman of the Labour Party, had pursued this policy. The third priority of the office is LGBT rights, which is an area of progress for UK women in the sense that few groups fight specifically for LGBT rights. For example, the main LGBT group is the LGBT wing of Amnesty International. Still, the protected status of LGBT citizens is part of the Government Equalities Office's duty. The elimination of violence against women is the office's fourth priority, which matches the second priority of women's organizations. Other office priorities aim to bring about improvements for women, but at the level of individual court cases and in the private rather than public or political sectors. With this broad portrait of the top policy priorities of women, we can look to see if specific differences emerge in policy priorities in England, Scotland, Wales, and Northern Ireland.

The United Kingdom exhibits considerable subnational variation in women's policy priorities, as do Poland and Pakistan. In England, the top four priorities of women's organizations were public awareness campaigns about women's equality, public sector cuts, women in political decision making, and migrant women. In England, women have mobilized against budget cuts more prominently, led by the Fawcett Society. In Scotland, women's groups reported that their policy priorities were public awareness campaigns about women's equality, eliminating violence against women, gender budgeting, and legal assistance to women. As we see through comparison, women's organizations in England and Scotland placed a higher priority on migrant and BAME women than organizations in Wales and Northern Ireland, because the former nations are more urban and industrialized and have higher levels of immigration than the latter. The top four policy priorities for Welsh women in 2011 were eliminating violence against women, legal assistance for women, female leadership, and a tie between promoting women in higher education and assisting rural women. So in Wales, women's organizations gave higher importance to eliminating violence against women and female leadership. The Equality and Human Rights Commission in Wales reported the appointment of the first female deputy vice chancellor, Elizabeth Treasure, at Cardiff University, an important milestone for women in Wales.

Top priorities for women's organizations in Northern Ireland were adult education and literacy, public awareness campaigns about women's equality, job training for women in the workforce, and eliminating violence against women. These priorities in Northern Ireland reflect that its women's labor force participation is the lowest in the United Kingdom. For example, a women's organization leader in Northern Ireland noted:

> The lack of equality starts at a young age. At our center we pick up the pieces of many women; they have no confidence in themselves, whether because they've been at home six to eight years, suffer from mild depression, or worse. It's like a wave keeps churning out this kind of person. Without organizations like ourselves, there would be more casualties. Women don't get focus back in their lives, and our system doesn't recognize it. The state says we have child care; you can go back to work if you want to, but that's not addressing lack of confidence [that hinders getting] into the system again. We have in our system one lady who just went back to work in human resources. She said she felt nervous about going back to work after just six to

eight weeks of being off. Mums can get reskilled by signing up for a course; one to two hours for ten weeks can help. Women are 90 to 95 percent of those who stay at home after birth of children.[8]

By and large, the policy priorities of devolved gender equality policy makers matched the unique priorities of women in their meso units as well or better than the national Government Equalities Office. In Scotland, Wales, and Northern Ireland, most gender equality policy makers matched women's organizations on two of their four policy priorities. Scotland's MWPA matched women's organizations on two priorities—eliminating violence against women and gender budgeting—but had two unique priorities: reduction of gender-based occupational segregation and inclusion of adults with disabilities, gypsy travelers, and LGBT students. The Wales MWPA matched women's organizations' focus on female leadership and women in higher education but had three unique priorities of embedding the Equality Act of 2010, assessing the gendered impact of budget cuts, and raising awareness about gender-based employment discrimination. The Northern Ireland MWPA did not directly align with women's organizations, instead prioritizing addressing the gender pay gap, encouraging child care, promoting women in political decision making, and ending pregnancy discrimination.

In interviews with women's organization leaders, many women pointed to progress for women that occurred under the leftist Labour governments. For example, they discussed progress represented by the Equality Act of 2006 (which covers England and Wales), the Equality Act in Scotland, and subsequent changes embodied in the 2010 Equality Act. Leftist governments produced consistent advances for women in pay equality, particularly by requiring businesses to keep detailed pay statistics that government agencies could audit. After the 2010 general election, Government Equalities Office Minister Theresa May announced that the government would not enforce these pay equity measures. Many women's groups expressed concern that the 2006 Equality Act had been hollowed out.

Comparison across the meso-level units shows that the most favorable situation for women's descriptive and substantive representation occurs when statutory gender quotas that apply to the meso level are passed along with gender-mainstreaming and gender-budgeting policy at the meso level. This brings more women into the policy-making process, leading to more policies that reduce gender inequalities. Even the architectural structures of the new devolved assemblies—on-site day care and the physical layout of assembly

---

8. Telephone interview by the author, March 2011.

rooms—foster greater inclusiveness of female members than the confrontational style and layout of Westminster.

Assessment of Women's Descriptive and Substantive Representation

Before activists within the Labour Party successfully pushed for devolution in the United Kingdom and all-women shortlists, the percentage of women in the House of Commons was just 9 percent (1992), but it boosted to 18 percent in the 1997 elections (Apostolova and Cracknell 2016, 22). Women's descriptive representation in the devolved assemblies has shown impressive highs, including gender parity in the Welsh Assembly in 2003. As of 2011, women's descriptive representation was just under 20 percent in Northern Ireland, 30 percent in Scotland, and 40 percent in Wales. Though more can be done to safeguard quotas, women have won increased descriptive representation in the United Kingdom through devolution. When we compare the policy priorities that women's groups expressed in Scotland, Wales, and Northern Ireland with the substantive policies actually passed in their respective legislatures (see Appendix 6), we find mixed results for women in terms of substantive representation. Between 1999 and 2011, the Scottish Parliament passed significant legislation on violence against women. As of 2016, the Scottish Equalities Unit contains a very influential Equality and Budget Advisory Group that works regularly with feminist members of the Scottish Parliament to implement gender budgeting in Scotland. See Figure 5.3.

Scottish Parliament members have also drafted legislation to offer public assistance to refugee women who have had to stay in violent relationships because they are ineligible for public assistance. The Scottish Parliament has thus acted on three of the four policy areas that women care about in Scotland: eliminating violence against women, gender budgeting, and legal assistance for women. Also, Karen Celis, Fiona Mackay, and Petra Meier (2013) show that under the Conservative–Liberal Democrat government in Westminster, Scottish women's organizations have focused their work on the more favorable Scottish parliamentary context.

In Wales, the Welsh assembly has acted on, to a lesser degree, women's top policy priorities. As Appendix 6 shows, the main policy action has been on children's issues, new legislation for caregivers, and a new equality duty passed in 2011. The percentage of women in the Welsh assembly fell in spring 2011 elections from its former parity, but it remains high. The Welsh assembly has not acted on violence against women, assisting women from rural areas, or public awareness campaigns about women's equality. However, the Welsh government has acted on getting more women in higher education, and the equality duty may have widespread effects in terms of legal assistance

Figure 5.3 Angela O'Hagan, convenor of the Scottish Women's Budget Group

for women. As a result, the Welsh assembly has acted on two issues women's organization leaders have prioritized in Wales.

Aside from some broad measures to expand the job opportunities that have not been gendered, the Northern Irish government has not acted on women's organizations' priorities and has been the least responsive of the subnational parliaments to women's issues. Rather than gender, race, or class issues, sectarian issues between Catholics and Protestants dominate much of the political discourse in the Northern Ireland Assembly. The Women's Coalition in Northern Ireland formed, but this party did not remain competitive in later elections, and former members have won elections at mixed rates through other, related parties. Even across religious lines, female interviewees reported the importance of electing women from the other religious traditions because they often effectively argued for women's issues within their own party caucus. In total, the Northern Ireland Assembly addressed only one of four priorities of its female constituents.

Conclusion

The United Kingdom went through asymmetric decentralization around 1998, allowing the Scottish Parliament to form and the Welsh assembly to be created. In the intervening fifteen years, the presence of the three nodes

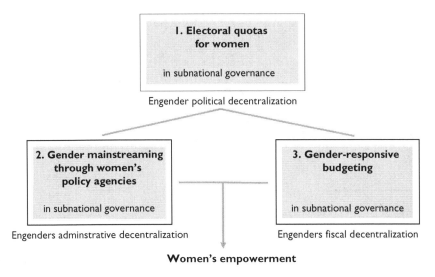

Figure 5.4 The gender policy trifecta in the United Kingdom. A shaded box means the node is present; an unshaded box means it is not.

of the gender policy trifecta has led to significant improvements in women's empowerment in the United Kingdom (see Figure 5.4).

The British Labour Party, Scottish and Welsh nationalists, and many women's organizations advocated decentralization and participated in movements specifically supporting devolution. The initial drivers of decentralization, supporting women's representation themselves, helped bring about more engendered politics at the meso level, particularly in Scotland and Wales. The case of the United Kingdom affirmatively answers the second guiding question: more women were elected to meso-level assemblies with gender quotas than those where there were none. When decentralization occurred, meso units with strong support for the Labour Party elected more women than ever to assembly positions, and these elected women frequently advocated feminist policy outcomes, particularly in Wales and Scotland. Leftist parties have done more to advance quotas, centrist parties have adopted weaker targets for women's candidacies, and conservative parties have eschewed formal quotas while using informal tactics to encourage women to stand for election. MWPAs in Scotland, Wales, and Northern Ireland emerged and advocated gender mainstreaming across government agencies. Gender-responsive budgeting also cropped up at the meso level, helping women's organizations gain a foothold.

Even as the gender policy trifecta engenders women's representation across institutions, it requires maintenance. The gender policy trifecta cannot ensure on its own that women will be equally well represented across meso units. In Northern Ireland, strong Catholic norms on gender roles and low election rates for women show that women have not yet effectively penetrated meso-level institutions. Policy priorities in Northern Ireland have emphasized reducing pregnancy discrimination and bringing women into the workforce, and women's participation in Northern Ireland still lags other meso-level units in the United Kingdom.

In spite of active women's policy agencies and feminist members of the Scottish Parliament and the Welsh assembly, the 2010 and 2015 election of Conservative-led governments and low levels of fiscal decentralization have affected women's representation. When Westminster leaned to the political right and pursued budget cuts, these cuts constrained the ability of gender equality agencies and the devolved assemblies. As Scotland and eventually Wales gain more fiscal decentralization powers and as Wales exercises its power of initial legislation won in a March 2011 referendum, policy implementations in these meso units might diverge further from Westminster. Even when the United Kingdom participated in the European Union, the EU played a small role in pushing for decentralization because the United Kingdom had been a member long before it pursued decentralization.

In terms of policy recommendations, this research suggests that Westminster and devolved assemblies should consider statutory gender quotas to durably establish gains in women's descriptive representation, that female politicians should establish succession plans to mentor female aspirants to take up the mantle after one generation retires from office, and that the devolved assemblies should make further strides toward fiscal decentralization. The United Kingdom has two nodes of the gender policy trifecta firmly in place and a third that needs further support.

For the first node, during the first twenty years of decentralization, some political parties adopted voluntary quotas, creating a gender policy trifecta at times in Wales and Scotland. For the second, active women's policy agencies engage in gender mainstreaming at the national and subnational level. For the third, some of its meso units have gender-responsive budgeting, particularly Scotland. Interestingly, voluntary quotas and decentralization have emerged in the same time frame in the United Kingdom as Labour sought new strategies to win power in the mid-1990s. In some ways, it seems a contagion has spread from the Labour to the Conservative Party in terms of revamping candidate selection processes to encourage female candidates (such as Cameron's A-list). Surprisingly, the percentage of women in UK meso-level assemblies is higher under its voluntary quota system than Pakistan's percentage under its system of meso-level reserved seats for women. However, the costs for women of holding office may be greater in Pakistan than in the United Kingdom (Rincker, Aslam, and Isani 2016). On the other hand, Poland has held meso-level elections with its 35 percent statutory quota in place only since

2014, so support for voluntary quotas in the United Kingdom over statutory quotas may be premature. Statutory quotas prevent parties from shirking their democratic duty of identifying and cultivating women to participate in politics at all levels of governance; they also prevent parties sympathetic to greater inclusion of women from backpedaling when they encounter quota critics. Quota critics imply that all male candidates are inherently qualified for office; that no unidentified, qualified female candidates exist; and that no changes can be made to party or official duties that make elected office more attractive to female candidates.

A dispersed and well-maintained gender policy trifecta could lead to passage of policies specific to the priorities of women's groups in each area: policies to advance black, Asian, minority, and ethnic women in Scotland; job-training programs in Northern Ireland; policies to promote women to positions in higher education in Wales; and measures to support women after public sector cuts in England. The adoption of statutory gender quotas, gender-responsive budgeting, and gender mainstreaming across all subnational units, including Northern Ireland, would enable passage of policies responsive to the diverse priorities of women in the United Kingdom.

Part III

6

Global Assessment of the Gender Policy Trifecta

Under what conditions does decentralization lead to women's empowerment? I argue in this book that women's empowerment means greater responsiveness to women's policy priorities, more women in politics, and cross-institutional collaboration on feminist policy outcomes. In this final chapter, I revisit the evidence on the three guiding questions, provide readers (including policy makers and activists) insights on where in the world the gender policy trifecta is operating, and identify countries with missing nodes. This book shows that what women want—in terms of women's organization policy priorities—varies as much within each of the three countries studied as it does across the three countries. This evidence constitutes a strong, new argument in favor of decentralization. As an analogy to clarify this point, consider Georges Seurat's famous painting *A Sunday Afternoon on the Island of La Grande Jatte* (Figure 6.1).[1] At first glance, the most important diversity in colors comes from comparing people in the park: the earthy red shirt of a workman lying back on his elbows, the vibrant blue bustle of a woman standing with a parasol. But if we look at just one individual—like the young girl at the center of the painting—in this pointillist work, we notice the remarkable variety of blue, pink, yellow, brown, and gray hues Seurat used to paint one figure. Similarly, this book demonstrates that we must be as attentive to within-country diversity in women's policy priorities as across-country diversity.

---

1. A color image of the painting is available at http://en.wikipedia.org/wiki/A_Sunday_ Afternoon_on_the_Island_of_La_Grande_Jatte#mediaviewer/File:A_Sunday_on_La_Grande_ Jatte,_Georges_Seurat,_1884.jpg.

Figure 6.1 *A Sunday Afternoon on the Island of La Grande Jatte,* by Georges Seurat (1884)

This research also updates the work of Friedrich Hayek (1945) and Charles Tiebout (1956), which shows that subnational politicians are more informed about (male) constituents' preferences than national politicians are. I show that meso-level politicians must work in an engendered environment of the gender policy trifecta before they can develop information advantages about the diverse priorities of groups traditionally marginalized in political life, like women. To recognize the policy preferences of all its citizens, a fully democratized society cannot just decentralize; it must also engender its political institutions. Women's substantive representation does not increase with decentralization alone. Women's empowerment increases in the presence of the gender policy trifecta. I begin this chapter by revisiting the three guiding questions and reflecting on how decentralization has affected women's empowerment across three country cases. Then, on the basis of my findings on decentralization and women's empowerment in the country case chapters, I present data identifying countries around the world that possess the gender policy trifecta and countries with gaps. I close by discussing contributions of this book to ongoing debates in political science.

Assessing the Three Guiding Questions

A comparison of the hybrid survey-interview data from across the three countries of study answers yes to the first guiding question: *Do women's policy priorities vary as much within countries as across countries?* Surprisingly, when aggregated to the national level, women in very different countries share similar top public policy priorities. Comparing women's organizations' top four policy priorities aggregated to the country level in Poland (Table 3.2), Pakistan (Table 4.3), and the United Kingdom (Table 5.2), we find that women in the United Kingdom, Pakistan, and Poland share two: the elimination of violence against women and public awareness campaigns about women's equality. In fact, Pakistan and the United Kingdom also prioritize education and literacy, but in the United Kingdom it is for adult women and in Pakistan for school-age girls. Despite these two countries having different levels of freedom, experience with democracy, and economic development, they share two out of four policy priorities. Poland also shares two of its top four aggregated policy priorities with the United Kingdom and Pakistan: public campaigns for women's equality and the elimination of violence against women. It is also important to note that each country had policy priorities aggregated to the country level that were not highly ranked in the other countries. In Poland, women's groups placed unique emphasis on assisting women from rural areas and raising awareness about gender-based employment discrimination. This could be attributable to larger urban-rural disparities in women's rights and the effort by the European Union to eliminate gender-based employment discrimination. Women's organizations in Pakistan highly prioritized getting women into political decision making, and in the United Kingdom, women's organizations prioritized female leadership. But the key finding is that women's organizations across these three extremely different countries share 50 percent of their top policy priorities. Across the globe, women's organizations want to see far more public awareness campaigns that remind citizens that women and girls are equal to men and boys and policies to eliminate violence against women. The results in this book suggest that women's organizations can pursue gender equality through regional, transnational, and international organizations like the United Nations. The analysis thus contributes to meso-level theory building, because it connects the political behavior of individual women's organizations and leaders to larger political organizations and agendas. The hybrid survey-interview data show particularly the connections between micro-level data on women's organizations' priorities in Poland, Pakistan, and the United Kingdom and macro-level realities. For example, the United Nations passed near-unanimous resolutions to eliminate violence against women in United Nations Security Council Resolution 1325 (United States Institute of Peace, n.d.) and to increase roles for women in political decision making in Millennium Development Goal 3: promote gender equality and empower women (United Nations, n.d.).

This research for the first time demonstrates that women's policy priorities vary as much within individual countries as across them. I show this result first by comparing the percentages of priorities shared across a particular country's provinces with the percentage of priorities that country shares with the other two nations in this study. Look at the data on women's policy priorities aggregated to the meso level in Poland (Figure 3.3), Pakistan (Figure 4.2), and the United Kingdom (Figure 5.2). In the United Kingdom, women's organizations in Scotland, Northern Ireland, Wales, and England share eight of sixteen (50 percent) top policy priorities. The remaining 50 percent of women's policy priorities in these meso units diverge from one another, meaning that women's policy priorities vary as much within the United Kingdom as they do with Poland and Pakistan (50 percent). Looking at the Polish case, we find that seven of twelve priorities (58 percent) are shared among the provinces of Pomorskie, Wielkopolskie, and Mazowieckie. This means that women's organization leaders differ on their policy priorities about as much within the country as they do with women's organization leaders in the United Kingdom and Pakistan.

In Pakistan, women's organizations in Khyber Pakhtunkhwa and Punjab Provinces and the capital Islamabad share as many as nine of twelve (75 percent) top policy priorities, aggregated to the meso level. The strong cross-provincial convergence in what Pakistani women want makes Pakistan's lack of democratization for women even more striking. This finding highlights women's organizations' frustration that national women's policy machinery did not put eliminating violence against women on their list of top four policy priorities. I argue that violence against women is an issue too volatile and too fraught with legal consequences for any women's policy agency (WPA) to deal with alone. Civil society activists are admirably giving attention to this issue despite threats of retributive violence against them by Islamic militants. Pakistani legislators, in particular, have to be willing to enforce current laws and to amend the Hudood Ordinances despite resistance, especially from religious quarters that see activism on this issue as alignment with the United States and the West. Although within-country variance is less than across-country variance in Pakistan, provincial variance in policy priorities does occur. For example, Khyber Pakhtunkhwa prioritizes reproductive choice services and awareness, Islamabad women's organizations prioritize raising awareness about gender-based job discrimination, and women's groups in Punjab push for public awareness campaigns about women's equality.

The second way I demonstrate within-country variance in policy priorities is from the perspective of national and meso-level women's policy agencies. Table 6.1 shows the top four policy priorities reported by women's organizations in each country, followed by the top four reported by the national women's policy agency and all top four policy priorities reported by the meso-level women's policy agencies (MWPAs) in a country. Two main findings emerge. First, the MWPA priorities tend to match those of women's organizations as well as or better than the national WPA priorities. Second,

Table 6.1 Policy priorities of women's organizations and national and meso-level WPAs in Poland, Pakistan, and the United Kingdom

Country	Women's organization policy priorities	National WPA priorities	Additional priorities addressed by MWPAs
Poland	Public awareness campaigns for women's equality (13) Eliminating violence against women (13) Assisting women from rural areas (12) Raising awareness about gender employment discrimination (11)	Promoting women in the labor market *Raising awareness about gender-based employment discrimination* Family-friendly policy Reconciliation of work and family life	Family-friendly policy Education of school-age girls Foster care *Public awareness campaigns for women's equality* *Assisting women from rural areas* *Raising awareness about gender-based employment discrimination* Promoting women in labor market *Eliminating violence against women* Job training for women Work-family reconciliation Physical fitness Promoting health of family and women Legal assistance for women Grant writing for capacity building Supporting women-led NGOs Women as political leaders Advice for victims of mobbing Lectures on EU law
Pakistan	Eliminating violence against women (15) Public awareness campaigns for women's equality (10) Education and literacy for school-age girls (10) Women in political decision making (10)	Women's entrepreneurship and microcredits for women *Education and literacy for school-age girls* Food assistance for girls and women *Women in political decision making*	Reconstruction from earthquake Forest, greenery, and technical skills Promoting women in labor market *Eliminating violence against women* Legal assistance for women Economic empowerment Rehabilitation of female beggars and job training for women Shelters for women (*dar-ul-aman* system) Raising awareness about gender-based employment discrimination Eliminating female trafficking
United Kingdom	Eliminating violence against women (16) Public awareness campaigns for women's equality (14) Female leadership (7) Adult education and literacy for women (6)	Promoting women in the labor market Ending gender-based employment discrimination LGBT rights *Eliminating violence against women*	*Adult education and literacy for women* *Public awareness campaigns about women's equality* *Eliminating violence against women* Assisting women from rural areas *Female leadership* Women's entrepreneurship and micro-credits for women Promoting women in the labor market Raising awareness about gender-based employment discrimination Family-friendly policy Reconciliation of work and family life Gender mainstreaming in public policy Encouraging women's associationalism and social participation LGBT rights Encouraging women's political participation Quality of life and social cohesion

Note: Numbers in parentheses are the number of women's organizations that listed the item as a top four priority. Italic text indicates where WPA priorities match women's organization priorities.

the existence of MWPAs allows the state to address a wider diversity of women's policy priorities. MWPAs in Poland, Pakistan, and the United Kingdom each identified between ten and eighteen issues as within the realm of their top four policy priorities. So together, national and meso-level WPAs cover many of the policy priorities of women's organizations, but decentralization or existence of MWPAs allows them to respond to diverse within-country variance. As Table 6.1 shows, MWPAs display widely varying priorities that reflect local cultures and conditions.

This finding does not contradict the first finding of global commonalities but rather shows that, in smaller spatial areas, between one and three unique policy priorities emerge. Therefore, as Tiebout argues (1956), a decentralized governance structure that allows policies to be crafted to match unique policy priorities inherent to the territorial unit will be the most efficient. However, we cannot expect that politicians will necessarily listen or respond to female citizens as intently as to male citizens, who tend to have more economic power and experience interacting in formal channels of political participation. I substantially augment Tiebout's argument by demonstrating that a gender policy trifecta is necessary to engender subnational political institutions and their practices in legislative assemblies and bureaucracies and in their interactions with civil society groups, particularly in creating budgets.

Hybrid survey-interviews with MWPA leaders demonstrated their sensitivity to local needs and concerns that a national WPA leader would need to push aside in the interest of coherent national policy. MWPA leaders in Belfast, Northern Ireland, report job training for women as a top priority, in an atmosphere of traditional Catholic values and the expectation that women will not rejoin the workforce after childbirth. In London, WPA leaders mention LGBT rights as central, reflecting greater concentration of organized LGBT citizens in this global city. MWPA leaders report antitrafficking measures as crucial in Khyber Pakhtunkhwa, while leaders in Azad Jammu and Kashmir report that access to forest resources is a top priority, reflecting the need to engender specific resources in Muzaffarabad, capital of Azad Jammu and Kashmir. That women within the same country have very different priorities for public money provides an important and overlooked justification for decentralization. Decentralization is a more accurate way to represent women's diverse policy priorities. This research builds on John Carey's (2000), showing the process of aggregating citizen preferences to different scales—from local to meso to national. I also show that it takes additional outreach, advocacy, and critical change within institutions to aggregate the preferences of groups historically marginalized from politics on new scales of governance. Decentralization reforms must target these groups and make them feel that their issues will be heard. In contrast to G. Bingham Powell Jr. and Georg Vanberg (2000), my results show that proportional representation systems (as in Pakistan and Poland) are not necessarily more responsive than single-member-district systems (as in the United Kingdom); rather, the presence of gender quotas is crucial to getting women's issues on national and meso-level agendas.

Therefore, examination of the diverse cases of Poland, Pakistan, and the United Kingdom also answers yes to the second guiding question: *Is women's representation higher in meso-level assemblies that have gender quotas than those that do not?* Pakistan's provincial assemblies had 17 percent women under its quota system; when quotas expired they had zero. Similarly in Poland, quotas raised the average percentage of women in government from 14 to 22 percent. The United Kingdom's devolved assemblies with stronger Labour Party support have a higher percentage of women than assemblies in which parties supporting voluntary quotas are absent. It is notable that women's descriptive representation is higher in the United Kingdom's meso-level assemblies with voluntary quotas than in Poland and Pakistan with their mandatory quotas. This is an area where further research is needed: do voluntary or mandatory gender quotas produce more lasting gains in women's descriptive representation, or should voluntary quotas at some point be made mandatory? Chapters 3, 4, and 5 also answer yes to the third guiding question: *Are MWPAs and women's organizations important sites of representation of women's policy priorities in decentralizing countries?* Women's organizations serve women most directly and bring their issues to meso-level legislators and WPAs in their advocacy of gender budgeting and mainstreaming. Similarly, from semistructured interviews, I found that WPAs are very important in raising awareness within government circles of top priorities for women's organizations and in linking women's organization leaders to elected officials.

Reflecting across the Country Cases

In this section, I look across Poland, Pakistan, and the United Kingdom to reflect more broadly on women's empowerment. Only one node of the gender policy trifecta was present in Poland, MWPAs, which took a vocal role on issues like violence against women. Not until 2011 did Poland adopt subnational gender quotas, and it held its first round of local elections in which these applied in 2014. The European Union applied pressure to encourage the passage of this gender quota bill, and rightist President Komorowski signed it into law. As of 2015, Poland does not have gender-responsive budgeting in place. However, the supranational pressure exerted on Poland is a reminder that decentralization does not occur in a vacuum and organizations like the European Union can impose it from a level above the national. Women's descriptive and substantive representation could take hold in the coming years, especially in wealthier provinces.

In Pakistan, there are only two nodes of the gender policy trifecta at the meso level: 17 percent gender quotas and MWPAs. The Gender Reform Action Plan provides gender-responsive budgeting and even more substantial quotas at the municipal (30 percent) and national (20 percent) levels. Women are more mobilized into groups in wealthier provinces. In the absence of strong gender quotas, neither women's descriptive nor substantive representation advances through meso-level legislatures. The Eighteenth Amendment gives responsibility for gender rights to provinces, but women are relatively weakest at this level of governance, calling into question the motives of politicians. Are they placating religious leaders at the meso level? Women's substantive representation is therefore mixed. Surprisingly, WPAs provide increased representation in some unexpected provinces, like Khyber Pakhtunkhwa. Pakistan's partly free status reminds us that quotas matter little if local elections are not held consistently.

In the United Kingdom, all three nodes of the gender policy trifecta have been in effect. It had gender quotas operating at the subnational level, active MWPAs engaging in gender mainstreaming, and gender-responsive budgeting. Still, women are not equally situated; women in Northern Ireland have not yet achieved gains in descriptive or substantive representation in the Northern Ireland Assembly. The case also reminds us that the gender policy trifecta must be maintained, gains for women like electoral quotas must be protected, and fiscal decentralization sustained.

Moving to Larger Lessons: The Gender Policy Trifecta around the Globe

On one hand, the European Union, the Asian Development Bank, the World Bank, and the International Monetary Fund argue that decentralization is a positive reform because meso units within countries differ from one another and a one-size policy does not fit all. These international organizations have mostly assumed that decentralization reforms on their own will lead to women's empowerment. Yet as I show in Chapter 2, indicators of political, fiscal, and administrative decentralization were not, on their own, strongly associated with gender equality. This book has drawn on the decentralization literature and gender and politics literature to identify the gender policy trifecta. Its central aim is to understand the conditions under which decentralization leads to women's empowerment, when women are more active in decentralized political institutions and when their policy preferences are better represented.

My approach was based on evaluating what women wanted and what politicians at different levels of government believed were the top policy priorities of women in their jurisdictions. In countries that varied on the gender policy trifecta, I asked women's organizations about their policy priorities. Using over one hundred structured interviews across Poland, Pakistan, and the United Kingdom, I show that what women want differs in different geographic parts of a country, just as what men want differs. Decentralization reforms between 1998 and 2000 in Poland, Pakistan, and the United Kingdom produced many new spots for elected office, bureaucratic decision making, and new taxing and spending patterns. Crucially, that the top four policy priorities for women's organizations have not been fully enacted across all meso units in the study suggests women's policy priorities diverge from men's priorities in their respective political units. That such policies were not passed in decentralized institutions, despite men and women holding office who both ostensibly face pressures to represent the needs of their constituents, reinforces the need for the gender policy trifecta.

Decentralization reforms must themselves be engendered for women to have access to these reforms in Poland, Pakistan, and the United Kingdom. Women were most able to access decentralization in the United Kingdom, where the gender policy trifecta was met through electoral gender quotas, gender-mainstreaming WPAs, and gender-responsive budgeting at the subnational level of governance (see Appendix 6). When one or even two of the trifecta nodes were missing, public policy in Poland and Pakistan remained largely status quo or was even retrograde for women (see Appendixes 4 and 5). When Poland and Pakistan acquired nodes of the gender policy trifecta, women's descriptive and substantive representation at some levels of subnational governance improved, although neither Poland nor Pakistan at this writing possess all three nodes of the trifecta at the relevant level of governance necessary and sufficient for women's empowerment in a decentralized country.

Global Assessments of the Gender Policy Trifecta

I have built an argument, by looking broadly at the literatures on decentralization and women and politics, that at a given level of governance the gender policy trifecta must be present and include the following:

1. *Electoral gender quotas* to open subnational legislative offices to women and engender political decentralization
2. *Gender mainstreaming* enforced by MWPAs, which constitute a bureaucratic home for gendered analysis of all public policy issues
3. *Gender-responsive budgeting*, which requires that taxing and spending policies incorporate the views of both male and female citizens and those of women's organization leaders. The country case chapters crescendo from one node of the trifecta (Poland) to

two nodes (Pakistan) to all three nodes (United Kingdom). In the United Kingdom, decentralization with the full gender policy trifecta leads to women's empowerment. I have substantiated my argument that one or two nodes is insufficient and that all three nodes are necessary and sufficient for women's empowerment.

The natural next question for readers, policy makers, and activists is whether these findings apply worldwide. How many countries in the world that are decentralized have a gender policy trifecta in place? For the countries that are decentralized but do not have a gender policy trifecta in place, which nodes need to be activated and strengthened? In this chapter, I report cross-national data showing which countries possess all three nodes and where gaps in nodes lie. I view this data as particularly useful for policy makers, activists, and students.

Table 6.2 collects evidence of the gender policy trifecta worldwide. As of January 2013, the United Nations recognized 193 sovereign states in the world. The Global Database of Quotas for Women reported in 2014 that 64 out of 193 countries, or 33.2 percent, have passed some form of subnational gender quotas.[2] Table 6.2 shows 64 countries that have adopted some form of subnational gender quota. This in and of itself is interesting information. One-third of all countries recognize that merely having subnational political elected office is not sufficient to ensure women's descriptive representation in local levels of politics. All 64 countries have local-level quotas for women, but only half of these have meso-level quotas. Only 30 countries worldwide, about 15 percent of all countries, have subnational gender quotas that apply to the meso level of politics.

Of countries that have a subnational gender quota, at either meso or local level, gender-responsive budgeting is active in many of them, while the establishment of subnational women's policy machinery is not widespread. As Table 6.2 shows, among the 64 countries that have some form of subnational gender quota, 37 also have gender-responsive budgeting projects, but just 11 have active meso-level women's policy machinery. Finally, just 5 countries (France, Mexico, Brazil, the United Kingdom, and Spain) have a meso-level gender policy trifecta. A few countries (Afghanistan and Uruguay) are in the process of establishing meso-level women's policy machinery needed for a gender policy trifecta. Additionally, some countries have established a gender policy trifecta at other levels of governance, like India at the municipal, or panchayat, level. These results thus show that there is a long way to go to advance women's political representation in countries around the globe. Table 6.2 identifies which areas of the gender policy trifecta are missing.

---

2. The database is available at http://www.quotaproject.org.

Table 6.2 Global assessment of subnational gender policy trifectas, 2014

Country	Watts (2008) federation type	Freedom House (2014) rating	Earliest year of legislated quotas	Legislated municipal quotas by 2014	Number of meso units	Legislated meso-level quotas by 2014	Meso-level quota type (% specified)	Gender-responsive budgeting	Active women's policy machinery in all meso units	Meso-level gender policy trifecta
Afghanistan	unitary	nf	2005	x	34 provinces	x	statutory (20)	x	in progress	no
Albania	unitary	pf	2008	x	12 prefectures	x	statutory (30)	x		no
Algeria	unitary	nf	2012	x	48 wilayas	x	statutory-R (30)		x	no
Bangladesh	unitary	pf	2001	x	7 districts					no
Bolivia	unitary	pf	2010	x	9 departments		statutory-R (50)	x		no
Burkina Faso	unitary	pf	2009	x	13 regions					no
Burundi	unitary	pf	2005	x	17 provinces			x		no
Cape Verde	unitary	f	2010	x	22 municipalities	x	statutory (25)	x		no
Costa Rica	unitary	f	1999	x	7 provinces	x	statutory (40)		x	no
Dominican Rep.	unitary	f	1997	x	31 provinces					no
DR of Congo	unitary	nf	2006	x	26 provinces	x	constitutional (50)			no
East Timor	unitary	pf	2002	x	13 districts			x		no
Ecuador	unitary	pf	2000	x	24 provinces			x	x	no
El Salvador	unitary	f	2013	x	14 departments			x	x	no
Eritrea	unitary	nf	1994	x	6 districts	x	statutory (30)			no
France	unitary	f	2009	x	27 regions	x	statutory (50)	x	x	yes
Guinea	unitary	pf	2010	x	8 regions					no
Greece	unitary	f	2010	x	13 regions	x	statutory (30)	x		no
Honduras	unitary	pf	2000	x	18 departments			x		no
Iraq	unitary	nf	2005	x	18 provinces	x	statutory-R (30)	x		no
Jordan	unitary	nf	2003	x	12 governorates					no
Kenya	unitary	pf	2010	x	47 counties	x	constitutional-R (30)	x		no
Korea	unitary	f	2000	x	8 provinces					no
Lesotho	unitary	f	2005	x	10 districts					no
Macedonia	unitary	pf	2008	x	84 municipalities	x	statutory (30)	x		no
Mauritania	unitary	nf	2006	x	12 regions			x		no

(continued)

Table 6.2 continued

Country	Watts (2008) federation type	Freedom House (2014) rating	Earliest year of legislated quotas	Legislated municipal quotas by 2014	Number of meso units	Legislated meso-level quotas by 2014	Meso-level quota type (% specified)	Gender-responsive budgeting	Active women's policy machinery in all meso units	Meso-level gender policy trifecta
Mauritius	unitary	f	2011	x	9 districts					no
Mongolia	unitary	f	2012	x	21 provinces					no
Montenegro	unitary	f	1998	x	23 municipalities	x	statutory (30)	x		no
Morocco	unitary	pf	2012	x	16 regions			x		no
Nepal	unitary	pf	1999	x	75 districts					no
Nicaragua	unitary	pf	2008	x	17 departments			x		no
Niger	unitary	pf	2011	x	8 regions					no
Paraguay	unitary	pf	1996	x	17 departments			x		no
Peru	unitary	f	1997	x	26 regions			x		no
Philippines	unitary	pf	1991	x	17 regions			x		no
Poland	unitary	f	2011	x	16 provinces	x			x	no
Rep. of Congo	unitary	nf	2007	x	12 departments					no
Rwanda	unitary	nf	2003	x	5 provinces			x		no
Senegal	unitary	f	2010	x	14 regions	x		x		no
Sierra Leone	unitary	f	2004	x	4 regions					no
Slovenia	unitary	f	2006	x	211 municipalities					no
S. Sudan	unitary	nf	2011	x	10 states	x	constitutional-R (25)	x		no
Uganda	unitary	pf	1995	x	109 counties			x		no
United Kingdom	unitary	f	1997	x	4 regions	x	voluntary (40–50)	x	x	yes
Uruguay	unitary	f	2015	x	19 departments	x	statutory (30)	x	in progress	no
Uzbekistan	unitary	nf	2004	x	12 provinces	x				no
Colombia	hybrid union	pf	2011	x	32 departments	x		x		no
Indonesia	hybrid union	pf	2012	x	34 provinces	x		x		no
Italy	hybrid union	f	2003	x	20 regions	x	statutory (12 of 20 regions)	x		no

Namibia	hybrid union	f	1992	x	13 regions					no
Portugal	hybrid union	f	2006	x	18 districts					no
Tanzania	hybrid union	pf	1995	x	30 regions			x		no
Vanuatu	hybrid union	f	2013	x	6 provinces					no
Argentina	federal	f	1991	x	23 departments	x	statutory (30)	x		no
Belgium	federal	f	1994	x	10 provinces	x	statutory (50)		x	no
Bosnia	federal	pf	1998	x	10 cantons	x	statutory (40)	x		no
Brazil	federal	f	1995	x	27 states	x	statutory (30)	x	x	yes
India	federal	f	1996	x	28 states	x		x		no
Mexico	federal	pf	1996	x	31 states	x	statutory (40)	x	x	yes
Pakistan	federal	pf	2001	x	6 provinces	x	constitutional-R (17)		x	no
Serbia	federal	f	2004	x	29 districts	x	statutory (30)	x		no
South Africa	federal	f	1998	x	9 provinces	x	statutory (50)	x		no
Spain	federal	f	2007	x	17 autonomous communities	x	statutory (40)	x	x	yes
TOTAL	47 unitary; 7 hybrid union; 10 federal	29 f; 24 pf; 11 nf		64 (33.2% of all 193 countries)		30 (15.5% of all 193 countries)	22 statutory; 4 constitutional; 1 voluntary	37	11	5 yes

Sources: Global Database of Quotas for Women. http://www.quotaproject.org; Htun and Piscopo 2014; UN Women, n.d., 2013.

Note: In June 2014, the Global Database of Quotas for Women listed 125 (of 193, or 64.7 percent) countries with constitutional, electoral, or party quotas. From that list, I selected all the countries that have legislated subnational gender quotas. There were 64 countries total (33.2 percent of 193). Of that list, I noted which subnational level gender quotas applied to (e.g., provincial, departmental, regional, municipal, etc.). Matching that textual information with information on the names of subnational tiers from Internet sources, I determined whether the subnational quota was one level below the national level. f = free, pf = partly free, nf = not free, R = reserved seats.

While quite a few countries have gender-responsive budgeting, very few have passed meso-level gender quotas, and the most common oversight is a lack of meso-level women's policy machineries to provide women's organizations with influence and access in meso-level policy-making processes.

International organizations encourage and fund mid- and small-size unitary states to democratize their political systems through decentralization. They often argue that the reforms themselves will create new, closer, accessible spaces for women. Yet in the absence of subnational quotas, women's descriptive representation is lower than at the national level, and subnational quotas are few and far between. The most successful cases of decentralization—adopted in countries that vary dramatically in level of economic development, cultural support for women in politics, and even religious heritage—make evident that decentralization policies must be engendered across all sectors through policies at the subnational level for electoral gender quotas, mainstreaming WPAs, and gender-responsive budgeting. A 2004 report by the United Nations Division for the Advancement of Women notes that the creation of meso- and local-level agencies is one of the most important developments in the bureaucratic sector (United Nations Division for the Advancement of Women 2004). To my knowledge, cross-national reports on countries with MWPAs have not been published. Women's organizations play a crucial aggregating role in forwarding the needs of women to political actors, because women's organization leaders and staff interact with women every day and see their needs over time. They are an important link between women constituents and political institutions.

Some might expect worldwide meso-level politics to shy away from gender leadership quotas when legislative quotas remain so controversial and women hesitate to lay claim to their 50 percent of the legislative pie. For example, the political agenda in the countries studied will not likely include quotas mandating women's representation at one-third of governors in Poland or one-third of cabinet ministers in the United Kingdom. Without leadership quotas for women at the subnational level, women should strive to reduce the inequalities that prevent greater recruitment and advancement of women in politics and to seek policies that meet what women want. Lasting progress in women's rights as human rights will be seen with on-the-ground transformations in women's economic, political, and educational status and then from decentralization reforms they can participate in equally.

Theoretical and Empirical Contributions

This mixed-methods study of three countries that decentralized in the late 1990s provides three main theoretical contributions and four key empirical contributions. First, it offers a new way of conceptualizing good representation as a representative who is able to identify and match the policy priorities of a constituent group. This conceptualization allows representatives to have delegate-like responsiveness to citizens' policy priorities and trustee roles in forming solutions and knowing what policy solutions will have political support. Second, it shows that decentralization itself does not itself increase the power of groups traditionally marginalized from politics because local political offices are lower status than national office or require less travel time for members of these groups. Reformers have to explicitly make meso-level institutions more representative by creating those reforms along with decentralization. Third, it advances the idea that decentralization involves trade-offs between representation and equality. The gender policy trifecta means that each of three decentralization sectors (political, administrative, and fiscal) has been engendered. This concept explains where and why decentralization has worked for women in contexts very different in terms of economic development levels and cultural support for women leaders. Whether in more unitary or more federal decentralizing states, the gender policy trifecta is the key takeaway in explaining how to enhance women's empowerment. For example, India, Australia, and Spain (federations) and the United Kingdom (unitary with decentralized features) all passed gender quotas applying at the subnational level (the political node), implemented gender-responsive budgeting to benefit women's organizations (the fiscal node), and created subnational WPAs furthering gender mainstreaming (the administrative node), achieving this trifecta for a given time and level of governance.

This book offers four empirical contributions to political science and policy studies of decentralization. First, it provides for the first time cross-national evidence of relationship between sectors of decentralization and women's empowerment. Second, using the same structured survey-interview in three very different countries reveals that women's policy priorities differ as much within a country as across countries. Women in the capital cities of very different countries share many policy priorities, whereas women in urban and rural parts of the same country report widely divergent policy priorities. While part of a feminist empirical and integrative approach (see Mazur 2012), this book examines governmental knowledge of the policy priorities of women's groups, both feminist and nonfeminist (Baldez 2002) but also measures the conditions under which governments adopt feminist policies. Third, the policy analysis in each country chapter shows that substantive representation of women does not come without pressure to tangibly increase women's descriptive representation. Fourth, the results regarding subnational variation in women's preferences constitute a new reason to decentralize, to meet the diverse needs of women. In this book I show that decentralization in and of itself is not an institutional reform that brings about women's empowerment. Centralization to a strong feminist dictator might bring about increased gender equality, though not democracy or representation for diverse women's interests. Rather, institutional reforms that send political power to spaces where women are already strong or have allies will lead to more women-responsive outcomes. Women's groups in the United Kingdom knew they were well-positioned for strength under decentralization; this is why women's movements for decentralization emerged in the United Kingdom and not in Poland or Pakistan. What matters with any institutional reform, including decentralization, is that political actors question and reform institutional arenas for equality through means such as quotas, mainstreaming, and gender-responsive budgeting practices.

However, one can argue for decentralization for women (as well as men) by stating that women as a constituency have diverse preferences and that local politicians have more accurate information about those preferences than national politicians. In some cases, those local politicians also have the requisite administrative capacity to respond to those preferences. But in most scenarios, increasing the diversity of descriptive representation will be necessary to provide policy responsiveness to all groups in society. In all, this book identifies the conditions under which decentralization brings about increased numbers of women in subnational political office and the realization of women's policy priorities.

Continuing the Conversation on Democratization and Women's Empowerment

This book contributes to a number of areas of scholarship in applied policy, decentralization, comparative democratization, and the comparative politics of gender, quotas, state architecture, representation, and aggregation. With respect to applied policy, this book shows that new institutions at any level of governance require actors and outsiders to discuss gender and gender inequalities in a sustained way to engender new practices. This book adds to the decentralization literature, providing empirical evidence for Tiebout's (1956) assertion that local politicians have better information about their constituents than their national counterparts. However, I add that the gender policy trifecta is necessary to engender subnational institutions, through (1) subnational-level electoral gender quotas to boost the descriptive representation of women, (2) MWPAs to coordinate gender mainstreaming across government agencies, and (3) subnational-level gender-responsive budgeting to examine taxing and spending policies and enhance funding opportunities for women's organizations in civil society.

In terms of comparative democratization, this book shows that decentralization can help countries along a path to democratization but that it can also be a façade for democratization, as in Pakistan, where other issues such as internal security, external sovereignty, and destabilizing competition of elites over parties present hurdles for democratization. If women in decentralized governance get increased training and literacy through grassroots mobilization that is not tied to Western influence, decentralization can help Pakistan in the near term. Also, regular local elections in Pakistan would show legitimacy of decentralized institutions. In the United Kingdom, decentralization has increased democracy, as it has in Poland, but in Poland it was supplemented by pressure from the European Union. This book adds to the field of comparative politics of gender, demonstrating the common logic to decentralization across a wide variety of developed and developing countries, provided that reforms are engendered. Decentralization benefits women in very different cases, ranging from the United Kingdom to India, from Australia to Spain.

This book contributes to and supports the burgeoning literature on gender quotas and favors their expansion to the subnational level, despite the limitations of unequally treated women, for their symbolic effect and their improvement of women's political skills. Some may wonder if changes to women's numbers in office matter more at the low level than at the high level. As Appendix 3 shows, women's descriptive representation 2010–2013 in the national parliaments of Poland, Pakistan, and the United Kingdom averaged 20–23 percent. At the subnational level it varied least in Pakistan, more in the United Kingdom, and the most in Poland. In my opinion, having national and meso-level gender quotas to ensure minimum levels of women's descriptive representation is at least as important as getting women's representation up to at least 25 percent. While an imperfect solution, institutionalization of women's seats in legislatures through gender quotas helps protect gains made in women's status and voice. These gains are often hard fought and can easily slip away a few years later in the absence of a gender quota. Gender quotas will help women, improve public policy making, and encourage the next generation of young women to run for office.

In terms of state architecture, this book supports existing conditional and cross-institutional work on women in federations and decentralizing unitary states (see Chappell 2006; Haussman, Sawer, and Vickers 2010) showing that we must examine women's opportunities and challenges in legislatures, bureaucracies, and particularly civil society (see Banaszak 2010) if we conceive of decentralization as a multisectoral reform with political, administrative, and fiscal sectors. In literature on state architecture, feminist men and women can create a subnational "logic of appropriateness" (Chappell 2006) that involves advancing the gender policy trifecta as countries consider decentralization programs. This work also shows that we need to carefully specify the levels of governance to which powers are decentralized and whether advances for women, like quotas, gender-responsive budgeting, and WPAs, occur on the level of governance to which power shifted. Otherwise, gender norms may undergird state institutions (Vickers 2013) in ways that exclude women.

In terms of representation, we see firsthand through this research that national politicians face tough challenges of aggregating preferences across a diverse citizenry and rural and urban units. The policy priorities of constituents in the urban capital can be the loudest and easiest to hear, while rural constituents' priorities are overlooked. Additionally, policy priorities of women residing in urban areas of very different countries have structural similarities. This research gives us the micro-level women's organization evidence for why we sometimes see policy priority alignment across countries at an international forum like the UN Commission on the Status of Women, in UN work to eliminate violence against women, and in the 1979 adoption of CEDAW. This book also contributes to unique conceptualization of good representation: knowing the policy priorities of a group within a constituency, even if all sources of substantive representation are "contingent and contestable, [and] all share problems and dilemmas of authorization and accountability, [and] . . . are interactive and relational" (Mackay 2008, 135). This book supports Fiona Mackay's finding that "effective [substantive representation of women] requires institutional reform and innovation, including the creation of arrangements that foster the norm of participatory parity and the opportunity to contest and negotiate the meanings and content of [the substantive representation of women] over time" (135). The gender policy trifecta is just such an example of institutional reform for women. The higher degree of policy matching provided by MWPA leaders shows that decentralizing governance adds value for women. Meso-level femocrats (feminist bureaucrats) are necessary but insufficient to successfully engender decentralization reforms going on in some form in 80 percent of the world's countries. Femocrats, a little-used tool to build women's political activism in nongovernmental organizations, can be crucial in building women's organization capacity and can be important liaisons between women's organizations and politicians at any level of government.

Women can benefit from decentralized political institutions if quotas boost their numbers in office in the first few election cycles. However, not all women have the time or resources to devote to determining what policy areas need the most political work. Women's organizations play a crucial aggregating role in drawing political actors' attention to needs of women such as literacy, shelters for victims of domestic violence, or reproductive technologies, because these organizations know their needs. This research is along the line of that of Mala Htun and Laurel Weldon (2012), who show that feminist organizations worldwide are critical political actors in bringing about policies that represent women's interests.

When implemented according to the gender policy trifecta, decentralization shifts political power to subnational units, ensuring that women are included in all institutional pathways of representation. These processes in turn lead to policy innovations such as those in Scotland, United Kingdom; Punjab, Pakistan; and Pomorskie, Poland. It is also worth noting that an increase in women's representation through the gender policy trifecta in these subnational units has not lessened men's representation but broadened and deepened democracy and representation for all.

Empowered by Design demonstrates that international organizations, decentralization enthusiasts, pundits, and policy makers must recognize that women have diverse policy priorities. Subnational politicians have more accurate information about these priorities than national politicians. When the gender policy trifecta is in place, at least 25 to 30 percent of subnational legislators are themselves women, and all subnational legislators have the capacity to respond to those preferences because they craft policy on the basis of gender-responsive budgeting and with the input of MWPA. Thus the gender policy trifecta means the people and processes of making public policy are more fully responsive to men and women, rural and urban citizens, and public policy can better represent all interests. With a deeper understanding of the conditions under which decentralization increases women in subnational political offices, responsiveness to women's diverse policy priorities, and the possibility of feminist policy outcomes, citizens and policy makers can embark on a path to more fully democratize states around the globe.

Appendix 1

Hybrid Survey–Structured Interview Method

In this book I introduce a new, significant data set on women and politics in Poland, Pakistan, and the United Kingdom. This data set covers information about women's organizations' capacities, allies, and policy priorities and the policy priorities of meso-level government ministers regarding women's and girls' empowerment. The hybrid survey–structured interview format uses original survey questionnaires, "Survey of Women's Organization Leaders" and "Survey of Gender Equality Policy Makers," developed by Candice Ortbals and me, which collected responses at the national and the meso levels. The English-language questionnaires were translated into Urdu (for Pakistan) and Polish (for Poland) by a professional translation service. The translated questionnaires and the English-language questionnaires were then sent to two native speakers of Urdu and Polish, respectively, both holding master's degrees and being fluent in English. The native speakers first read the translated survey and then read the English-language survey and identified discrepancies in underlying meaning between the two versions. These discrepancies were sent back to the translation service and the process repeated until a final translation was reached. In the three countries where the questionnaires were fielded, the researcher marked answers on a paper copy of the relevant survey questionnaire and entered the results into SurveyGizmo (http://www.surveygizmo.com) for ease of reporting and analysis in Excel and other statistical packages.

On the women's organization side, I used existing handbooks to compile a list of women's organizations to contact. My criteria were to interview eight to ten women's organization leaders in each capital city and six to ten women's organization leaders in two subnational capitals of roughly equal gross domestic product per capita, and I sought to include one left-leaning and one right-leaning meso unit.

In Poland, I developed a letter of introduction with an online survey link. I followed the letter with phone calls to women's organizations and officials. My research assistant and I used the *Directory of Women's Organizations and Initiatives in Poland*

(Centrum Promocji Kobiet 1997, 2001, 2002, 2005) to contact women's organization leaders in the capital city of Warsaw in Mazowieckie Province, the more left-leaning city of Gdańsk in Pomorskie Province, and in Poznań, a more traditional right-leaning city in south-central Wielkopolskie Province. My research assistant interviewed women's organization leaders from these three meso units and ministers from national and meso-level women's policy agencies. A meso-level women's policy agency minister from each of the sixteen provinces participated in the survey, so we can see if there is meaningful variance in what different gender equality ministers would do in different parts of the same country.

In Pakistan, I had difficulty tracking down listings of women's organizations, as the government claims not to register nonprofit organizations. However, I combined listings from the *Encyclopedia of Women's Associations Worldwide* (Barrett and Malonis 1993) with the online "Women Rights NGOs in Pakistan" (KGM Consultants, n.d.). My research assistant and I contacted eight women's organizations in the capital Islamabad, in the more left-leaning meso-unit capital of Lahore in Punjab Province, and the right-leaning meso-unit capital of Peshawar in North-West Frontier Province (now Khyber Pakhtunkhwa). A representative of the national Ministry of Women Development participated in the structured interview as did officials from meso-level ministries of women's development in Punjab, North-West Frontier Province, Sindh, Balochistan, and Azad Jammu and Kashmir. A total of six ministers participated in structured interviews. The research assistant, as in Poland and the United Kingdom, was female; to secure her personal safety and in accordance with Pakistani norms, a male relative accompanied her to the interviews.

In the United Kingdom, to obtain a number of meso-level units comparable to Poland's and Pakistan's, I contacted women's organizations in England, Scotland, Wales, and Northern Ireland. I used the regrettably abolished Women's National Commission website (Women's National Commission, n.d.) to identify women's groups in London, Edinburgh, Cardiff, and Belfast. I e-mailed a letter of introduction with a link to the online survey to each of these groups and followed up with a phone call to set up an appointment for an interview. In each case, I contacted a variety of right-wing and left-wing groups, groups explicitly representing women of color, women's business and labor groups, and groups representing women of different ages, physical abilities, and sexual orientations. Likewise, I wrote a letter of introduction to gender equality policy makers, including the Government Equalities Office and the Equality and Human Rights Commission offices in London, Cardiff, Edinburgh, and Belfast. This yielded thirty structured interviews with women's organization leaders across the United Kingdom. I interviewed participants in person except those in Northern Ireland; I interviewed participants in Northern Ireland over the phone while interviewees read the survey online. I also conducted four structured interviews with gender equality policy makers, one at the national level in London and one each in Scotland, Wales, and Northern Ireland.

The structured interview method provides numerous advantages. It allows researchers to collect comparable data on the same questions across many different contexts, allowing generalization across countries that have thus far not been systematically compared. Beyond online surveys, the structured interview also allows passage of fine-grained substantive knowledge from the interviewee to the interviewer. The social dynamic of the in-person interview allows interviewees to expand more specifically on questions they believe matter more or to interrogate dynamics not covered directly in the questionnaire, particularly for the final question, asking for comments on equality, decentralization, and other matters in the interviewee's country.[1]

Finally, to discern the women's organization policy priorities reported in the country chapters, I took the following steps. Survey questions dealt with policy priorities for women, one question asking respondents to indicate which out of a list of thirty-four policy areas their group serves. In the follow-up question, respondents were asked to rank, from one to four, one being most important, their top four policy priorities for women. I asked these same questions of national- and meso-level women's policy agencies. The tables in the country chapters on women's policy priorities note the frequency that women's groups mentioned a given policy area as one of their top four priorities. I use frequencies rather than a probabilistic model to find policy priorities because I am more interested in whether an issue is among the top four for women's groups and women's policy agencies than whether the groups and agencies rank issues in the same order. However, when two priorities tied, the priority that landed more frequently in the top two priorities broke the tie. After compiling the total number of unique policy priorities in each country (those listed in the top four for a meso-level agency but not a national agency), in Chapter 6 I report the matches between women's organization priorities, the priorities of the national women's policy agency, and the priorities expressed by meso-level women's policy agencies, thus showing the new possible benefit of decentralization for women: a broader diversity of women's issues being addressed.

The comparability of the survey–structured interview questionnaire allows discerning what women's organizations, a key part of the triangle of women's empowerment (see, for example, Ortbals, Rincker, and Montoya 2011), describe as the top priorities for women, or what they want out of their political system. By asking the same questions of the meso-level and national bureaucrats most responsible for gender equality policy and by examining resultant policy, I show that across the countries I surveyed the meso level of government tends to have better information and better match local preferences, as Charles Tiebout (1956) predicts. However, the capacity and will of meso-level legislators to enact such policy varies across country by method of decentralization.

---

1. Appendix 2 includes copies of the survey questionnaire for Scotland and the United Kingdom.

Appendix 2

Sample Survey Questionnaires

his section contains an example of my "Survey of Women's Organization Leaders" and "Survey of Gender Equality Policy Makers." I made separate versions of the surveys for Poland, Pakistan, and the United Kingdom.[1] I used responses to these surveys to determine women's policy priorities and the extent to which women's policy agency ministers' policy priorities match them. Research assistants translated responses in languages other than English.

Survey of Women's Organization Leaders

This interview questionnaire comes to you from Dr. Meg Rincker, Assistant Professor of Political Science, Purdue University, USA. I am carrying out an academic study of women's organizations and what they want out of politics for publication in a book I am writing. Your name has been selected from publicly available information because of your leadership role in a women's organization in Scotland.

I would like to ask your views on a number of subjects pertaining to women's organizations and politics in Scotland. Your input will be treated strictly confidential, but it will contribute to a better understanding of what women's organizations want out of politics in different parts of the world.

If you choose to participate in the study, it will involve answering about 40 questions, which should take about 25 minutes. I will talk you through the questionnaire, so you can ask me questions anytime if something is unclear or you would like to add on to the area we are

---

1. The first example survey questionnaire included in this appendix is one for women's organizations in Scotland. Similar survey questionnaires were fielded in Poland, Pakistan, England, Wales, and Northern Ireland. The second is one for the national women's policy agency (and its gender equality policy makers) in the United Kingdom. Likewise, I created separate survey questionnaires for gender equality policy makers in Poland and Pakistan. Because of space constraints, I do not reproduce all the surveys in this appendix, but I provide an illustration of the two types. Those wishing further details on other survey questionnaires used for this study can contact me.

discussing. If you have any questions after we speak, feel free to contact me at mrincker@purduecal.edu. Thank you very much for your time!

1. In what decade was your organization founded?
   - [ ] before 1900
   - [ ] 1901–1909
   - [ ] 1910–1919
   - [ ] 1920–1929
   - [ ] 1930–1939
   - [ ] 1940–1949
   - [ ] 1950–1959
   - [ ] 1960–1969
   - [ ] 1970–1979
   - [ ] 1980–1989
   - [ ] 1990–1999
   - [ ] 2000–2009
   - [ ] 2010–present
   - [ ] Don't know

2. Approximately how many members are in your organization?
   - [ ] 0–10 members
   - [ ] 11–24 members
   - [ ] 25–49 members
   - [ ] 50–99 members
   - [ ] More than 100 members

3. How would you describe the organization that you represent? Check all that apply.
   - [ ] Women's rights organization
   - [ ] Feminist organization
   - [ ] Housewives association
   - [ ] Association for rural women
   - [ ] Cultural or literary association
   - [ ] Religious association
   - [ ] Small business or micro-credit organization
   - [ ] Health association
   - [ ] Other

4. What is the geographic scope of your organization's activities?
   - [ ] International
   - [ ] National
   - [ ] Subnational
   - [ ] City
   - [ ] Neighborhood
   - [ ] Other

5. Of the following policy areas, which would you say your women's organization addresses? Check all that apply.
   - [ ] A-Food assistance for girls and women
   - [ ] B-Public awareness campaigns about women's equality
   - [ ] C-Adult education and literacy for women
   - [ ] D-Recreation for women
   - [ ] E-Education and literacy for school-age girls
   - [ ] F-Promotion of female students and faculty in higher education
   - [ ] G-Eliminating violence against women
   - [ ] H-Improving treatment of women in jails
   - [ ] I-Combating *swara/vanni* and honor killings

☐ J-Legal assistance for women
☐ K-Information on prenatal care
☐ L-Information on women's screening for mammograms
☐ M-Information/screening on osteoporosis
☐ N-Information/screening for cervical cancer
☐ O-Women's access to immunizations
☐ P-Financial support for raising children
☐ Q-Development of nurseries/child care centers
☐ R-Reproductive choice services or awareness
☐ S-Physical fitness
☐ T-Promotion of foster care
☐ U-Assisting women from rural areas
☐ V-Female leadership
☐ W-Migrant women
☐ X-Gender budgeting (assessing subnational budgetary impact on women)
☐ Y-Women in political decision making
☐ Z-Women's entrepreneurship and microcredits for women
☐ AA-Job training for women in the workforce
☐ BB-Promoting women in the labor market
☐ CC-Raising awareness about gender-based employment discrimination
☐ DD-Family-friendly policy
☐ EE-Reconciliation of work and family life
☐ FF-Advancement for women of color
☐ GG-Lesbian, gay, bisexual, or transgender rights
☐ HH-Sex workers' rights
☐ II-Other 1
☐ JJ-Other 2
☐ Don't know

6. What is your organization's first policy priority for women?
☐ A-Food assistance for girls and women
☐ B-Public awareness campaigns about women's equality
☐ C-Adult education and literacy for women
☐ D-Recreation for women
☐ E-Education and literacy for school-age girls
☐ F-Promotion of female students and faculty in higher education
☐ G-Eliminating violence against women
☐ H-Improving treatment of women in jails
☐ I-Combating *swara/vanni* and honor killings
☐ J-Legal assistance for women
☐ K-Information on prenatal care
☐ L-Information on women's screening for mammograms
☐ M-Information/screening on osteoporosis
☐ N-Information/screening for cervical cancer
☐ O-Women's access to immunizations
☐ P-Financial support for raising children
☐ Q-Development of nurseries/child care centers
☐ R-Reproductive choice services or awareness
☐ S-Physical fitness
☐ T-Promotion of foster care
☐ U-Assisting women from rural areas
☐ V-Female leadership
☐ W-Migrant women
☐ X-Gender budgeting (assessing subnational budgetary impact on women)
☐ Y-Women in political decision making
☐ Z-Women's entrepreneurship and microcredits for women

☐ AA-Job training for women in the workforce
☐ BB-Promoting women in the labor market
☐ CC-Raising awareness about gender-based employment discrimination
☐ DD-Family-friendly policy
☐ EE-Reconciliation of work and family life
☐ FF-Advancement for women of color
☐ GG-Lesbian, gay, bisexual, or transgender rights
☐ HH-Sex workers' rights
☐ II-Other 1
☐ JJ-Other 2
☐ Don't know

7. What is your organization's second policy priority for women?
☐ A-Food assistance for girls and women
☐ B-Public awareness campaigns about women's equality
☐ C-Adult education and literacy for women
☐ D-Recreation for women
☐ E-Education and literacy for school-age girls
☐ F-Promotion of female students and faculty in higher education
☐ G-Eliminating violence against women
☐ H-Improving treatment of women in jails
☐ I-Combating *swara/vanni* and honor killings
☐ J-Legal assistance for women
☐ K-Information on prenatal care
☐ L-Information on women's screening for mammograms
☐ M-Information/screening on osteoporosis
☐ N-Information/screening for cervical cancer
☐ O-Women's access to immunizations
☐ P-Financial support for raising children
☐ Q-Development of nurseries/child care centers
☐ R-Reproductive choice services or awareness
☐ S-Physical fitness
☐ T-Promotion of foster care
☐ U-Assisting women from rural areas
☐ V-Female leadership
☐ W-Migrant women
☐ X-Gender budgeting (assessing subnational budgetary impact on women)
☐ Y-Women in political decision making
☐ Z-Women's entrepreneurship and microcredits for women
☐ AA-Job training for women in the workforce
☐ BB-Promoting women in the labor market
☐ CC-Raising awareness about gender-based employment discrimination
☐ DD-Family-friendly policy
☐ EE-Reconciliation of work and family life
☐ FF-Advancement for women of color
☐ GG-Lesbian, gay, bisexual, or transgender rights
☐ HH-Sex workers' rights
☐ II-Other 1
☐ JJ-Other 2
☐ Don't know

8. What is your organization's third policy priority for women?
☐ A-Food assistance for girls and women
☐ B-Public awareness campaigns about women's equality
☐ C-Adult education and literacy for women

☐ D-Recreation for women
☐ E-Education and literacy for school-age girls
☐ F-Promotion of female students and faculty in higher education
☐ G-Eliminating violence against women
☐ H-Improving treatment of women in jails
☐ I-Combating *swara/vanni* and honor killings
☐ J-Legal assistance for women
☐ K-Information on prenatal care
☐ L-Information on women's screening for mammograms
☐ M-Information/screening on osteoporosis
☐ N-Information/screening for cervical cancer
☐ O-Women's access to immunizations
☐ P-Financial support for raising children
☐ Q-Development of nurseries/child care centers
☐ R-Reproductive choice services or awareness
☐ S-Physical fitness
☐ T-Promotion of foster care
☐ U-Assisting women from rural areas
☐ V-Female leadership
☐ W-Migrant women
☐ X-Gender budgeting (assessing subnational budgetary impact on women)
☐ Y-Women in political decision making
☐ Z-Women's entrepreneurship and microcredits for women
☐ AA-Job training for women in the workforce
☐ BB-Promoting women in the labor market
☐ CC-Raising awareness about gender-based employment discrimination
☐ DD-Family-friendly policy
☐ EE-Reconciliation of work and family life
☐ FF-Advancement for women of color
☐ GG-Lesbian, gay, bisexual or transgender rights
☐ HH-Sex workers' rights
☐ II-Other 1
☐ JJ-Other 2
☐ Don't know

9. What is your organization's fourth policy priority for women?
☐ A-Food assistance for girls and women
☐ B-Public awareness campaigns about women's equality
☐ C-Adult education and literacy for women
☐ D-Recreation for women
☐ E-Education and literacy for school-age girls
☐ F-Promotion of female students and faculty in higher education
☐ G-Eliminating violence against women
☐ H-Improving treatment of women in jails
☐ I-Combating *swara/vanni* and honor killings
☐ J-Legal assistance for women
☐ K-Information on prenatal care
☐ L-Information on women's screening for mammograms
☐ M-Information/screening on osteoporosis
☐ N-Information/screening for cervical cancer
☐ O-Women's access to immunizations
☐ P-Financial support for raising children
☐ Q-Development of nurseries/child care centers
☐ R-Reproductive choice services or awareness
☐ S-Physical fitness

☐ T-Promotion of foster care
☐ U-Assisting women from rural areas
☐ V-Female leadership
☐ W-Migrant women
☐ X-Gender budgeting (assessing subnational budgetary impact on women)
☐ Y-Women in political decision making
☐ Z-Women's entrepreneurship and microcredits for women
☐ AA-Job training for women in the workforce
☐ BB-Promoting women in the labor market
☐ CC-Raising awareness about gender-based employment discrimination
☐ DD-Family-friendly policy
☐ EE-Reconciliation of work and family life
☐ FF-Advancement for women of color
☐ GG-Lesbian, gay, bisexual, or transgender rights
☐ HH-Sex workers' rights
☐ II-Other 1
☐ JJ-Other 2
☐ Don't know

10. Please rate the level of your organization's effectiveness on the four policy priorities you indicated above.

Priority	Very successful	Moderately successful	No change	Moderately unsuccessful	Very unsuccessful	Don't know
	☐	☐	☐	☐	☐	☐
	☐	☐	☐	☐	☐	☐
	☐	☐	☐	☐	☐	☐
	☐	☐	☐	☐	☐	☐

11. Of the following policy areas, which would you say the UK Government Equalities Office (managed by the Right Honorable Minister Theresa May) addresses? Check all that apply.
☐ A-Food assistance for girls and women
☐ B-Public awareness campaigns about women's equality
☐ C-Adult education and literacy for women
☐ D-Recreation for women
☐ E-Education and literacy for school-age girls
☐ F-Promotion of female students and faculty in higher education
☐ G-Eliminating violence against women
☐ H-Improving treatment of women in jails
☐ I-Combating *swara/vanni* and honor killings
☐ J-Legal assistance for women
☐ K-Information on prenatal care
☐ L-Information on women's screening for mammograms
☐ M-Information/screening on osteoporosis
☐ N-Information/screening for cervical cancer
☐ O-Women's access to immunizations
☐ P-Financial support for raising children
☐ Q-Development of nurseries/child care centers
☐ R-Reproductive choice services or awareness
☐ S-Physical fitness
☐ T-Promotion of foster care
☐ U-Assisting women from rural areas

☐ V-Female leadership
☐ W-Migrant women
☐ X-Gender budgeting (assessing subnational budgetary impact on women)
☐ Y-Women in political decision making
☐ Z-Women's entrepreneurship and microcredits for women
☐ AA-Job training for women in the workforce
☐ BB-Promoting women in the labor market
☐ CC-Raising awareness about gender-based employment discrimination
☐ DD-Family-friendly policy
☐ EE-Reconciliation of work and family life
☐ FF-Advancement for women of color
☐ GG-Lesbian, gay, bisexual, or transgender rights
☐ HH-Sex workers' rights
☐ II-Other 1
☐ JJ-Other 2
☐ Don't know

12. What would you consider to be the UK Government Equalities Office's first policy priority for women?
☐ A-Food assistance for girls and women
☐ B-Public awareness campaigns about women's equality
☐ C-Adult education and literacy for women
☐ D-Recreation for women
☐ E-Education and literacy for school-age girls
☐ F-Promotion of female students and faculty in higher education
☐ G-Eliminating violence against women
☐ H-Improving treatment of women in jails
☐ I-Combating *swara/vanni* and honor killings
☐ J-Legal assistance for women
☐ K-Information on prenatal care
☐ L-Information on women's screening for mammograms
☐ M-Information/screening on osteoporosis
☐ N-Information/screening for cervical cancer
☐ O-Women's access to immunizations
☐ P-Financial support for raising children
☐ Q-Development of nurseries/child care centers
☐ R-Reproductive choice services or awareness
☐ S-Physical fitness
☐ T-Promotion of foster care
☐ U-Assisting women from rural areas
☐ V-Female leadership
☐ W-Migrant women
☐ X-Gender budgeting (assessing subnational budgetary impact on women)
☐ Y-Women in political decision making
☐ Z-Women's entrepreneurship and microcredits for women
☐ AA-Job training for women in the workforce
☐ BB-Promoting women in the labor market
☐ CC-Raising awareness about gender-based employment discrimination
☐ DD-Family-friendly policy
☐ EE-Reconciliation of work and family life
☐ FF-Advancement for women of color
☐ GG-Lesbian, gay, bisexual, or transgender rights
☐ HH-Sex workers' rights
☐ II-Other 1
☐ JJ-Other 2
☐ Don't know

13. What would you consider to be the UK Government Equalities Office's second policy priority for women?

☐ A-Food assistance for girls and women
☐ B-Public awareness campaigns about women's equality
☐ C-Adult education and literacy for women
☐ D-Recreation for women
☐ E-Education and literacy for school-age girls
☐ F-Promotion of female students and faculty in higher education
☐ G-Eliminating violence against women
☐ H-Improving treatment of women in jails
☐ I-Combating *swara/vanni* and honor killings
☐ J-Legal assistance for women
☐ K-Information on prenatal care
☐ L-Information on women's screening for mammograms
☐ M-Information/screening on osteoporosis
☐ N-Information/screening for cervical cancer
☐ O-Women's access to immunizations
☐ P-Financial support for raising children
☐ Q-Development of nurseries/child care centers
☐ R-Reproductive choice services or awareness
☐ S-Physical fitness
☐ T-Promotion of foster care
☐ U-Assisting women from rural areas
☐ V-Female leadership
☐ W-Migrant women
☐ X-Gender budgeting (assessing subnational budgetary impact on women)
☐ Y-Women in political decision making
☐ Z-Women's entrepreneurship and microcredits for women
☐ AA-Job training for women in the workforce
☐ BB-Promoting women in the labor market
☐ CC-Raising awareness about gender-based employment discrimination
☐ DD-Family-friendly policy
☐ EE-Reconciliation of work and family life
☐ FF-Advancement for women of color
☐ GG-Lesbian, gay, bisexual, or transgender rights
☐ HH-Sex workers' rights
☐ II-Other 1
☐ JJ-Other 2
☐ Don't know

14. What would you consider to be the UK Government Equalities Office's third policy priority for women?

☐ A-Food assistance for girls and women
☐ B-Public awareness campaigns about women's equality
☐ C-Adult education and literacy for women
☐ D-Recreation for women
☐ E-Education and literacy for school-age girls
☐ F-Promotion of female students and faculty in higher education
☐ G-Eliminating violence against women
☐ H-Improving treatment of women in jails
☐ I-Combating *swara/vanni* and honor killings
☐ J-Legal assistance for women
☐ K-Information on prenatal care
☐ L-Information on women's screening for mammograms
☐ M-Information/screening on osteoporosis
☐ N-Information/screening for cervical cancer

☐ O-Women's access to immunizations
☐ P-Financial support for raising children
☐ Q-Development of nurseries/child care centers
☐ R-Reproductive choice services or awareness
☐ S-Physical fitness
☐ T-Promotion of foster care
☐ U-Assisting women from rural areas
☐ V-Female leadership
☐ W-Migrant women
☐ X-Gender budgeting (assessing subnational budgetary impact on women)
☐ Y-Women in political decision making
☐ Z-Women's entrepreneurship and microcredits for women
☐ AA-Job training for women in the workforce
☐ BB-Promoting women in the labor market
☐ CC-Raising awareness about gender-based employment discrimination
☐ DD-Family-friendly policy
☐ EE-Reconciliation of work and family life
☐ FF-Advancement for women of color
☐ GG-Lesbian, gay, bisexual, or transgender rights
☐ HH-Sex workers' rights
☐ II-Other 1
☐ JJ-Other 2
☐ Don't know

15. What would you consider to be the UK Government Equalities Office's fourth policy priority for women?
☐ A-Food assistance for girls and women
☐ B-Public awareness campaigns about women's equality
☐ C-Adult education and literacy for women
☐ D-Recreation for women
☐ E-Education and literacy for school-age girls
☐ F-Promotion of female students and faculty in higher education
☐ G-Eliminating violence against women
☐ H-Improving treatment of women in jails
☐ I-Combating *swara/vanni* and honor killings
☐ J-Legal assistance for women
☐ K-Information on prenatal care
☐ L-Information on women's screening for mammograms
☐ M-Information/screening on osteoporosis
☐ N-Information/screening for cervical cancer
☐ O-Women's access to immunizations
☐ P-Financial support for raising children
☐ Q-Development of nurseries/child care centers
☐ R-Reproductive choice services or awareness
☐ S-Physical fitness
☐ T-Promotion of foster care
☐ U-Assisting women from rural areas
☐ V-Female leadership
☐ W-Migrant women
☐ X-Gender budgeting (assessing subnational budgetary impact on women)
☐ Y-Women in political decision making
☐ Z-Women's entrepreneurship and microcredits for women
☐ AA-Job training for women in the workforce
☐ BB-Promoting women in the labor market
☐ CC-Raising awareness about gender-based employment discrimination
☐ DD-Family-friendly policy

☐ EE-Reconciliation of work and family life
☐ FF-Advancement for women of color
☐ GG-Lesbian, gay, bisexual, or transgender rights
☐ HH-Sex workers' rights
☐ II-Other 1
☐ JJ-Other 2
☐ Don't know

16. Please rate the level of effectiveness of the UK Government Equalities Office on its four policy priorities you indicated above.

Priority	Very successful	Moderately successful	No change	Moderately unsuccessful	Very unsuccessful	Don't know
	☐	☐	☐	☐	☐	☐
	☐	☐	☐	☐	☐	☐
	☐	☐	☐	☐	☐	☐
	☐	☐	☐	☐	☐	☐

17. What are the reasons for communication between the UK Government Equalities Office and your women's organization? Check all that apply.
☐ To communicate about activities for women hosted by the agency
☐ To communicate about activities hosted by this women's organization
☐ To offer organized input and feedback on the agency's actions
☐ To collaborate with women's organizations on joint initiatives for women
☐ To connect women's groups to avenues of financial support
☐ To brainstorm and develop equality plans
☐ To assist women's organizations in their dealings with Scottish political officials and institutions
☐ To assist women's organizations in their dealings with UK political officials and institutions
☐ To assist women's organizations in their dealings with international political officials, institutions, and funding sources
☐ Don't know
☐ Other

18. How often does the UK Government Equalities Office communicate with your women's organization?
☐ Frequently
☐ Occasionally
☐ Sometimes
☐ Never
☐ Don't know

19. How many members of this organization have participated in activities hosted by the UK Government Equalities Office (for example, conferences, meetings, job training, campaigns, etc.)?
☐ 75 to 100 percent of the organization's members have participated in activities hosted by the UK Government Equalities Office.
☐ Roughly 50 to 74 percent of the organization's members have participated in activities hosted by the UK Government Equalities Office.
☐ Between 25 and 49 percent of the organization's members have participated in activities hosted by the UK Government Equalities Office.
☐ Less than 24 percent of this organization's members have participated in activities hosted by the UK Government Equalities Office.

20. In your opinion, has the UK Government Equalities Office changed since the May 2010 elections?
- ☐ Yes
- ☐ No
- ☐ Don't know

21. How has the UK Government Equalities Office changed as a result of the May 2010 British general election?
- ☐ The UK Government Equalities Office is more effective now than it was before the May 2010 election.
- ☐ The UK Government Equalities Office is less effective now than it was before the May 2010 election.

Please elaborate:

22. Of the following policy areas, which would you say the Scottish Government Equality Unit (managed by Minister Nicola Sturgeon) addresses? Check all that apply.
- ☐ A-Food assistance for girls and women
- ☐ B-Public awareness campaigns about women's Equality
- ☐ C-Adult education and literacy for women
- ☐ D-Recreation for women
- ☐ E-Education and literacy for school-age girls
- ☐ F-Promotion of female students and faculty in higher education
- ☐ G-Eliminating violence against women
- ☐ H-Improving treatment of women in jails
- ☐ I-Combating *swara/vanni* and honor killings
- ☐ J-Legal assistance for women
- ☐ K-Information on prenatal care
- ☐ L-Information on women's screening for mammograms
- ☐ M-Information/screening on osteoporosis
- ☐ N-Information/screening for cervical cancer
- ☐ O-Women's access to immunizations
- ☐ P-Financial support for raising children
- ☐ Q-Development of nurseries/child care centers
- ☐ R-Reproductive choice services or awareness
- ☐ S-Physical fitness
- ☐ T-Promotion of foster care
- ☐ U-Assisting women from rural areas
- ☐ V-Female leadership
- ☐ W-Migrant women
- ☐ X-Gender budgeting (assessing subnational budgetary impact on women)
- ☐ Y-Women in political decision making
- ☐ Z-Women's entrepreneurship and microcredits for women
- ☐ AA-Job training for women in the workforce
- ☐ BB-Promoting women in the labor market
- ☐ CC-Raising awareness about gender-based employment discrimination
- ☐ DD-Family-friendly policy
- ☐ EE-Reconciliation of work and family life
- ☐ FF-Other 1
- ☐ GG-Other 2
- ☐ Don't know

23. Considering the Scottish Government Equality Unit, what would you say seems to be its first policy priority for women?
- ☐ A-Food assistance for girls and women
- ☐ B-Public awareness campaigns about women's equality

☐ C-Adult education and literacy for women
☐ D-Recreation for women
☐ E-Education and literacy for school-age girls
☐ F-Promotion of female students and faculty in higher education
☐ G-Eliminating violence against women
☐ H-Improving treatment of women in jails
☐ I-Combating *swara/vanni* and honor killings
☐ J-Legal assistance for women
☐ K-Information on prenatal care
☐ L-Information on women's screening for mammograms
☐ M-Information/screening on osteoporosis
☐ N-Information/screening for cervical cancer
☐ O-Women's access to immunizations
☐ P-Financial support for raising children
☐ Q-Development of nurseries/child care centers
☐ R-Reproductive choice services or awareness
☐ S-Physical fitness
☐ T-Promotion of foster care
☐ U-Assisting women from rural areas
☐ V-Female leadership
☐ W-Migrant women
☐ X-Gender budgeting (assessing subnational budgetary impact on women)
☐ Y-Women in political decision making
☐ Z-Women's entrepreneurship and microcredits for women
☐ AA-Job training for women in the workforce
☐ BB-Promoting women in the labor market
☐ CC-Raising awareness about gender-based employment discrimination
☐ DD-Family-friendly policy
☐ EE-Reconciliation of work and family life
☐ FF-Advancement for women of color
☐ GG-Lesbian, gay, bisexual, or transgender rights
☐ HH-Sex workers' rights
☐ II-Other 1
☐ JJ-Other 2
☐ Don't know

24. Considering the Scottish Government Equality Unit, what would you say seems to be its second policy priority for women?
☐ A-Food assistance for girls and women
☐ B-Public awareness campaigns about women's equality
☐ C-Adult education and literacy for women
☐ D-Recreation for women
☐ E-Education and literacy for school-age girls
☐ F-Promotion of female students and faculty in higher education
☐ G-Eliminating violence against women
☐ H-Improving treatment of women in jails
☐ I-Combating *swara/vanni* and honor killings
☐ J-Legal assistance for women
☐ K-Information on prenatal care
☐ L-Information on women's screening for mammograms
☐ M-Information/screening on osteoporosis
☐ N-Information/screening for cervical cancer
☐ O-Women's access to immunizations
☐ P-Financial support for raising children
☐ Q-Development of nurseries/child care centers
☐ R-Reproductive choice services or awareness

☐ S-Physical fitness
☐ T-Promotion of foster care
☐ U-Assisting women from rural areas
☐ V-Female leadership
☐ W-Migrant women
☐ X-Gender budgeting (assessing subnational budgetary impact on women)
☐ Y-Women in political decision making
☐ Z-Women's entrepreneurship and microcredits for women
☐ AA-Job training for women in the workforce
☐ BB-Promoting women in the labor market
☐ CC-Raising awareness about gender-based employment discrimination
☐ DD-Family-friendly policy
☐ EE-Reconciliation of work and family life
☐ FF-Advancement for women of color
☐ GG-Lesbian, gay, bisexual, or transgender rights
☐ HH-Sex workers' rights
☐ II-Other 1
☐ JJ-Other 2
☐ Don't know

25. Considering the Scottish Government Equality Unit, what seems to be its third policy priority for women?
☐ A-Food assistance for girls and women
☐ B-Public awareness campaigns about women's equality
☐ C-Adult education and literacy for women
☐ D-Recreation for women
☐ E-Education and literacy for school-age girls
☐ F-Promotion of female students and faculty in higher education
☐ G-Eliminating violence against women
☐ H-Improving treatment of women in jails
☐ I-Combating *swara/vanni* and honor killings
☐ J-Legal assistance for women
☐ K-Information on prenatal care
☐ L-Information on women's screening for mammograms
☐ M-Information/screening on osteoporosis
☐ N-Information/screening for cervical cancer
☐ O-Women's access to immunizations
☐ P-Financial support for raising children
☐ Q-Development of nurseries/child care centers
☐ R-Reproductive choice services or awareness
☐ S-Physical fitness
☐ T-Promotion of foster care
☐ U-Assisting women from rural areas
☐ V-Female leadership
☐ W-Migrant women
☐ X-Gender budgeting (assessing subnational budgetary impact on women)
☐ Y-Women in political decision making
☐ Z-Women's entrepreneurship and microcredits for women
☐ AA-Job training for women in the workforce
☐ BB-Promoting women in the labor market
☐ CC-Raising awareness about gender-based employment discrimination
☐ DD-Family-friendly policy
☐ EE-Reconciliation of work and family life
☐ FF-Advancement for women of color
☐ GG-Lesbian, gay, bisexual, or transgender rights
☐ HH-Sex workers' rights

☐ II-Other 1
☐ JJ-Other 2
☐ Don't know

26. Considering the Scottish Government Equality Unit, what seems to be its fourth policy priority for women?
☐ A-Food assistance for girls and women
☐ B-Public awareness campaigns about women's equality
☐ C-Adult education and literacy for women
☐ D-Recreation for women
☐ E-Education and literacy for school-age girls
☐ F-Promotion of female students and faculty in higher education
☐ G-Eliminating violence against women
☐ H-Improving treatment of women in jails
☐ I-Combating *swara/vanni* and honor killings
☐ J-Legal assistance for women
☐ K-Information on prenatal care
☐ L-Information on women's screening for mammograms
☐ M-Information/screening on osteoporosis
☐ N-Information/screening for cervical cancer
☐ O-Women's access to immunizations
☐ P-Financial support for raising children
☐ Q-Development of nurseries/child care centers
☐ R-Reproductive choice services or awareness
☐ S-Physical fitness
☐ T-Promotion of foster care
☐ U-Assisting women from rural areas
☐ V-Female leadership
☐ W-Migrant women
☐ X-Gender budgeting (assessing subnational budgetary impact on women)
☐ Y-Women in political decision making
☐ Z-Women's entrepreneurship and microcredits for women
☐ AA-Job training for women in the workforce
☐ BB-Promoting women in the labor market
☐ CC-Raising awareness about gender-based employment discrimination
☐ DD-Family-friendly policy
☐ EE-Reconciliation of work and family life
☐ FF-Advancement for women of color
☐ GG-Lesbian, gay, bisexual, or transgender rights
☐ HH-Sex workers' rights
☐ II-Other 1
☐ JJ-Other 2
☐ Don't know

27. Please rate the level of effectiveness of the Scottish Government Equality Unit on its four policy priorities you indicated above.

Priority	Very successful	Moderately successful	No change	Moderately unsuccessful	Very unsuccessful	Don't know
	☐	☐	☐	☐	☐	☐
	☐	☐	☐	☐	☐	☐
	☐	☐	☐	☐	☐	☐
	☐	☐	☐	☐	☐	☐

28. In what ways does the Scottish Government Equality Unit interact with women's organizations in Scotland? Check all that apply.
- ☐ The commission regularly organizes meetings to bring together agency personnel and members from women's organizations.
- ☐ The commission organizes meetings on an ad hoc basis to bring together agency personnel and women's organizations.
- ☐ The commission personnel occasionally attend the meetings or events of women's organizations.
- ☐ The commission personnel interacts with women's organizations when a representative from an organization attends a meeting.
- ☐ The commission personnel relate to women's organization via mail or telecommunications (phone, fax, e-mail, etc.).
- ☐ The commission largely does not interact with women's organizations.
- ☐ Don't know
- ☐ Other

29. How many members of your organization have participated in activities hosted by the Scottish Government Equality Unit (for example, conferences, meetings, job training, campaigns, etc.)?
- ☐ Every member (or almost every member) of the organization has participated in activities hosted by the gender equality unit.
- ☐ More than 50 percent of the organization's members have participated in activities hosted by the devolved gender equality commission.
- ☐ Between 25 and 50 percent of the organization's members have participated in activities hosted by the devolved gender equality commission
- ☐ Zero to 24 percent of the members of this organization members have participated in activities hosted by the devolved gender equality commission.
- ☐ Don't know

30. In general, in which of the following ways has the Scottish Government Equality Unit contributed the achievement of this organization's goals?
- ☐ The Scottish Government Equality Unit has positively influenced the achievement of this organization's goals.
- ☐ The Scottish Government Equality Unit has negatively influenced the achievement of this organization's goals.
- ☐ The Scottish Government Equality Unit has not influenced the achievement of this organization's goals.
- ☐ Don't know

Explain further if you wish:

31. Which gender equality office does your women's organization interact with most?
- ☐ United Nations Division for Advancement of Women/UN Entity for Women
- ☐ European Institute for Gender Equality
- ☐ UK Government Equalities Office
- ☐ Scottish Government Equality Unit
- ☐ City-level gender equality unit
- ☐ Other

32. Why this level of government?
- ☐ This is the level of government which most affects my organization.
- ☐ This organization has allies at this level of government.
- ☐ Don't know
- ☐ Other

33. Is your organization formally affiliated with a political party?
☐ Yes
☐ No

34. If yes to question 33, which political party?
☐ Labour Party
☐ Conservative Party
☐ Liberal Democrat Party
☐ Scottish National Party
☐ Don't know
☐ Other

35. In your opinion, which of the following political parties does *the least* to create equality between the sexes in political, economic, and social life?
☐ Labour Party
☐ Conservative Party
☐ Liberal Democrat Party
☐ Scottish National Party
☐ Don't know
☐ Other

36. In your opinion, which of the following political parties is the *most likely* to help this organization achieve its goals?
☐ Labour Party
☐ Conservative Party
☐ Liberal Democrat Party
☐ Scottish National Party
☐ Don't know
☐ Other

37. In your opinion, which of the following political parties is the *least likely* to help this organization to achieve its goals?
☐ Labour Party
☐ Conservative Party
☐ Liberal Democrat Party
☐ Scottish National Party
☐ Don't know
☐ Other

38. In your opinion, which of the following political parties is *most likely* to block the achievement of this organization's goals?
☐ Labour Party
☐ Conservative Party
☐ Liberal Democrat Party
☐ Scottish National Party
☐ Don't know
☐ Other

39. Which legislators does your women's organization interact with most?
☐ Members of European Parliament
☐ Members of Parliament at Westminster
☐ Members of the Scottish Parliament
☐ Local councilors
☐ Other

40. Why does your organization interact most with these legislators?
    ☐ These legislators most affect my organization.
    ☐ My organization has allies at this level of government.
    ☐ Don't know
    ☐ Other

41. Finally, you are invited to give your opinion about equality politics in this meso-level unit, equality politics in the United Kingdom as a whole, or any other topic mentioned in this questionnaire.

_____

_____

_____

_____

Survey of Gender Equality Policy Makers

Hello. This survey comes to you from Dr. Meg Rincker, Assistant Professor of Political Science, Purdue University, USA. I am carrying out a study of women's policy agencies in the United Kingdom and their role in gender equality policy making. Your name has been selected from publicly available information because of your leadership role in a women's policy agency in the United Kingdom.

I'd like to ask your views on a number of subjects pertaining to gender equality policy making and politics in the United Kingdom. Your input will be treated strictly confidential, but it will contribute to a better understanding of what women's policy agencies do in different parts of the world.

If you choose to participate in the study, it will involve filling out roughly 60 questions, which should take about 25 minutes. Note that if you skip to a later page in the survey and then jump back to an earlier page, the software will not save your answers. So it's easiest if you answer questions in the order presented. If you have any questions, feel free to contact me at mrincker@purduecal.edu. Thank you very much for your time!

1. Please indicate the office you lead.
    ☐ UK Government Equalities Office
    ☐ Scottish Government Equality Unit
    ☐ Welsh Equal Opportunities Commission
    ☐ Northern Ireland Gender Equality Unit
    ☐ Other

2. Please indicate your sex.
    ☐ Female
    ☐ Male
    ☐ No response

3. In what decade was your organization founded?
    ☐ before 1900
    ☐ 1901–1909
    ☐ 1910–1919
    ☐ 1920–1929
    ☐ 1930–1939
    ☐ 1940–1949
    ☐ 1950–1959
    ☐ 1960–1969
    ☐ 1970–1979
    ☐ 1980–1989

☐ 1990–1999
☐ 2000–2009
☐ 2010–present
☐ Don't know

4. By what legal means was your agency established?
    ☐ By a Public Law
    ☐ By Executive Decree
    ☐ Other

5. At the time your agency was established, who in your opinion were the greatest proponents of this agency?

_____

_____

_____

_____

6. At the time your agency was established, who in your opinion were the greatest opponents of this agency?

_____

_____

_____

_____

7. Currently, what individuals or organizations (in your opinion) are the most active supporters of gender equality work? Please explain.

_____

_____

_____

_____

8. Currently, in your opinion, who are the greatest opponents of this agency?

_____

_____

_____

_____

9. Is your agency a stand-alone ministry (that is, not located underneath another ministry— e.g., an organ of the ministry of social services, health, etc.)?
    ☐ Yes
    ☐ No
    ☐ Don't know

10. If your agency is under another ministry, which area is it?
    ☐ Social services
    ☐ Health
    ☐ Not applicable
    ☐ Don't know
    ☐ Other

11. Which of the following political parties leads your government?
  - ☐ Labour Party
  - ☐ Conservative Party
  - ☐ Liberal Democratic Party
  - ☐ Scottish National Party
  - ☐ Don't know
  - ☐ Other

12. Of the following policy areas, which would you say your agency addresses pertaining to women? Check all that apply.
  - ☐ A-Food assistance for girls and women
  - ☐ B-Public awareness campaigns about women's equality
  - ☐ C-Adult education and literacy for women
  - ☐ D-Recreation for women
  - ☐ E-Education and literacy for school-age girls
  - ☐ F-Promotion of female students and faculty in higher education
  - ☐ G-Eliminating violence against women
  - ☐ H-Improving treatment of women in jails
  - ☐ I-Combating *swara/vanni* and honor killings
  - ☐ J-Legal assistance for women
  - ☐ K-Information on prenatal care
  - ☐ L-Information on women's screening for mammograms
  - ☐ M-Information/screening on osteoporosis
  - ☐ N-Information/screening for cervical cancer
  - ☐ O-Women's access to immunizations
  - ☐ P-Financial support for raising children
  - ☐ Q-Development of nurseries/child care centers
  - ☐ R-Reproductive choice services or awareness
  - ☐ S-Physical fitness
  - ☐ T-Promotion of foster care
  - ☐ U-Assisting women from rural areas
  - ☐ V-Female leadership
  - ☐ W-Migrant women
  - ☐ X-Gender budgeting (assessing subnational budgetary impact on women)
  - ☐ Y-Women in political decision making
  - ☐ Z-Women's entrepreneurship and microcredits for women
  - ☐ AA-Job training for women in the workforce
  - ☐ BB-Promoting women in the labor market
  - ☐ CC-Raising awareness about gender-based employment discrimination
  - ☐ DD-Family-friendly policy
  - ☐ EE-Reconciliation of work and family life
  - ☐ FF-Advancement for women of color
  - ☐ GG-Lesbian, gay, bisexual, and transgender rights
  - ☐ HH-Sex workers' rights
  - ☐ II-Other 1
  - ☐ JJ-Other 2
  - ☐ Don't know

13. What is your agency's first policy priority for women?
  - ☐ A-Food assistance for girls and women
  - ☐ B-Public awareness campaigns about women's equality
  - ☐ C-Adult education and literacy for women
  - ☐ D-Recreation for women
  - ☐ E-Education and literacy for school-age girls
  - ☐ F-Promotion of female students and faculty in higher education
  - ☐ G-Eliminating violence against women

- ☐ H-Improving treatment of women in jails
- ☐ I-Combating *swara/vanni* and honor killings
- ☐ J-Legal assistance for women
- ☐ K-Information on prenatal care
- ☐ L-Information on women's screening for mammograms
- ☐ M-Information/screening on osteoporosis
- ☐ N-Information/screening for cervical cancer
- ☐ O-Women's access to immunizations
- ☐ P-Financial support for raising children
- ☐ Q-Development of nurseries/child care centers
- ☐ R-Reproductive choice services or awareness
- ☐ S-Physical fitness
- ☐ T-Promotion of foster care
- ☐ U-Assisting women from rural areas
- ☐ V-Female leadership
- ☐ W-Migrant women
- ☐ X-Gender budgeting (assessing subnational budgetary impact on women)
- ☐ Y-Women in political decision making
- ☐ Z-Women's entrepreneurship and microcredits for women
- ☐ AA-Job training for women in the workforce
- ☐ BB-Promoting women in the labor market
- ☐ CC-Raising awareness about gender-based employment discrimination
- ☐ DD-Family-friendly policy
- ☐ EE-Reconciliation of work and family life
- ☐ FF-Advancement for women of color
- ☐ GG-Lesbian, gay, bisexual, or transgender rights
- ☐ HH-Sex workers' rights
- ☐ II-Other 1
- ☐ JJ-Other 2
- ☐ Don't know

14. What is your agency's second policy priority for women?
    - ☐ A-Food assistance for girls and women
    - ☐ B-Public awareness campaigns about women's equality
    - ☐ C-Adult education and literacy for women
    - ☐ D-Recreation for women
    - ☐ E-Education and literacy for school-age girls
    - ☐ F-Promotion of female students and faculty in higher education
    - ☐ G-Eliminating violence against women
    - ☐ H-Improving treatment of women in jails
    - ☐ I-Combating *swara/vanni* and honor killings
    - ☐ J-Legal assistance for women
    - ☐ K-Information on prenatal care
    - ☐ L-Information on women's screening for mammograms
    - ☐ M-Information/screening on osteoporosis
    - ☐ N-Information/screening for cervical cancer
    - ☐ O-Women's access to immunizations
    - ☐ P-Financial support for raising children
    - ☐ Q-Development of nurseries/child care centers
    - ☐ R-Reproductive choice services or awareness
    - ☐ S-Physical fitness
    - ☐ T-Promotion of foster care
    - ☐ U-Assisting women from rural areas
    - ☐ V-Female leadership
    - ☐ W-Migrant women
    - ☐ X-Gender budgeting (assessing subnational budgetary impact on women)

☐ Y-Women in political decision making
☐ Z-Women's entrepreneurship and microcredits for women
☐ AA-Job training for women in the workforce
☐ BB-Promoting women in the labor market
☐ CC-Raising awareness about gender-based employment discrimination
☐ DD-Family-friendly policy
☐ EE-Reconciliation of work and family life
☐ FF-Advancement for women of color
☐ GG-Lesbian, gay, bisexual, or transgender rights
☐ HH-Sex workers' rights
☐ II-Other 1
☐ JJ-Other 2
☐ Don't know

15. What is your agency's third policy priority for women?
☐ A-Food assistance for girls and women
☐ B-Public awareness campaigns about women's equality
☐ C-Adult education and literacy for women
☐ D-Recreation for women
☐ E-Education and literacy for school-age girls
☐ F-Promotion of female students and faculty in higher education
☐ G-Eliminating violence against women
☐ H-Improving treatment of women in jails
☐ I-Combating *swara/vanni* and honor killings
☐ J-Legal assistance for women
☐ K-Information on prenatal care
☐ L-Information on women's screening for mammograms
☐ M-Information/screening on osteoporosis
☐ N-Information/screening for cervical cancer
☐ O-Women's access to immunizations
☐ P-Financial support for raising children
☐ Q-Development of nurseries/child care centers
☐ R-Reproductive choice services or awareness
☐ S-Physical fitness
☐ T-Promotion of foster care
☐ U-Assisting women from rural areas
☐ V-Female leadership
☐ W-Migrant women
☐ X-Gender budgeting (assessing subnational budgetary impact on women)
☐ Y-Women in political decision making
☐ Z-Women's entrepreneurship and microcredits for women
☐ AA-Job training for women in the workforce
☐ BB-Promoting women in the labor market
☐ CC-Raising awareness about gender-based employment discrimination
☐ DD-Family-friendly policy
☐ EE-Reconciliation of work and family life
☐ FF-Advancement for women of color
☐ GG-Lesbian, gay, bisexual, or transgender rights
☐ HH-Sex workers' rights
☐ II-Other 1
☐ JJ-Other 2
☐ Don't know

16. What is your agency's fourth policy priority for women?
☐ A-Food assistance for girls and women
☐ B-Public awareness campaigns about women's equality

☐ C-Adult education and literacy for women
☐ D-Recreation for women
☐ E-Education and literacy for school-age girls
☐ F-Promotion of female students and faculty in higher education
☐ G-Eliminating violence against women
☐ H-Improving treatment of women in jails
☐ I-Combating *swara/vanni* and honor killings
☐ J-Legal assistance for women
☐ K-Information on prenatal care
☐ L-Information on women's screening for mammograms
☐ M-Information/screening on osteoporosis
☐ N-Information/screening for cervical cancer
☐ O-Women's access to immunizations
☐ P-Financial support for raising children
☐ Q-Development of nurseries/child care centers
☐ R-Reproductive choice services or awareness
☐ S-Physical fitness
☐ T-Promotion of foster care
☐ U-Assisting women from rural areas
☐ V-Female leadership
☐ W-Migrant women
☐ X-Gender budgeting (assessing subnational budgetary impact on women)
☐ Y-Women in political decision making
☐ Z-Women's entrepreneurship and microcredits for women
☐ AA-Job training for women in the workforce
☐ BB-Promoting women in the labor market
☐ CC-Raising awareness about gender-based employment discrimination
☐ DD-Family-friendly policy
☐ EE-Reconciliation of work and family life
☐ FF-Advancement for women of color
☐ GG-Lesbian, gay, bisexual, or transgender rights
☐ HH-Sex workers' rights
☐ II-Other 1
☐ JJ-Other 2
☐ Don't know

17. Please rate the level of your organization's effectiveness on the four policy priorities you indicated above.

Priority	Very successful	Moderately successful	No change	Moderately unsuccessful	Very unsuccessful	Don't know
	☐	☐	☐	☐	☐	☐
	☐	☐	☐	☐	☐	☐
	☐	☐	☐	☐	☐	☐
	☐	☐	☐	☐	☐	☐

18. Of the following policy areas, which would you say the United Kingdom Gender Equalities Office (managed by the Right Honorable Minister Theresa May) addresses? Check all that apply.
☐ A-Food assistance for girls and women
☐ B-Public awareness campaigns about women's equality
☐ C-Adult education and literacy for women
☐ D-Recreation for women
☐ E-Education and literacy for school-age girls
☐ F-Promotion of female students and faculty in higher education

☐ G-Eliminating violence against women
☐ H-Improving treatment of women in jails
☐ I-Combating *swara/vanni* and honor killings
☐ J-Legal assistance for women
☐ K-Information on prenatal care
☐ L-Information on women's screening for mammograms
☐ M-Information/screening on osteoporosis
☐ N-Information/screening for cervical cancer
☐ O-Women's access to immunizations
☐ P-Financial support for raising children
☐ Q-Development of nurseries/child care centers
☐ R-Reproductive choice services or awareness
☐ S-Physical fitness
☐ T-Promotion of foster care
☐ U-Assisting women from rural areas
☐ V-Female leadership
☐ W-Migrant women
☐ X-Gender budgeting (assessing budgetary impact on women)
☐ Y-Women in political decision making
☐ Z-Women's entrepreneurship and microcredits for women
☐ AA-Job training for women in the workforce
☐ BB-Promoting women in the labor market
☐ CC-Raising awareness about gender-based employment discrimination
☐ DD-Family-friendly policy
☐ EE-Reconciliation of work and family life
☐ FF-Other 1
☐ GG-Other 2
☐ Don't know

19. What would you consider to be the UK Gender Equalities Office's first policy priority for women?
☐ A-Food assistance for girls and women
☐ B-Public awareness campaigns about women's equality
☐ C-Adult education and literacy for women
☐ D-Recreation for women
☐ E-Education and literacy for school-age girls
☐ F-Promotion of female students and faculty in higher education
☐ G-Eliminating violence against women
☐ H-Improving treatment of women in jails
☐ I-Combating *swara/vanni* and honor killings
☐ J-Legal assistance for women
☐ K-Information on prenatal care
☐ L-Information on women's screening for mammograms
☐ M-Information/screening on osteoporosis
☐ N-Information/screening for cervical cancer
☐ O-Women's access to immunizations
☐ P-Financial support for raising children
☐ Q-Development of nurseries/child care centers
☐ R-Reproductive choice services or awareness
☐ S-Physical fitness
☐ T-Promotion of foster care
☐ U-Assisting women from rural areas
☐ V-Female leadership
☐ W-Migrant women
☐ X-Gender budgeting (assessing budgetary impact on women)
☐ Y-Women in political decision making
☐ Z-Women's entrepreneurship and microcredits for women

☐ AA-Job training for women in the workforce
☐ BB-Promoting women in the labor market
☐ CC-Raising awareness about gender-based employment discrimination
☐ DD-Family-friendly policy
☐ EE-Reconciliation of work and family life
☐ FF-Advancement for women of color
☐ GG-Lesbian, gay, bisexual, or transgender rights
☐ HH-Sex workers' rights
☐ II-Other 1
☐ JJ-Other 2
☐ Don't know

20. What would you consider to be the UK Gender Equality Office's second policy priority for women?
☐ A-Food assistance for girls and women
☐ B-Public awareness campaigns about women's equality
☐ C-Adult education and literacy for women
☐ D-Recreation for women
☐ E-Education and literacy for school-age girls
☐ F-Promotion of female students and faculty in higher education
☐ G-Eliminating violence against women
☐ H-Improving treatment of women in jails
☐ I-Combating *swara/vanni* and honor killings
☐ J-Legal assistance for women
☐ K-Information on prenatal care
☐ L-Information on women's screening for mammograms
☐ M-Information/screening on osteoporosis
☐ N-Information/screening for cervical cancer
☐ O-Women's access to immunizations
☐ P-Financial support for raising children
☐ Q-Development of nurseries/child care centers
☐ R-Reproductive choice services or awareness
☐ S-Physical fitness
☐ T-Promotion of foster care
☐ U-Assisting women from rural areas
☐ V-Female leadership
☐ W-Migrant women
☐ X-Gender budgeting (assessing budgetary impact on women)
☐ Y-Women in political decision making
☐ Z-Women's entrepreneurship and microcredits for women
☐ AA-Job training for women in the workforce
☐ BB-Promoting women in the labor market
☐ CC-Raising awareness about gender-based employment discrimination
☐ DD-Family-friendly policy
☐ EE-Reconciliation of work and family life
☐ FF-Advancement for women of color
☐ GG-Lesbian, gay, bisexual, or transgender rights
☐ HH-Sex workers' rights
☐ II-Other 1
☐ JJ-Other 2
☐ Don't know

21. What would you consider to be the UK Gender Equality Office's third policy priority for women?
☐ A-Food assistance for girls and women
☐ B-Public awareness campaigns about women's equality

☐ C-Adult education and literacy for women
☐ D-Recreation for women
☐ E-Education and literacy for school-age girls
☐ F-Promotion of female students and faculty in higher education
☐ G-Eliminating violence against women
☐ H-Improving treatment of women in jails
☐ I-Combating *swara/vanni* and honor killings
☐ J-Legal assistance for women
☐ K-Information on prenatal care
☐ L-Information on women's screening for mammograms
☐ M-Information/screening on osteoporosis
☐ N-Information/screening for cervical cancer
☐ O-Women's access to immunizations
☐ P-Financial support for raising children
☐ Q-Development of nurseries/child care centers
☐ R-Reproductive choice services or awareness
☐ S-Physical fitness
☐ T-Promotion of foster care
☐ U-Assisting women from rural areas
☐ V-Female leadership
☐ W-Migrant women
☐ X-Gender budgeting (assessing budgetary impact on women)
☐ Y-Women in political decision making
☐ Z-Women's entrepreneurship and microcredits for women
☐ AA-Job training for women in the workforce
☐ BB-Promoting women in the labor market
☐ CC-Raising awareness about gender-based employment discrimination
☐ DD-Family-friendly policy
☐ EE-Reconciliation of work and family life
☐ FF-Advancement for women of color
☐ GG-Lesbian, gay, bisexual, or transgender rights
☐ HH-Sex workers' rights
☐ II-Other 1
☐ JJ-Other 2
☐ Don't know

22. What would you consider to be the UK Gender Equality Office's fourth policy priority for women?
☐ A-Food assistance for girls and women
☐ B-Public awareness campaigns about women's equality
☐ C-Adult education and literacy for women
☐ D-Recreation for women
☐ E-Education and literacy for school-age girls
☐ F-Promotion of female students and faculty in higher education
☐ G-Eliminating violence against women
☐ H-Improving treatment of women in jails
☐ I-Combating *swara/vanni* and honor killings
☐ J-Legal assistance for women
☐ K-Information on prenatal care
☐ L-Information on women's screening for mammograms
☐ M-Information/screening on osteoporosis
☐ N-Information/screening for cervical cancer
☐ O-Women's access to immunizations
☐ P-Financial support for raising children
☐ Q-Development of nurseries/child care centers
☐ R-Reproductive choice services or awareness

☐ S-Physical fitness
☐ T-Promotion of foster care
☐ U-Assisting women from rural areas
☐ V-Female leadership
☐ W-Migrant women
☐ X-Gender budgeting (assessing budgetary impact on women)
☐ Y-Women in political decision making
☐ Z-Women's entrepreneurship and microcredits for women
☐ AA-Job training for women in the workforce
☐ BB-Promoting women in the labor market
☐ CC-Raising awareness about gender-based employment discrimination
☐ DD-Family-friendly policy
☐ EE-Reconciliation of work and family life
☐ FF-Advancement for women of color
☐ GG-Lesbian, gay, bisexual, or transgender rights
☐ HH-Sex workers' rights
☐ II-Other 1
☐ JJ-Other 2
☐ Don't know

23. Please rate the level of effectiveness of the UK Gender Equalities Office on its four policy priorities you indicated above.

Priority	Very successful	Moderately successful	No change	Moderately unsuccessful	Very unsuccessful	Don't know
	☐	☐	☐	☐	☐	☐
	☐	☐	☐	☐	☐	☐
	☐	☐	☐	☐	☐	☐
	☐	☐	☐	☐	☐	☐

24. Which of the following best describes gender equality policies within the United Kingdom?
☐ All policy units within the United Kingdom have developed similar gender equality policies.
☐ Gender equality policies differ slightly from one nation to another nation.
☐ Gender equality policies differ moderately from one nation to another nation.
☐ Gender equality policies differ greatly from one nation to another nation.
☐ Other

25. How often does the UK Gender Equality Office communicate with your women's organization?
☐ Frequently
☐ Occasionally
☐ Sometimes
☐ Never
☐ Don't know

26. Please check any ways in which gender equality policies differ from one nation in the United Kingdom to another.
☐ Some nations have more advanced equality policies than other nations.
☐ Some nations pursue more socially progressive equality policies than other nations.
☐ Some nations pursue more socially conservative equality policies than other nations.
☐ Some nations devote more money to gender equality policies than other nations.

☐ Some nations have institutionally stronger women's policy agencies than other nations.
☐ Nations do not differ in any noticeable way.
☐ Other

27. What was your agency's operating budget for the most recent year you remember? Please specify the year as well.

_____
_____
_____
_____

28. Please estimate the percentage of your budget that comes from each of the following sources.
Westminster: _____
National government: _____
European Union: _____
Other international sources: _____
Nongovernmental organizations: _____
Other: _____

29. How many full-time employees work in your agency?
☐ 1–9
☐ 10–19
☐ 20–29
☐ 29–49
☐ more than 50

30. How many part-time employees work in your agency?
☐ 1–9
☐ 10–19
☐ 20–29
☐ 29–49
☐ more than 50

31. Does your agency director have significant control over how the agency budget is spent?
☐ Yes
☐ No
☐ Don't know

32. Does your agency have its own office space?
☐ Yes
☐ No
☐ Don't know

33. What percentage of the national budget would you estimate is spent on gender equality policy?

_____

34. What is the background of the agency's director? Please check all that apply.
☐ Civil servant
☐ Politician
☐ Academic
☐ Women's movement activist
☐ Other

35. Please complete the following phrase: Our women's policy agency is staffed with people with:
- ☐ Extensive experience in women's organizations
- ☐ Moderate experience in women's organizations
- ☐ Limited experience in women's organizations

36. How many women's organizations would you estimate are in your meso-level unit?
- ☐ 5–10
- ☐ 11–30
- ☐ 31–50
- ☐ 51–100
- ☐ 101–250
- ☐ 251–500
- ☐ 501–750
- ☐ 751–1,000
- ☐ Over 1,000

37. In your opinion, are women's organizations in your meso-level unit strong and active?
- ☐ Yes
- ☐ No
- ☐ Don't know

38. Compared to those of other meso-level units in the United Kingdom, do you believe your women's organizations have large memberships?
- ☐ Yes
- ☐ No
- ☐ Don't know

39. Women's organizations may work on a variety of issues and may serve women in a variety of ways. In your estimation, to what degree is there a unified perspective among women's organizations in this meso-level unit?
- ☐ Women's organizations in our meso-level unit are extremely unified.
- ☐ Women's organizations in our meso-level unit are very unified.
- ☐ Women's organizations in our meso-level unit are somewhat divided.
- ☐ Women's organizations in our meso-level unit are very divided.
- ☐ Women's organizations in our meso-level unit are extremely divided.

40. Do women's organizations in your meso-level unit interact much with government officials?
- ☐ Yes
- ☐ No
- ☐ Don't know

41. How would you describe the frequency of communication between your agency and the women's organizations in the meso-level unit?
- ☐ Never
- ☐ Very infrequent
- ☐ Infrequent
- ☐ Occasional
- ☐ Frequent
- ☐ Very frequent

42. What are the reasons for communication between this agency and women's organizations in the meso-level unit? Check all that apply.
- ☐ To communicate about activities for women hosted by this agency
- ☐ To communicate about activities hosted by women's organizations
- ☐ To coordinate with women's organizations about the details of programs and activities

☐ To brainstorm and develop equality plans for this meso-level unit
☐ To discuss the role of women in this meso-level unit and ways to improve women's lives in this meso-level unit
☐ To discuss policies that affect women in this meso-level unit
☐ To communicate about the agency's facilities in this meso-level unit
☐ To communicate about subsidies for women's organizations
☐ To assist women's organizations in their dealings with meso political officials and institutions
☐ To assist women's organizations in their dealings with national political officials and institutions
☐ To assist women's organizations in their dealings with international political officials, and institutions, international political bodies, or funding sources
☐ Other

43. In what ways does your agency interact with women's organizations in your meso-level unit? Please check all that apply.
☐ Our agency regularly organizes meetings to bring together women's organizations in our meso-level unit.
☐ Our agency organizes meetings on an ad hoc basis to bring together agency personnel and women's organizations in our meso-level unit.
☐ Our agency personnel occasionally attend the meetings or events held by women's organizations in our meso-level unit.
☐ Our agency personnel interacts with women's organizations when an representative from an organization visits the agency's headquarters.
☐ Our agency personnel relate to women's organization via mail or telecommunications (phone, fax, e-mail, etc.).
☐ Our agency rarely interacts with women's organizations in our meso-level unit.
☐ Other

44. Which legislators does your agency interact with most?
☐ Members of the European Parliament
☐ Members of Parliament at Westminster
☐ Members of the meso-level assembly
☐ Local councilors
☐ Other

45. Why does your agency interact most with these legislators?
☐ These legislators most affect my agency.
☐ My agency has allies at this level of government.
☐ Don't know
☐ Other

46. Generally speaking, meso-level political parties support the work of the agency.
☐ Strongly agree
☐ Agree
☐ Disagree
☐ Strongly disagree
☐ Don't know

47. In what ways, if any, do the meso-level parties support the work of the agency? (If relevant, specify which political party or parties apply.) Please check all that apply.
☐ Meso-level parties include women's policy goals on their party programs.
☐ Women's sections in political parties advance the women's policy agency goals.
☐ Parties in meso-level legislature advocate women's policy legislation.
☐ Meso-level parties advocate for resources to fund women's policy legislation.
☐ Meso-level parties do little or nothing to advance women's policy agency goals.
☐ Other

48. Generally speaking, the first minister of my country supports the work of the agency.
   ☐ Strongly agree
   ☐ Agree
   ☐ Disagree
   ☐ Strongly disagree
   ☐ Don't know

49. In what ways, if any, does the meso-level first minister support the work of the agency? Please check all that apply.
   ☐ The meso-level first minister ensures reasonably adequate funding for the agency.
   ☐ The meso-level first minister generally backs initiatives and programs of the agency.
   ☐ The meso-level first minister attends events organized by the women's policy agency.
   ☐ The meso-level first minister participates in formation of gender equality policy.
   ☐ Other

50. In what ways, if any, does the meso-level parliament support the work of the agency? Please check all that apply.
   ☐ The meso-level legislature works to propose legislation favorable to the agency.
   ☐ The meso-level legislature works to pass legislation favorable to the agency.
   ☐ The meso-level legislature works to secure funding from the meso-level budget for the agency.
   ☐ The meso-level legislature works to secure funding from international organizations for the agency.
   ☐ The meso-level legislature works to refer issues or problems to your agency.
   ☐ Other
   ☐ Don't know

51. Please identify the legislators who are the greatest advocates for the agency, and describe the nature of their advocacy in two to three sentences.

_____

_____

_____

_____

52. Meso-level legislatures have been a good avenue for women to get involved in politics in the United Kingdom.
   ☐ Strongly agree
   ☐ Agree
   ☐ Disagree
   ☐ Strongly disagree
   ☐ Don't know
   ☐ Other

53. Please identify any meso-level executive agencies you work with in order to further equality policy. Please check all that apply
   ☐ Ministry of Health
   ☐ Ministry of Social Welfare
   ☐ Ministry of Education
   ☐ Ministry of Labor
   ☐ Ministry of Justice
   ☐ Ministry of Agriculture
   ☐ Bureau of Statistics
   ☐ Our agency does not work with other meso-level executive agencies at this time.
   ☐ Other

54. If elections to Westminster were held and power changed hands to the political opposition, how much would your agency change in terms of *agency personnel*?
- ☐ Agency personnel would completely change.
- ☐ Agency personnel would change moderately.
- ☐ Agency personnel changes would be minor.
- ☐ Agency personnel would not change.

55. If elections to Westminster were held and power changed hands to the political opposition, how much would your agency change in terms of *agency mission*?
- ☐ Agency mission would completely change.
- ☐ Agency mission would change moderately.
- ☐ Agency mission changes would be minor.
- ☐ Agency mission would not change.

56. If national assembly elections (i.e., Scottish Parliament) were held and power changed hands to the political opposition, how much would your agency change in terms of *agency personnel*?
- ☐ Agency personnel would completely change.
- ☐ Agency personnel would change moderately.
- ☐ Agency personnel changes would be minor.
- ☐ Agency personnel would not change.

57. If national assembly elections (i.e., Scottish Parliament) were held and power changed hands to the political opposition, how much would your agency change in terms of *agency mission*?
- ☐ Agency mission would completely change.
- ☐ Agency mission would change moderately.
- ☐ Agency mission changes would be minor.
- ☐ Agency mission would not change.

58. What policies, programs, activities, or institutional procedures on gender equality have been successful in this meso-level unit?

_____

_____

_____

_____

59. What gender equality policies are lacking in this meso-level unit? What about the agency needs to change?

_____

_____

_____

_____

60. Meso-level women's policy agencies have improved the status of women in this meso-level unit.
- ☐ Strongly agree
- ☐ Agree
- ☐ Disagree
- ☐ Strongly disagree
- ☐ Don't know

61. Finally, you are invited to give your opinion about equality politics in this meso-level unit, equality politics in the United Kingdom as a whole, or any other topic mentioned in this questionnaire.

_____

_____

_____

_____

Appendix 3

Women's Descriptive Representation (%) in Decentralized Poland, Pakistan, and the United Kingdom

Poland	1997	2001	2005	2011
Sejm	13.0	20.2	20.4	23.9
Meso-level average	10.4	14.2	16.9	25.3
Meso unit				
Dolnośląskie	7.0	16.7	16.7	33.3
Kujawsko-Pomorskie	16.0	21.2	15.2	24.2
Lubelskie	10.0	18.2	21.2	15.8
Lubuskie	4.4	6.7	10.0	23.3
Łódzkie	14.5	22.2	16.7	44.4
Małopolskie	10.0	17.9	28.2	17.9
Mazowieckie	16.3	17.6	23.5	39.2
Opolskie	13.3	20.0	13.3	16.7
Podkarpackie	6.0	6.1	12.1	15.2
Podlaskie	4.4	10.0	3.3	13.3
Pomorskie	20.0	18.2	21.2	27.3
Śląskie	16.0	14.6	10.4	31.3
Świętokrzyskie	2.2	3.3	10.0	19.2
Warmińsko-Mazurskie	6.7	6.7	23.3	23.3
Wielkopolskie	6.7	10.3	28.2	17.9
Zachodniopomorskie	13.3	16.7	16.7	30.0
Pakistan	**1997**	**2002**	**2008**	**2013**
National Assembly	2.3	21.3	22.5	20.5
Meso-level average	0	16.0	17.2	19.4
Meso unit				
Balochistan	0	16.9	18.8	18.5
Punjab	0	17.8	20.0	20.5
Sindh	0	17.3	17.3	18.5
Khyber Pakhtunkhwa	0	17.7	17.7	17.7
Azad Jammu and Kashmir	0	10.2	12.2	12.5
United Kingdom	**1997**	**2001**	**2005**	**2014**
House of Commons	18.2	17.9	19.8	22.0
Meso-level average	30.4	34.5	32.3	28.2
Meso unit				
Scotland	37.2	39.5	33.3	30.2
Wales	40.0	50.0	46.7	41.7
Northern Ireland	13.9	14.0	16.7	18.5

Note: National representation pertains to lower houses of parliament.

Appendix 4

Policies and Events Directly Affecting Women in Poland, 1993–2014

Unit	Policies and events	Description
National level	Family Planning, Human Embryo Protection and Conditions of Permissibility of Abortion Act of 7 January 1993	• Although women had possessed the right to abortion since 1956, the January 7, 1993, law makes abortion illegal unless (1) the mother's health is endangered, (2) there is strong evidence that the pregnancy resulted from a crime, or (3) prenatal tests show the fetus is severely or irreversibly damaged. The law also restricts access to prenatal testing. • The abortion law was liberalized under a leftist government in 1997 and allowed an additional acceptable reason for abortion—economic hardship of the woman—but added a required three-day wait period before the operation. The Constitutional Tribunal ruled this law unconstitutional on grounds of the state's responsibility for social justice and the view that life begins at the moment of conception. This decision was made very close to a visit by the Polish pontiff to Poland. • Under the law, the woman and doctor can serve up to three years in jail. Other changes to the penal code allow this sentencing in cases of abortion because of condition 2 or 3, in practice making *abortion punishable in every case except when the mother's life is endangered.* Limited sex education exists, as during the communist period, and during the communist period the state encouraged abortion, withdrawal, or rhythm as the primary birth control method; only an estimated 12 to 15 percent of Polish women used condoms, birth control pills, or intrauterine devices.
	Law on Equal Status of Women and Men (1996–2007)	• The law defined and made illegal direct or indirect gender discrimination; established procedures for workplace employment, promotion, equal pay, and prevention of sexual harassment; provided for equal access to social insurance and health care; gave attention to public ads and textbooks; and created national and local ombudspersons. Ośrodek Informacji Środowisk Kobiecych (OSKA; Women's Information Center Environments) formed as a citizen's bill,

(continued)

Unit	Policies and events	Description
		with a hundred thousand signatures, but the Solidarity-successor-party (Akcja Wyborcza Solidarność) government disagreed with 40 percent quotas. A second conference of women supporting quotas led by Kongress Kobiet was held in 1999. • The 2007 Department for Women, Family and Counteracting Discrimination passed a basic definition of sexual harassment to meet EU deadlines by 2008, but only unions and work-related groups, not women's groups, were invited to consultations on the definition.
	Law on Counteracting Violence in the Family (2005)	This legislation requires police to remove from the household a perpetrator of violence against a family member and bans future contact between the perpetrator and victims.
	Amendment to the Domestic Violence Law (2010)	This amendment bans corporal punishment, provides for restraining orders against perpetrators, and requires central and local awareness raising and services.
	Quota Law (2011)	President Komorowski signed a law on January 5, 2011, requiring that the number of candidates of either gender on the electoral lists may not be lower than 35 percent of the overall number of candidates on this list, and for lists that include three candidates, there must be at least one candidate of each gender. This law applies only to city/village (*gmina*), county (*powiat*), Sejm, and European Parliament elections.
	Equal Treatment Law (2011)	This law establishes an Equality Unit as a ministerial cabinet, responsible for protection from discrimination in all fields except employment for the protected categories of race, gender, and ethnicity or nationality.
	Act on Care for a Child under the Age of 3 and 4 (2011)	This act establishes crèches for up to ten hours a day of care, children's clubs for up to five hours a day of care, and nanny care. Local governments (*gmina*) are responsible for regulating crèches and children's clubs, which are not considered public health institutions but do have to fulfill safety requirements.
	Proposed zipper for electoral lists (2014)	This proposal requires that party candidate lists alternate by gender all the way through the list to prevent clustering women in the bottom of electoral lists in unwinnable slots.
	Proposed change to definition of a young scientist (2014)	This proposal sought to change the definition of "young scientist" to specify years since the individual obtained his or her doctorate. The previous definition specified the age of thirty-five, which may discriminate against women who delay training to accommodate childbirth but who, in terms of years of experience, are a few years out from their doctorate.
Meso level		No meso-level assembly resolution titles visibly addressing women's policy priorities were reported in surveys.

Sources: Bojarski 2010; Dabrowksa 2007; Global Database of Quotas for Women 2016c; Nowakowska 2000; Republic of Poland Human Rights Council 2011; UN Women 2006.

Note: Most resolutions passed during this time frame dealt with changes in status of different hospitals, roads, cultural institutions, budgetary amendments, and scholarship requirements.

Appendix 5

Policies and Events Directly Affecting Women in Pakistan, 1973–2013

Unit	Policies and events	Description
National level	1973 Constitution of Pakistan	After the secession of East Pakistan, supported by India, Pakistan enacted this constitution.
	1979 Law of Evidence (Qanoon-e-Shahadat) and the Hudood Ordinances	These laws, passed by Zia-ul-Haq, were targeted at reducing theft, alcohol consumption, and adultery (*zina*). In practice many women were charged with and imprisoned on the basis of alleged *zina* without proof. Under the Hudood Ordinances, rape had to be witnessed by four adult males, and a woman who charged rape and failed to prove it could be charged with *zina* (adultery). Women's Action Forum was organized by Asma Jahangir and other activists to fight Hudood Ordinances.
	2000 Gender Reform Action Plan (GRAP)	In February 2000 Musharraf requested that the Asian Development Bank, in concert with the Ministry of Women Development, prepare the GRAP, which consists of four provincial-level GRAP plans and one national GRAP plan. The four components of these plans are administrative restructuring, women's employment in the public sector, political empowerment, and budgetary/policy reform.
	2001 Local Government Ordinance	This ordinance effectively abolished the Office of the Divisional Commissioner, a centrally appointed bureaucrat who arguably undermined local politics. The Balochistan Board of Revenue challenged the ordinance, saying the divisional commissioner strengthened provincial governance, helped people caught between local governments, and improved tax collection abilities.
	2001 Devolution of Power Program	General Pervez Musharraf, to gain legitimacy after the 1999 coup and Legal Framework Order, reinstated local elections.
	2002 Small Claims and Minor Offences Courts Ordinance; Prevention and Control of Human Trafficking Ordinance; Protection of Breast Feeding and Visitation Ordinance	These ordinances set up small claims courts so that women's cases do not languish in the courts, provide harsher sentences for human trafficking, and protect women's right to breast-feed.

(continued)

Unit	Policies and events	Description
	2004 Crimes in the Name of Honour Amendment Bill	This bill requires senior police officers to investigate charges of honor killing and ends previous protection for the accused that applied if he could prove he was provoked into committing the crime. The bill also increases the minimum sentencing for convictions from seven to ten years. This is a limited version of the original bill, authored by PPP senator Sherry Rehman, who among others noted that the watered-down version fails to punish a whole range of honor crimes short of murder and hold close relatives of the deceased accountable.
	Ministry of Women Development	This ministry was opened in 2005 to coordinate all policy related to gender equality initiatives, coordinate research on women's equality, encourage implementation of GRAP, reduce violence against women, and encourage women's financial independence, among other things.
	2005 Muzaffarabad earthquake	This magnitude 7.6 earthquake affected the spending priorities of the Ministry of Women Development.
	2006 Protection of Women Act	This act amends the Penal Code, moving rape cases from Islamic Sharia courts to criminal courts and removing the need for four adult male witnesses to substantiate rape charges. It makes nonmarital consensual sex punishable by five years in prison. Adultery is still tried in Sharia courts and punishable by stoning. Rape committed by an individual is punished by ten to twenty-five years in prison; rape by two or more persons together is punished by death or life in prison. Sex with girls under sixteen is prohibited.
	2007 assassinations of Zilla Huma Usman and Benazir Bhutto	In 2007 Punjab Minister of Social Affairs Zilla Huma Usman was publicly assassinated in Gujranwala by Mohammad Sarwar for not wearing a head scarf and for participating in political affairs. Former prime minister Benazir Bhutto was assassinated while campaigning in Rawalpindi.
	2010 Protection against Harassment at Workplace Act	This act establishes definition of sexual harassment but needs further implementation mechanisms.
	2011 Supreme Court decision in Mukhtar Mai case	In 2002 Mukhtar Mai was gang raped by six Mastoi neighbors to settle a charge of illicit contact with their kinswoman by her brother. Mai received a compensation check for about US$8,000 from the Pakistan government. However, under Musharraf she was held under house arrest, her name was put on the Exit Control List, and her passport was confiscated in an effort to silence her. On April 21, 2011, the Supreme Court acquitted five attackers and upheld the life sentence of one.

Unit	Policies and events	Description
	2011 Amendment to Pakistani Penal Code	This law increases punishment for acid and burn crimes from fourteen years in prison to life in prison.
	2011 Acid Control and Acid Crime Prevention Act	This act requires police training in and investigation and reporting of acid and burn crimes; legal, medical, and social assistance for victims; data collection; and prevention authority. It was promoted by the National Commission on the Status of Women.
	2012 National Commission on the Status of Women Bill	This bill granted financial autonomy and authority for the commission to investigate women's rights violations.
Punjab	2009 women's caucus	In February 2009, a cross-party women's caucus was formed to work on women's issues.
	2009 parliamentary brawl	In June 2009, Minister of Prisons Chaudhry Abdul Ghafoor (a male) initiated a physical altercation with female assembly member Bushra Gardezi because he disliked a placard she held up. Parliamentary brawls such as this create a sense of intolerance and a chilly climate for women's participation in politics.
	2012 provincial board and fund for acid burn survivors; policy for home-based workers; women's career development centers; maternity leave policy	These developments provide financial and social assistance to acid burn survivors in Punjab, provide a legal framework of fair labor standards to protect an estimated 8.52 million home-based workers (primarily female) who do piecework like sewing footballs, set up job training centers for women, and establish maternity leave recommendations for employers.
Sindh	2003 law to create dar-ul-aman shelters for working women	Sindh Minister for Social Welfare and Women Development Saeeda Malik proposed a law that would create hostels for working women in unused Department of Social Welfare buildings.
	2004 law to end honor killing	A law to end honor killing (Karo-kari) was debated in the Sindh assembly by women in PML-Q. It was supported by President Suhaat Hussain of the PML-Q and PPP MP Mehreen Bhutto. But PPP women would not support PML-Q women because many of their husbands are vaderas (feudal lords) benefiting from traditional practices.
	2008 law to create women's courts	This law was proposed to create women's courts led by female judges.
	2013 Sindh Domestic Violence Act	This law enforces a one-year minimum prison sentence and 20,000-rupee fine for a person convicted of domestic violence.
	2013 Sindh Child Marriage Restraint Act	This law requires that both parties be at least eighteen years old to be married; otherwise, the parents of the bride and groom are sentenced to three years in prison and charged fines of 45,000 rupees.

(continued)

Unit	Policies and events	Description
Balochistan	Mainstreaming Gender and Development program	Influential provincial assembly member and wife of a governor Parveen Magsi supports the Mainstreaming Gender and Development program for women's leadership. Developed by the Institute for Development Studies and Practices, it includes 220 young Balochi women in curriculum, folk literature, and local government.
Khyber Pakhtunkhwa	2007 proposal for revised marriage forms	This was a proposal to revise marriage forms so that husbands and wives are required to list prior spouses or children.

Sources: Aurat Foundation, n.d.; Ghori 2013; Imran 2011; Masood 2011; "New 'Honour Killing' Law" 2004; "NWFP Women" 2007; Punjab Commission on the Status of Women, n.d.; Rauf 2005, 34; Tunio 2014; U.S. Department of State 2003; Violence against Women Watch Group 2010; Women Development Department, n.d.; Zahid 2007.

Note: The 2006 Protection of Women Act is available at http://www.pakistani.org/pakistan/legislation/2006/wpb.html. The National Policy on Home-Based Workers is available at http://www.homenetpakistan.org/draft_np_for_web.pdf.

Appendix 6

Policies and Events Directly Affecting Women in the United Kingdom, 1997–2014

Unit	Policies and events	Description
United Kingdom	1997 Labour Party All Women Shortlists	Party policy in which half of all winnable seats are assigned to women. The court ruled against all-women shortlists, citing 1975 Sexual Discrimination Act; already constructed lists led to the election of thirty-five Labour women. Now each party member gets one vote for a man, one for a woman.
	1999 Liberal Democrat Party institutes zipping for party lists	This party policy instituted zipping for European Parliament elections but retracted the practice for 2002 elections.
	2004 Domestic Violence Crime and Victims Act	This act extends provisions to combat domestic violence and creates the new offense of "causing or allowing the death of a child or vulnerable adult."
	2004 Civil Partnership Act	This act grants civil partnerships the same rights and responsibilities as marriage.
	2006 Conservative Party All Women Shortlists	This policy was proposed by David Cameron but failed.
	Equality Act 2006	This act creates and consolidates seven protected characteristics within the law: age, disability, gender, gender reassignment, race, religion or belief, and sexual orientation. The act defines and makes illegal direct discrimination, indirect discrimination, harassment, and victimization. This act also creates the Equality and Human Rights Commission from diverse commissions, paves the way for Sexual Orientation Regulations 2006, and most importantly *creates a gender equality duty*, or obligation of public authorities to promote equality in the provision of goods, facilities, and services and to carry out equality impact assessments. This duty is currently found in Equality Act 2010, section 1. Specifically, the Equality and Human Rights Commission has powers to set out strategic plans, investigate inequalities, require compliance with the gender equality duty by private and public sector entities, provide legal assistance to parties pursuing equalities, and intervene and use judicial review in legal proceedings.

(continued)

Unit	Policies and events	Description
	2006 Work and Families Act	This act provides for thirty-nine weeks of maternity leave, rights for caregivers of adults, and two weeks of paternity pay.
	2007 call for gender-neutral language in drafting legislation	This statement from the House of Commons requires that legislation not use the word "he" to mean men and women.
	2010 Equality Act (does not apply to Northern Ireland)	This act adds pregnancy and maternity as protected characteristics, requires employers to review salaries by gender and publish results, lists specific public bodies that have duty to consider how their policies affect people with protected characteristics, requires public agencies to consider socioeconomic disadvantage in strategic decision making, recognizes intersectionality in discrimination on more than one ground, creates greater property protection for civil partners in England and Wales and stops prohibition of registration of civil unions on religious premises, allows employers and public entities to take *positive action to achieve equality* on a protected category, and allows political parties to use all-women shortlists till 2030.
	Gender impact assessments for UK budgets after 2010	In August 1, 2010, the Fawcett Society applied for and was denied judicial review of United Kingdom 2010 Budget for the budget's not having "due regard" for need to eliminate sexual harassment and inequality, pursuant to 2006 Equality Act and 1975 Sexual Discrimination Act, and not promoting the equality of women. However, the Cameron government responded with voluntary gender impact assessment for all future budgets.
	Closure of Women's National Commission	In December 31, 2010, the Cameron government closed the Women's National Commission, an advisory body that reached across Northern Ireland, England, Scotland, and Wales for consultation with women's organizations and the Government Equalities Office.
	Marriage (Same Sex Couples) Act 2013	This act extends same-sex marriage to England and Wales; marriages in England or Wales are treated as civil partnerships in Northern Ireland and Scotland.
	International Development (Gender Equity Act) 2014	This act provides development and humanitarian assistance on the basis of gender equality principles.
Wales	Children's Commissioner	This position was created in response to reports from child protection agencies on mistreatment of children in group homes.
	Children and Families Measure 2010	This policy extends child care and play opportunities for children.
	Carers Strategies Measure 2010	This policy requires publication of strategies for caregivers.

Unit	Policies and events	Description
	Equality Act 2010, new duties in 2011	On March 30, 2011, amendments to the Equality Act 2010 extended equality duty to all public sector authorities, reformed procurement (government contracts for services) to affect private and voluntary sectors, and called for the use of equality impact assessments across eight protected identity categories.
	Marriage (Same Sex Couples) Act 2013	This act extends same-sex marriage to England and Wales and allows couples to keep civil partnerships if they choose; marriages in England or Wales are treated as civil partnerships in Northern Ireland and Scotland.
Scotland	Protection from Harassment Act 1997	Anyone who is being harassed can apply for a nonharassment order.
	Sexual Offences Act, amendment 2000	This amendment deals with issues arising from offenses committed against children by people in a position of trust.
	Protection from Abuse Act 2001	This act provides for power of arrest to be attached to an interdict regardless of the relationship between the abused and the abuser.
	Section 22 of the Criminal Justice Act 2003	This act provides that the maximum penalty for involvement in trafficking for the purpose of sexual exploitation is fourteen years' imprisonment on conviction on indictment. Sections 4 and 5 of the Asylum and Immigration (Treatment of Claimants) Act 2004 provide for a similar specific offense of involvement in human trafficking for other purposes.
	Prohibition of Female Genital Mutilation Act 2005	This act aims to protect women and girls from genital mutilation.
	Protection of Children and Prevention of Sexual Offences Act 2005	This act prohibits grooming a child under the age of sixteen for sexual purposes and meeting such a child following prior contact to engage in illegal sexual conduct.
	Prostitution (Public Places) Act 2007	This act covers soliciting and loitering in a public place to buy sex.
	Protection of Vulnerable Groups Act 2007	This act requires extensive background checks for those with regular contact with children.
	Sexual Offences Act 2009	This act creates a code of sexual offenses that reforms this area of the law and brings it into line with the Sexual Offences Act of 2003 covering England and Wales.
	The Criminal Justice and Licensing Act 2010	This act criminalizes stalking, makes nonharassment orders easier to get, criminalizes extreme pornography, and makes engaging in threatening or abusive behavior an offense.

(continued)

Unit	Policies and events	Description
	Domestic Abuse Act 2011	This act removes the requirement that there be previous abuse before issuing a nonharassment order in domestic abuse cases and criminalizes breach of interdict.
	Forced Marriage etc. (Protection and Jurisdiction) Act 2011	This act protects people from forced marriage.
Northern Ireland	2013 bill to disallow private abortions	The Northern Ireland Assembly debated this bill, which won a majority of votes but failed to pass because of a lack of cross-community (in this case nationalist or Catholic) support.
	2014 bill on human trafficking and exploitation	The Northern Ireland Assembly passed this bill, which criminalizes paying for sex.

Sources: "Domestic Violence" 2009; "Equality Act 2010: Explanatory Notes" 2010; Equality and Human Rights Commission 2009; Global Database of Quotas for Women 2013; "Human Trafficking Bill" 2014; "NI Assembly" 2013; "Sexual Offences" 2016; Women's Support Project, n.d.

Note: The Equality Act 2006 is available at http://www.legislation.gov.uk/ukpga/2006/3/pdfs/ukpga_20060003_en.pdf.

References

Agence France-Presse. 2014. "Verdict on Removing Musharraf's Name from ECL Today." Geo News, June 12. Available at http://www.geo.tv/article-150493 -Verdict-on-removing-Musharrafs-name-from-ECL-today.

Agrawal, Arun, Gautam Yadama, Raul Andrade, and Ajoy Bhattacharya. 2006. "Decentralization and Environmental Conservation: Gender Effects from Participation in Joint Forest Management." Collective Action and Property Rights Working Paper No. 53. Available at http://ebrary.ifpri.org/cdm/ref/collection/p15738coll2/ id/33217.

Ahmad, Sadaf, and Ali Khan, eds. 2010. *Pakistani Women: Multiple Locations and Competing Narratives.* Karachi, Pakistan: Oxford University Press.

Ahmed, Leila. 1992. *Women and Gender in Islam: Historical Roots of a Modern Debate.* New Haven, CT: Yale University Press.

Akhtar, Nasreen. 2006. "Women's Performance in National Legislature: A Comparative Study of Zia-ul-Haq and General Pervez Musharaf Regimes." Master's thesis, Quaid-i-Azam University, Islamabad, Pakistan.

Alvarez, Sonia. 1998. "The 'NGOization' of Latin American Feminisms." In *Cultures of Politics/Politics of Cultures*, edited by Sonia Alvarez, E. Dagnino, and Arturo Escobar, 306–324. Boulder, CO: Westview Press.

Apostolova, Vyara, and Richard Cracknell. 2016. "Women in Parliament and Government." House of Commons Library Briefing Paper no. SN01250. Available at http://researchbriefings.parliament.uk/ResearchBriefing/Summary/SN01250.

Araújo, Clara. 2003. "Quotas for Women in the Brazilian Legislative System." Paper presented at the IDEA "The Implementation of Quotas: Latin American Experiences" workshop, February 23–24, Lima, Peru. Available at http://aceproject.org/ ero-en/topics/parties-and-candidates/CS_Araujo_Brazil_25-11-2003.pdf.

Asia Pacific InfoServ Party. 2001. *International Directory of Women's Organizations.* Sydney: API.

Asian Development Bank. 2000. "Country Briefing Paper: Women in Pakistan." Available at https://www.adb.org/sites/default/files/institutional-document/32562/women-pakistan.pdf.

———. 2013. "Gender-Responsive Decentralized Governance in Asia." Available at http://www.adb.org/sites/default/files/project-document/78677/40314-012-reg-tacr-03.pdf.

Asian Development Bank, Department for International Development, and World Bank. 2004. "Devolution in Pakistan: Overview of the ADB/DfID/World Bank Study." Available at http://documents.worldbank.org/curated/en/578761468775577734/pdf/300830v110ENGL1ution0See0also029912.pdf.

Aslam, Ghazia. 2010. "Rationales of Implementing Decentralization in Pakistan." Paper presented at the Midwest Political Science Association meeting, April 3–5, Chicago.

Aslam, Ghazia, and Serdar Yilmaz. 2011. "Impact of Decentralization Reforms in Pakistan on Service Delivery: An Empirical Study." *Public Administration and Development* 31 (3): 159–171.

Aurat Foundation. n.d. "Citizens' Campaigns for Women's Participation in Local Government Elections 2001 and 2005: Backdrop, Glimpses of the Campaigns, Overall Results." Available at http://www.af.org.pk/Citizens%20Reports/Citizens%20campaigns.pdf (accessed August 16, 2016).

Bałandynowicz, Katarzyna. 2005. "Gdańsk Gender Budget Initiative." Available at http://gender-financing.unwomen.org/en/resources/g/e/n/gender-budget-initiative-in-gdansk-poland.

Baldez, Lisa. 2002. *Why Women Protest: Women's Movements in Chile.* Cambridge: Cambridge University Press.

———. 2007. "Primaries vs. Quotas: Gender and Candidate Nominations in Mexico." *Latin American Politics and Society* 49 (4): 69–96.

———. 2011. "The UN Convention to Eliminate All Forms of Discrimination against Women (CEDAW): A New Way to Measure Women's Interests." *Politics and Gender* 7 (3): 1–6.

———. 2014. *Defying Convention: U.S. Resistance to the U.N. Treaty on Women's Rights.* New York: Cambridge University Press.

Banaszak, Lee Ann. 1996. *Why Movements Succeed or Fail.* Princeton, NJ: Princeton University Press.

———. 2010. *The Women's Movement Inside and Outside the State.* New York: Cambridge University Press.

Banaszak, Lee Ann, Karen Beckwith, and Dieter Rucht. 2003. *Women's Movements Facing a Reconfigured State.* Cambridge: Cambridge University Press.

Banaszak, Lee Ann, and Laurel Weldon. 2011. "Informal Institutions, Protest, and Change in Gendered Federal Systems." *Politics and Gender* 7 (2): 262–273.

Bardhan, Pranab, and Dilip Mookherjee. 2005. "Decentralizing Antipoverty Program Delivery in Developing Countries." *Journal of Public Economics* 89:675–704. Available at http://people.bu.edu/dilipm/publications/BardhanMookherjee2005%20JPubE.pdf.

Barnes, Tiffany D., and Stephanie M. Burchard. 2013. "'Engendering' Politics: The Impact of Descriptive Representation on Women's Political Engagement in Sub-Saharan Africa." *Comparative Political Studies* 46 (7): 767–790.

Barrett, Jacqueline K., and Jane A. Malonis. 1993. *Encyclopedia of Women's Associations Worldwide*. London: Gale Research.

Beall, Jo. 2005. "Decentralization Government and Decentering Gender: Lessons from Local Government Reform in South Africa." *Politics and Society* 33 (2): 253–276.

Beckwith, Karen. 2005. "A Common Language of Gender." *Politics and Gender* 1 (1): 128–137.

———. 2006. "Moving to a Comparative Politics of Gender?" *Politics and Gender* 2 (2): 235–248.

———. 2010. "Comparative Politics and the Logic of a Comparative Politics of Gender." *Perspectives on Politics* 8 (1): 159–168.

Bennhold, Katrin. 2016. "'Glass Cliff,' Not Just Ceiling, Often Impedes Women Rising in Politics." *New York Times*, October 5. Available at http://www.nytimes.com/2016/10/05/world/europe/glass-cliff-uk-women-politics.html.

Bird, Richard Miller, and Francois Villancourt. 1998. *Fiscal Decentralization in Developing Countries*. Cambridge: Cambridge University Press.

Blair, Harry. 2000. "Participation and Accountability at the Periphery: Democratic Local Governance in Six Countries." *World Development* 28 (1): 21–39.

Bojarski, Łukasz. 2010. "News Report: New Law on Equal Treatment." Available at http://www.equalitylaw.eu/downloads/2325-pl-16-new-law-on-equal-treatment-passed-by-the-sejm.

Bowen, John. 2008. *Why the French Don't Like Headscarves: Islam, the State, and Public Space*. Princeton, NJ: Princeton University Press.

Brady, Henry, Kay Schlozman, and Sidney Verba. 1999. "Prospecting for Participants: Rational Expectations and the Recruitment of Political Activists." *American Political Science Review* 93 (1): 153–168.

Brancati, Dawn. 2009. *Peace by Design: Managing Intrastate Conflict through Decentralization*. Oxford: Oxford University Press.

Burness, Catriona. 2011. "Women and Parliaments in the UK." Available at https://www.activelearningcentre.org/wp-content/uploads/2013/11/Burness-Women-and-Parliaments-revised-July-2011.pdf.

Campbell, David E., and Christina Wolbrecht. 2006. "See Jane Run: Women Politicians as Role Models for Adolescents." *Journal of Politics* 68 (May): 233–247.

Carey, John. 2000. "Parchment, Equilibria, and Institutions." *Comparative Political Studies* 33 (6–7): 735–761.

Celis, Karen. 2009. "Substantive Representation of Women (and Improving It): What It Is and Should Be About?" *Comparative European Politics* 7:95–113.

———. 2013. "Representativity in Times of Diversity: The Political Representation of Women." *Women's Studies International Forum* 41:179–186.

Celis, Karen, Sarah Childs, Johanna Kantola, and Mona Lena Krook. 2008. "Rethinking Women's Substantive Representation." *Representation* 44 (2): 99–110.

Celis, Karen, Fiona Mackay, and Petra Meier. 2013. "Social Movement Organizations and Changing State Architectures: Comparing Women's Movement Organizing in Flanders and Scotland." *Publius* 43 (1): 44–67.

Celis, Karen, and Alison Woodward. 2003. "Do It Yourself and Do It Better? Regional Parliaments as Sites for Democratic Renewal and Gendered Representation." In *Regional Institutions and Governance in the European Union*, edited by Jose Maria Mangone, 173–191. Westport, CT: Praeger.

Center for Asia-Pacific Women in Politics. n.d. "Report on the State of Women in Urban Local Government: Pakistan." Available at http://www.capwip.org/reading room/pakistan.pdf (accessed November 24, 2016).

———. n.d. "State of Women in Urban Local Government: India." Available at http://www.capwip.org/readingroom/india.pdf (accessed December 30, 2016).

Centrum Promocji Kobiet [Center for the Advancement of Women]. 1997. *Informator o organizacjach I inicyatywach kobiecych w Polsce* [Directory of women's organizations and initiatives in Poland]. Warsaw: Warsaw University.

———. 2001. *Informator o organizacjach I inicyatywach kobiecych w Polsce* [Directory of women's organizations and initiatives in Poland]. Warsaw: Warsaw University.

———. 2002. *Informator o organizacjach I inicyatywach kobiecych w Polsce* [Directory of women's organizations and initiatives in Poland]. Warsaw: Warsaw University.

———. 2005. *Informator o organizacjach I inicyatywach kobiecych w Polsce* [Directory of women's organizations and initiatives in Poland]. Warsaw: Warsaw University.

Chaney, Paul, Fiona Mackay, and Laura McAllister, eds. 2007. *Women, Politics and Constitutional Change: The First Years of the National Assembly for Wales.* Cardiff: University of Wales Press.

Chappell, Louise. 2002. *Gendering Government: Feminist Engagement with the State in Australia and Canada.* Vancouver, BC: UBC Press.

———. 2006. "Comparing Political Institutions: Revealing the Gendered 'Logic of Appropriateness.'" *Politics and Gender* 2 (2): 223–235.

Chappell, Louise, and Kathleen Teghtsoonian. 2008. "The Rise and Decline of Women's Policy Machinery in British Columbia and New South Wales: A Cautionary Tale." *International Political Science Review* 29 (1): 29–51.

Chappell, Louise, and Jill Vickers. 2011. "Gender, Politics, and State Architecture: Introduction." *Politics and Gender* 7 (2): 251–254.

Chattopadhyay, Raghabendra, and Esther Duflo. 2004. "Evidence from a Randomized Policy Experiment in India." *Econometrica* 72 (5): 1409–1443.

Chaudhuri, Shubham. 2003. "What Difference Does a Constitutional Amendment Make? The 1994 Panchayati Raj Act and the Attempt to Revitalize Rural Local Government in India." Available at http://citeseerx.ist.psu.edu/viewdoc/download?doi=10.1.1.196.3636&rep=rep1&type=pdf.

Cheema, Ali, Asim Ijaz Khwaja, and Adnan Qadir. 2006. "Local Government Reform in Pakistan: Context, Content and Causes." In *Decentralization and Local Governance in Developing Countries: A Comparative Perspective,* edited by Pranab Bardhan and Dilip Mookherjee, 257–284. Boston: MIT Press.

Childs, Sarah. 2004. *New Labour's Women MPs: Women Representing Women.* London: Routledge.

Childs, Sarah, and Paul Webb. 2012. "Gender Politics and Conservatism: The View from the British Conservative Grassroots." *Government and Opposition* 47 (1): 21–48.

Chin, Mikyung. 2004. "Reflections on Women's Empowerment through Local Representation in South Korea." *Asian Survey* 44 (2): 295–315.

Conley, Hazel. 2012. "Using Equality to Challenge Austerity: New Actors, Old Problems." *Work Employment and Society* 26 (2): 349–359.

Conway, Margaret, Gertrude A. Steuernagel, and David W. Ahern. 2005. *Women and Public Policy: A Revolution in Progress.* 3rd ed. Washington, DC: CQ Press.

Crawford, Gordon. 2004. "Democratic Decentralisation in Ghana: Issues and Prospects." POLIS Working Paper No. 9. Available at http://www.polis.leeds.ac.uk/assets/files/research/working-papers/wp9crawford.pdf.

Cresswell, John W. 2007. *Qualitative Inquiry and Research Design: Choosing among Five Approaches.* 2nd ed. Thousand Oaks, CA: Sage.

Dabrowksa, Magdalena. 2007. "Issue Histories Poland: Series of Timelines of Policy Debates." Available at http://www.quing.eu/files/results/ih_poland.pdf.

Darcy, R., Susan Welch, and Janet Clark. 1994. *Women, Elections, and Representation.* Lincoln: University of Nebraska Press.

Darymple, William. 2007. "Pakistan's Flawed and Feudal Princess." *The Guardian,* December 30. Available at https://www.theguardian.com/commentisfree/2007/dec/30/pakistan.world.

David. 2009. "The Calman Report: Consolidating Asymmetrical Devolution." *Britology Watch* (blog), June 16. Available at http://britologywatch.wordpress.com/2009/06/16/the-calman-report-consolidating-asymmetrical-devolution.

Devika, J., and Binitha V. Thampi. 2012. *New Lamps for Old? Gender Paradoxes of Decentralisation in Kerala.* New Dehli: Zubaan.

"Devolution White Paper: Advancing the Arguments." 1997. *The Independent,* July 24. Available at http://www.independent.co.uk/news/devolution-white-paper-advancing-the-arguments-1252354.html.

"Domestic Violence, Crime and Victims Act 2004." 2009. *The Guardian,* January 19. Available at https://www.theguardian.com/commentisfree/libertycentral/2009/jan/13/domestic-violence-act.

Downs, Anthony. 1957. *An Economic Theory of Democracy.* New York: Addison-Wesley.

Drabsch, Talina. 2007. "Women, Parliament and the Media." NSW Parliamentary Library Briefing Paper No. 5/07. Available at https://www.parliament.nsw.gov.au/researchpapers/Documents/women-parliament-and-the-media/WomenParliamentMediaFinal.pdf.

Drakulic, Slavenka. 1993. *How We Survived Communism and Even Laughed.* New York: Harper Perennial.

Druciarek, Małgorzata, Małgorzata Fuszara, Aleksandra Niżyńska, and Jarosław Zbieranek. 2012. "Women on the Polish Political Scene." Available at http://pasos.org/wp-content/uploads/2012/05/womenpoland.pdf.

Duerst-Lahti, Georgia. 2005. "Institutional Gendering: Theoretical Insights into the Environment of Women Officeholders." In *Women and Elective Office: Past, Present and Future,* edited by Sue Thomas and Clyde Wilcox, 244–263. Oxford: Oxford University Press.

Eaton, Kent, and Larry Schroeder. 2010. "Measuring Decentralization." In *Making Decentralization Work: Democracy, Development, and Security,* edited by Ed Connerly, Kent Eaton, and Paul J. Smoke, 167–190. Boulder, CO: Lynne Rienner.

Ebel, Robert, and Serdar Yilmaz. 2002. "On the Measurement and Impact of Fiscal Decentralization." World Bank Policy Research Working Paper No. 2809. Available at http://www1.worldbank.org/publicsector/decentralization/decentralizationcorecourse2006/otherreadings/ebelyilmaz.pdf.

Eckstein, Harry. 1975. "Case Study and Theory in Political Science." In *The Handbook of Political Science,* vol. 7, edited by F. I. Greenstein and N. W. Polsby, 79–138. Reading, UK: Addison-Wesley.

Einhorn, Barbara. 1998. *Cinderella Goes to Market: Citizenship, Gender and Women's Movements in East Central Europe*. 2nd ed. New York: Verso.

Eisenstein, Hester. 1996. *Inside Agitators: Australian Femocrats and the State*. Philadelphia: Temple University Press.

"Equality Act 2010: Explanatory Notes." 2010. Available at http://www.legislation.gov.uk/ukpga/2010/15/pdfs/ukpgaen_20100015_en.pdf?view=plain.

Equality and Human Rights Commission. 2009. "Responding to Gender-Based Violence in Scotland." Available at http://www.womenssupportproject.co.uk/userfiles/responding_to_gender-based_violence_in_scotland_report.pdf.

Eurofound. 2010. "Subsidiarity." Available at http://www.eurofound.europa.eu/observatories/eurwork/industrial-relations-dictionary/subsidiarity.

European Union Election Observation Mission. 2008. "Islamic Republic of Pakistan: Final Report; National and Provincial Assembly Elections, 18 February 2008." Available at http://www.eods.eu/library/FR%20PAKISTAN%2016.04.2008_en.pdf.

Eurostat. 2016. "GDP at Regional Level." Available at http://ec.europa.eu/eurostat/statistics-explained/index.php/GDP_at_regional_level.

Falleti, Tulia. 2005. "A Sequential Theory of Decentralization: Latin American Cases in Comparative Perspective." *American Political Science Review* 99 (3): 327–346.

———. 2010. *Decentralization and Sub-national Politics in Latin America*. Cambridge: Cambridge University Press.

"Fawcett Society Loses Court Challenge to Legality of Budget." 2010. *The Guardian*, December 6. Available at http://www.guardian.co.uk/world/2010/dec/06/fawcett-society-loses-court-challenge-budget.

Fenno, Richard. 1978. *Homestyle: House Members in Their Districts*. New York: Harper Collins.

Fox, Richard L., and Jennifer L. Lawless. 2004. "Entering the Arena? Gender and the Decision to Run for Office." *American Journal of Political Science* 48:264–280.

Franceschet, Susan. 2011. "Gender Policy and State Architecture in Latin America." *Politics and Gender* 7 (2): 273–279.

———. 2012. "Federalism, Decentralization, and Reproductive Rights in Argentina and Chile." *Publius* 43 (1): 129–150.

Franceschet, Susan, Mona Lena Krook, and Jennifer M. Piscopo, eds. 2012. *The Impact of Gender Quotas*. New York: Oxford University Press.

Freedom House. 2014. "Map of Freedom." Available at http://www.freedomhouse.org/sites/default/files/MapofFreedom2014.pdf.

Freeland, Amy. 2015. "Girls and Women: The Key to Ending Poverty." *Global Citizen*, June 2. Available at https://www.globalcitizen.org/en/content/girls-women-the-key-to-ending-poverty.

Funk, Nanette, and Magda Mueller, eds. 1993. *Gender Politics and Post-Communism*. New York: Routledge.

Fuszara, Malgorzata. 2000. "New Gender Relations in Poland in the 1990s." In *Reproducing Gender: Politics, Publics, and Everyday Life after Socialism*, edited by Susan Gal and Gail Kligman, 259–285. Princeton, NJ: Princeton University Press.

Gal, Susan, and Gail Kligman, eds. 2000. *Reproducing Gender: Politics, Publics, and Everyday Life after Socialism*. Princeton, NJ: Princeton University Press.

Galligan, Yvonne, and Kathleen Knight. 2011. "Attitudes towards Women in Politics: Gender, and Party Identification in Northern Ireland." *Parliamentary Affairs* 64 (4): 585–611.

Garton Ash, Timothy. 2002. *The Polish Revolution: Solidarity.* 3rd ed. New Haven, CT: Yale University Press.

George, Alexander L., and Andrew Bennett. 2005. *Case Studies and Theory Development in the Social Sciences.* Boston: MIT Press.

Gerring, John. 2012. *Social Science Methodology: A Unified Framework.* Cambridge: Cambridge University Press.

Ghori, Habib Khan. 2013. "Sindh PA Adopts Bill to End Domestic Violence." *Dawn*, March 9. Available at http://www.dawn.com/news/791384.

Global Conference of Local Elected Women. 2013. "Paris Local and Regional Governments' Global Agenda for Equality of Women and Men in Local Life." Available at http://www.uclg.org/sites/default/files/ENG_Amended%20Paris%20Declaration%4031.pdf.

Global Database of Quotas for Women. n.d. "About the Project." Available at http://www.quotaproject.org/aboutProject.cfm (accessed August 16, 2016).

———. 2013. "United Kingdom." Available at http://www.quotaproject.org/country/united-kingdom.

———. 2014. "Pakistan." Available at http://www.quotaproject.org/country/pakistan.

———. 2015a. "India." Available at http://www.quotaproject.org/country/india.

———. 2015b. "South Africa." Available at http://www.quotaproject.org/country/south-africa.

———. 2016a. "Canada." Available at http://www.quotaproject.org/country/canada.

———. 2016b. "Korea, Republic of." Available at http://www.quotaproject.org/country/korea-republic-of.

———. 2016c. "Poland." Available at http://www.quotaproject.org/country/poland.

"Government of Wales Act 2006." 2016. *Wikipedia*, July 29. Available at https://en.wikipedia.org/wiki/Government_of_Wales_Act_2006#Schedule_5_of_the_Act.

Halsaa, Beatrice. 1998. "A Strategic Partnership for Women's Policies in Norway." In *Women's Movements and Public Policy in Europe, Latin America, and the Caribbean*, edited by Geertje Lycklama à Nijeholt, Virginia Vargas, and Saskia Wieringa, 167–189. New York: Garland.

Halvorson, Sarah J. 2005. "Growing Up in Gilgit: Exploring the Nature of Girlhood in Northern Pakistan." In *Geographies of Muslim Women: Gender, Religion and Space*, edited by Ghazi-Walid Falah and Caroline Nagel, 19–43. New York: Guilford.

Hancock, Ange-Marie. 2004. *The Politics of Disgust and the Public Identity of the "Welfare Queen."* New York: New York University Press.

Haussman, Melissa. 2005. *Abortion Politics in North America.* Boulder, CO: Lynne Rienner.

Haussman, Melissa, and Birgit Sauer, eds. 2007. *Gendering the State in the Age of Globalization: Women's Movements and State Feminism in Postindustrial Democracies.* New York: Rowman and Littlefield.

Haussman, Melissa, Marian Sawer, and Jill Vickers, eds. 2010. *Federalism, Feminism, and Multilevel Governance: Gender in a Global/Local World.* Surrey, UK: Ashgate.

Hayek, Friedrich. 1945. "The Use of Knowledge in Society." *American Economic Review* 35 (4): 519–530.

Hinojosa, Magda. 2012. *Selecting Women, Electing Women.* Philadelphia: Temple University Press.

Holli, Anne Maria. 2008. "Feminist Triangles: A Conceptual Analysis." *Representation* 44 (2): 169–185.

hooks, bell. 2000. *Feminism Is for Everybody: Passionate Politics.* Boston: South End Press.

Htun, Mala, and Mark Jones. 2002. "Engendering the Right to Participate in Decisionmaking: Electoral Quotas and Women's Leadership in Latin America." In *Gender and the Politics of Rights and Democracy in Latin America*, edited by Nikki Craske and Maxine Molyneux, 32–56. London: Palgrave.

Htun, Mala, and Jennifer Piscopo. 2014. "Women in Politics and Policy in Latin America and the Caribbean." Social Science Research Council CPPF Working Papers on Women in Politics No. 2. Available at http://webarchive.ssrc.org/working-papers/CPPF_WomenInPolitics_02_Htun_Piscopo.pdf.

Htun, Mala, and S. Laurel Weldon. 2012. "Civic Origins of Progressive Policy Change: Combating Violence against Women in Global Perspective." *American Political Science Review* 106 (3): 548–569.

"Human Trafficking Bill: Paying for Sex to Become a Crime in Northern Ireland." 2014. *BBC News*, December 9. Available at http://www.bbc.com/news/uk-northern-ireland-30404275.

Huntington, Samuel. 1991. *The Third Wave: Democratization in the Late Twentieth Century.* Norman: University of Oklahoma Press.

Imran, Myra. 2011. "Comprehensive Legislation to Support Victims Urged." *News International*, May 18. Available at https://www.thenews.com.pk/archive/print/301754-comprehensive-legislation-to-support-victims-urged.

Inglehart, Ronald, and Pippa Norris. 2003. *Rising Tide: Gender Equality and Cultural Change around the World.* Cambridge: Cambridge University Press.

International Monetary Fund. 1997. *International Finance Statistics Yearbook, 1997.* Washington, DC: IMF.

International Scientific Researchers. 2012. "Local Government System in Ghana." *International Advances in Engineering and Technology* 7 (July): 532–549.

Inter-Parliamentary Union. 2011. "Women in National Parliaments: World Classification." October 31. Available at http://www.ipu.org/wmn-e/arc/classif311011.htm.

———. 2016. "Women in National Parliaments: Averages." November 1. Available at http://www.ipu.org/wmn-e/world.htm.

Iqtidar, Humeira. 2011. *Secularizing Islamists? Jama'at-e-Islami and Jama'at-ud-Da'wa in Urban Pakistan.* Chicago: University of Chicago Press.

Jacquette, Jane, and Sharon L. Wolchik. 1998. *Women and Democracy: Latin American and Central and Eastern Europe.* Baltimore: Johns Hopkins University Press.

Jalalzai, Farida. 2013. *Shattered, Cracked, or Firmly Intact? Women and the Executive Glass Ceiling Worldwide.* Oxford: Oxford University Press.

Jamal, Amina. 2013. *Jamaat-e-Islami Women in Pakistan: Vanguard of a New Modernity?* Syracuse, NY: Syracuse University Press.

Javaid, Fakhra. 2006. "Women's Role in Pakistan's Provincial Legislature: The Case of Punjab, 1947–1999." Master's thesis, Quaid-i-Azam University.

Jones, Mark P. 1996. "Quota Legislation and the Election of Women: Learning from the Costa Rican Experience." *Journal of Politics* 66 (4): 1203–1233.

Kaiser, Kai. 2006. "Decentralization Reforms." In *Analyzing the Distributional Impact of Reforms*, edited by Aline Coudouel and Stefano Paternostro, 313–354. Washington, DC: World Bank.

Kanter, Rosabeth Moss. 1977. "Some Effects of Proportions on Group Life: Skewed Sex Ratios and Responses to Token Women." *American Journal of Sociology* 82 (5): 965–990.

Kathlene, Lyn. 1994. "Power and Influence in State Legislative Policymaking: The Interaction of Gender and Position in Committee Hearing Debates." *American Political Science Review* 88 (3): 560–576.

———. 1995. "Alternative Views of Crime: Legislative Policymaking in Gendered Terms." *Journal of Politics* 57 (3): 696–723.

Keefer, Philip E., Ambar Narayan, and Tara Vishwanath. 2006. "Decentralization in Pakistan: Are Local Governments Likely to Be More Accountable than Central Government?" In *Decentralization and Local Governance in Developing Countries*, 285–304. Boston: MIT Press.

Kenny, Meryl. 2013. *Gender and Political Recruitment: Theorizing Institutional Change.* New York: Palgrave Macmillan.

Kenny, Meryl, and Fiona Mackay. 2011a. "Gender and Devolution in Spain and the United Kingdom." *Politics and Gender* 7 (2): 280–286.

———. 2011b. "In the Balance: Women and the 2011 Scottish Parliament Elections." *Scottish Affairs* 76 (Summer): 74–90.

———. 2012. "Less Male, Pale and Stale? Women and the 2012 Scottish Local Government Elections." *Scottish Affairs* 80 (Summer): 20–32.

———. 2014. "When Is Contagion Not Very Contagious? Dynamics of Women's Political Representation in Scotland." *Parliamentary Affairs* 67 (4): 866–886.

Kenny, Meryl, and Tania Verge. 2013. "Decentralization, Political Parties, and Women's Representation: Evidence from Spain and Britain." *Publius* 43 (1): 109–128.

KGM Consultants. n.d. "Women Rights NGOs in Pakistan." Available at http://www.ngos.org.pk/rights/women_rights_ngos_pakistan.htm (accessed November 21, 2016).

Khan, Faraz. 2014. "TTP Claims Attack on ASF Hostel in Karachi." *Express Tribune*, June 8. Available at http://tribune.com.pk/story/719242/four-security-personnel-injured-in-attack-on-karachi-airport/.

Krook, Mona Lena. 2009. *Quotas for Women in Politics: Gender and Candidate Selection Reform Worldwide.* Oxford: Oxford University Press.

Krook, Mona Lena, and Fiona Mackay, eds. 2010. *Gender, Politics and Institutions: Towards a Feminist Institutionalism.* Basingstoke, UK: Palgrave Macmillan.

Krook, Mona Lena, and Diana Z. O'Brien. 2010. "The Politics of Group Representation: Quotas for Women and Minorities Worldwide." *Comparative Politics* 42 (3): 253–272.

Lakshminarayanan, Rama. 2003. "Decentralization and Its Implications for Reproductive Health: The Philippines Experience." *Reproductive Health Matters* 11 (21): 96–107.

Lawless, Jennifer, and Richard Fox. 2010. *It Still Takes a Candidate: Why Women Don't Run for Office.* New York: Cambridge University Press.

Lieberman, Evan. 2005. "Nested Analysis as a Mixed-Method Strategy for Comparative Research." *American Political Science Review* 99 (3): 435–452.

"List of Countries and Dependencies by Population." 2016. *Wikipedia*, August 12. Available at https://en.wikipedia.org/wiki/List_of_countries_and_dependencies _by_population.

Litvack, J., J. Ahmad, and R. M. Bird. 1998. *Rethinking Decentralization in Developing Countries.* Washington, DC: World Bank. Available at http://www1.worldbank .org/publicsector/decentralization/Rethinking%20Decentralization.pdf.

Lovenduski, Joni. 1986. *Women and European Politics: Contemporary Feminism and Public Policy.* Boston: University of Massachusetts Press.

———. 1999. "Sexing Political Behaviour in Britain." In *New Agendas for Women*, edited by Sylvia Wallby, 190–209. Basingstoke, UK: Macmillan.

Lovenduski, Joni, and Marila Guadagnini. 2010. "Political Representation." In *The Politics of State Feminism*, edited by Dorothy McBride and Amy Mazur, 164–192. Philadelphia: Temple University Press.

Luciak, Ilja A. 2005. "Party and State in Cuba: Gender Equality in Political Decision Making." *Politics and Gender* 1 (2): 241–264.

Lyall, Sarah, and Alan Cowell. 2010. "Britain Plans Deepest Cuts to Spending in 60 Years." *New York Times*, October 20. Available at http://www.nytimes .com/2010/10/21/world/europe/21britain.html.

Lycklama à Nijeholt, Geertje, Virginia Vargas, and Saskia Wieringa, eds. 1998. *Women's Movements and Public Policy in Europe, Latin America, and the Caribbean.* New York: Garland.

Macaulay, Fiona. 2006. *Gender Politics in Brazil and Chile: The Role of Parties in National and Local Policymaking.* New York: Palgrave Macmillan.

Mackay, Fiona. 2008. "'Thick' Conceptions of Substantive Representation: Women, Gender and Political Institutions." *Representation* 44 (2): 125–140.

Mackay, Fiona, and Meryl Kenny. 2011. "In the Balance: Women and the 2011 Scottish Parliament Elections." *Scottish Affairs* 76 (1): 74–86.

Mackay, Fiona, Fiona Myers, and Alice Brown. 2003. "Towards a New Politics? Women and the Scottish Change in Scotland." In *Women Making Constitutions*, edited by Alexandra Dobrolowsky and Vivien Hart, 84–98. Basingstoke, UK: Palgrave.

Malhotra, Anju, Sidney Ruth Schuler, and Carol Boender. 2002. "Measuring Women's Empowerment as a Variable in International Development." Paper prepared for World Bank "Poverty and Gender: New Perspectives" workshop, June 28, Washington, DC. Available at http://siteresources.worldbank.org/INTGENDER/ Resources/MalhotraSchulerBoender.pdf.

Masood, Salman. 2011. "Pakistan Top Court Upholds Acquittals in Notorious Rape Case." *New York Times*, April 21. Available at http://www.nytimes .com/2011/04/22/world/asia/22pakistan.html.

Matland, Richard, and Kathleen A. Montgomery. 2003. *Women's Access to Political Power in Post-communist Europe.* Oxford: Oxford University Press.

Matovu, George. 2002. "Africa and Decentralization: Enter the Citizens." *Development Outreach* 4 (1): 24–27.

Mayhew, David. 1975. *Congress: The Electoral Connection.* New Haven, CT: Yale University Press.

Mazur, Amy G. 2002. *Theorizing Feminist Policy*. Oxford: Oxford University Press.

——. 2005. "The Impact of Women's Participation and Leadership on Policy Outcomes: A Focus on Women's Policy Machineries." Paper prepared for UN Expert Group Meeting, October 24–27. Available at http://iknowpolitics.org/sites/default/files/ep.5_mazur.pdf.

——. 2012. "A Feminist Empirical and Integrative Approach in Political Science: Breaking Down the Glass Wall?" In *The Oxford Handbook of Philosophy of Social Science*, edited by Harold Kincaid, 553–558. Oxford: Oxford University Press.

McBride, Dorothy, and Amy G. Mazur, eds. 1995. *Comparative State Feminism*. Thousand Oaks, CA: Sage.

——. 2010. *The Politics of State Feminism: Innovation in Comparative Research*. Philadelphia: Temple University Press.

McGillivray, Mark, and J. Ram Pillarisetti. 2006. "Adjusting Human Well-Being Indices for Gender Disparity: Insightful Empirically?" In *Understanding Human Well-Being*, edited by Mark McGillivray and Matthew Clarke, 169–181. Tokyo: United Nations University Press.

McGrath, A. 1996. *The Destruction of Pakistan's Democracy*. Oxford: Oxford University Press.

McTavish, Duncan, ed. 2016. *Politics in Scotland*. Abingdon, UK: Routledge.

Mernissi, Fatima. 1992. *The Veil and the Male Elite: A Feminist Interpretation of Women's Rights in Islam*. New York: Perseus Book Group.

Mishra, Pankaj. 2012. "Imran Khan Must Be Doing Something Right." *New York Times*, August 16. Available at http://www.nytimes.com/2012/08/19/magazine/pakistans-imran-khan-must-be-doing-something-right.html.

Montinola, Gabriella, Yingyi Qian, and Barry Weingast. 1995. "Federalism, Chinese Style: The Political Basis for Economic Success in China." *World Politics* 48 (1): 50–81.

Montoya, Celeste. 2009. "International Initiative and Domestic Reforms: European Union Efforts to Combat Violence against Women." *Politics and Gender* 5 (3): 325–348.

——. 2013. *From Global to Grassroots: The European Union, Transnational Advocacy, and Combating Violence against Women*. New York: Oxford University Press.

Mumtaz, Khawar, and Farida Shaheed. 1988. *Women of Pakistan: Two Steps Forward, One Step Back*. London: Zed Books.

Murray, Rainbow. 2004. "Why Didn't Parity Work? A Closer Examination of the 2002 Election Results." *French Politics* 2 (3): 347–362.

Naples, Nancy A., and Manisha Desai, eds. 2002. *Women's Activism and Globalization: Linking Local Struggles and Transnational Politics*. New York: Routledge.

National Assembly for Wales. n.d. "Governance of Wales: Who Is Responsible for What?" Available at http://www.assembly.wales/en/abthome/role-of-assembly-how-it-works/Pages/governance-of-wales.aspx (accessed December 14, 2016).

"New 'Honour Killing' Law Does Not Go Far Enough: Rights Groups." 2004. *IRIN*, October 27. Available at http://www.irinnews.org/news/2004/10/27/new-honour-killing-law-does-not-go-far-enough-rights-groups.

"NI Assembly Fails in Bid to Change Abortion Law." 2013. *BBC News*, March 12. Available at http://www.bbc.com/news/uk-northern-ireland-21755507.

Norris, Pippa. 2008. *Driving Democracy*. Cambridge: Cambridge University Press.

Norris, Pippa, and Ronald Inglehart. 2005. "Women as Political Leaders Worldwide: Cultural Barriers and Opportunities." In *Women and Elective Office*. 2nd ed., edited by Sue Thomas and Clyde Wilcox, 244–263. Oxford: Oxford University Press.

Norris, Pippa, and Joni Lovenduski. 1995. *Political Recruitment: Gender, Race and Class in the British Parliament*. Cambridge: Cambridge University Press.

North South Inter-Parliamentary Association. 2015. "Women in Public Life." Available at http://www.niassembly.gov.uk/globalassets/documents/raise/publications/2015/northsouth/13715.pdf.

Nowakowska, Urszula, ed. 2000. *Polish Women in the 90s*. Warsaw: Women's Rights Center.

"NWFP Women Legislators Want Revised Nikahnama." 2007. *TwoCircles.net*, September 13. Available at http://twocircles.net/2007sep13/nwfp_women_legislators_want_revised_nikahnama.html#.WFhGRn0Xs-0.

Oates, Wallace E. 1972. "An Essay on Fiscal Federalism." *Journal of Economic Literature* 37 (3): 1120–1149.

"Only 6 of 150 Women Candidates Win NA Seats: Report." 2013. *Express Tribune*, May 16. Available at http://tribune.com.pk/story/550191/only-6-of-150-women-candidates-win-na-seats-report.

Open Society Institute. 2006. "Violence against Women: Does the Government Care in Poland?" Available at http://www.stopvaw.org/uploads/POLAND_VAW_FACT_SHEET_2006_3.pdf.

Ortbals, Candice D. 2008. "Sub-national Politics in Spain: New Avenues for Feminist Policymaking." *Politics and Gender* 4 (1): 93–119.

Ortbals, Candice D., and Meg E. Rincker. 2009a. "Embodied Researchers: Gendered Bodies, Research Activity, and Pregnancy in the Field." *PS: Political Science and Politics* 42 (2): 315–319.

———. 2009b. "Fieldwork, Identities, and Intersectionality: Negotiating Gender, Race, Class, and Age in the Research Field Abroad—Editors' Introduction." *PS: Political Science and Politics* 42 (2): 287–290.

Ortbals, Candice D., Meg E. Rincker, and Celeste Montoya. 2011. "Politics Close to Home: The Impact of Meso-Level Institutions on Women in Politics." *Publius* 42 (1): 78–107.

Outshoorn, Joyce, and Johanna Kantola, eds. 2007. *Changing State Feminism*. London: Palgrave Macmillan.

Pande, Rohini, and Deanna Ford. 2011. "Gender Quotas and Female Leadership: A Review." Available at http://scholar.harvard.edu/files/rpande/files/gender_quotas_-_april_2011.pdf.

Parliament of Canada. 2016. "Party Leaders and Standings." Available at www.parl.gc.ca/Parlinfo/compilations/ProvinceTerritory/PartyStandingsAndLeaders.aspx?Language=E.

Parry, Janine. 2005. "Women's Policy Agencies: The Women's Movement and Representation in the USA." In *State Feminism and Political Representation*, edited by Joni Lovenduski, 239–259. Cambridge: Cambridge University Press.

Penn, Shana. 2005. *Solidarity's Secret: The Women Who Defeated Communism in Poland*. Ann Arbor: University of Michigan Press.

Phillips, Anne. 1995. *The Politics of Presence*. Oxford: Oxford University Press.

————. 2002. "Feminism and the Politics of Difference; Or, Where Have All the Women Gone?" In *Visible Women: Essays on Feminist Legal Theory and Political Philosophy*, edited by Susan James and Stephanie Palmer, 11–28. Oxford: Hart.

Pini, Barbara, and Paula McDonald, eds. 2011. *Women and Representation in Local Government: International Case Studies*. New York: Routledge.

Pitkin, Hannah. 1967. *The Concept of Representation*. Berkeley: University of California Press.

"Poland's Women: Sisters Are Doin' It for Themselves." 2014. *The Economist*, May 21. Available at http://www.economist.com/blogs/easternapproaches/2014/05/polands-women.

Praveen, Rai. 2011. "Electoral Participation of Women in India: Key Determinants and Barriers." *Economic and Political Weekly*, January 14, pp. 47–55.

Public Opinion Research Center. 2000. "Czechs, Hungarians and Poles on the European Union." *Polish Public Opinion*, September 2000. Available at http://www.cbos.pl/PL/publikacje/public_opinion/2000/09_2000.pdf.

Punjab Commission on the Status of Women. n.d. "The Acid Control and Acid Crime Prevention Act, 2011." Available at http://pcsw.punjab.gov.pk/acid_crime_prevention (accessed November 27, 2016).

Putnam, Robert. 1993. *Making Democracy Work: Civic Traditions in Modern Italy*. Princeton, NJ: Princeton University Press.

Raja, Shafait, and Katharine Houreld. 2014. "Pakistan PM Condemns 'Brutal Killing' of Pregnant Woman." *Mail and Guardian*, May 29. Available at http://mg.co.za/article/2014-05-29-pakistan-pm-condemns-brutal-killing-of-pregnant-woman.

Randall, Vicky. 1987. *Women and Politics: An International Perspective*. London: Taylor and Francis.

Rankin, L. Pauline, and Jill Vickers. 2001. "Women's Movements and State Feminism: Integrating Diversity into Public Policy." Available at http://citeseerx.ist.psu.edu/viewdoc/download?doi=10.1.1.558.2901&rep=rep1&type=pdf.

————. 2010. "Locating Women's Politics." In *Women and Political Representation in Canada*, edited by Caroline Andrew and Manon Tremblay, 341–372. Ottawa, ON: University of Ottawa Press.

Rauf, Shazia. 2005. "Role of Women in the Politics of NWFP: 1988–02." Master's thesis, Quaid-i-Azam University.

Regulska, Joanna. 1992. "Women and Power in Poland." In *Women Transforming Politics*, edited by Jill Bystydzienski, 175–191. Bloomington: Indiana University Press.

————. 1998. "Transition to Local Democracy: Do Polish Women Have a Chance?" In *Women in the Politics of Postcommunist Eastern Europe*, edited by Marilyn Rueschmeyer. 2nd ed. Armonk, NY: M. E. Sharpe.

Regulska, Joanna, and Anne Graham. 1997. "Expanding Political Space for Women in Poland: An Analysis of Three Communities." *Communist and Post-Communist Studies* 30:65–82.

Regulski, Jerzy. 2003. *Decentralization in Poland: An Insider's Story*. Budapest: Open Society Institute.

Reif, Megan. 2009. "Making Democracy Safe: Explaining the Causes, Rise, and Decline of Coercive Campaigning and Election Violence in Old and New Democracies." Paper presented at American Political Science Association annual meeting, September 3–6, Toronto. Available at http://papers.ssrn.com/sol3/papers .cfm?abstract_id=1449176.

Republic of Poland Human Rights Council. 2011. "Universal Periodic Review: Mid-term Progress Report by Poland." Available at lib.ohchr.org/HRBodies/UPR/ Documents/Session1/PL/Poland_mid-term_report.pdf.

Reyes, Socorro L. 2002. "Quotas for Women for Legislative Seats at the Local Level in Pakistan." Available at http://www.idea.int/publications/wip/upload/CS _Pakistan_Reynes.pdf.

Rincker, Meg E. 2006. *Women's Access to the Decentralized State: Engendering Regional-Level Government in Poland*. Ph.D. diss., Washington University in St. Louis.

———. 2009. "Masculinized or Marginalized: Decentralization and Women's Status in Regional Polish Institutions." *Journal of Women, Politics and Policy* 30 (1): 46–69.

———. 2013. "Anti-elite, Anti-drone Cricket Star Is Best Hope for Pakistan Election—and for US." *Christian Science Monitor*, May 10. Available at http://www .csmonitor.com/Commentary/Opinion/2013/0510/Anti-elite-anti-drone-cricket -star-is-best-hope-for-Pakistan-election-and-for-US.

Rincker, Meg, Ghazia Aslam, and Mujtaba Isani. 2016. "Crossed My Mind, but Ruled It Out: Gender and Political Ambition in the Pakistani Lawyers' Movement, 2007–2009." *International Political Science Review*, June 1. Available at http://ips .sagepub.com/content/early/2016/06/01/0192512116642219.abstract.

Rincker, Meg, and Martin Battle. 2011. "Dissatisfied with Decentralization: Explaining Citizen Evaluations of Poland's 1998 Health Care Reforms." *Journal of East European Politics and Societies* 12 (3): 340–357.

Rincker, Meg E., and Candice D. Ortbals. 2009. "Leaders or Laggards: Engendering Sub-national Governance through Women's Policy Agencies in Spain and Poland." *Democratization* 16 (2): 269–297.

Rodden, Jonathan, and Erik Wibbels. 2002. "Beyond the Fiction of Federalism: Macroeconomic Management in Multi-tiered Systems." *World Politics* 54 (4): 494–531.

Rodriguez, Victoria E. 1997. *Decentralization in Mexico: From Reforma Municipal to Solidaridad to Nuevo Federalismo.* Boulder, CO: Westview.

Rondinelli, Dennis A., John R. Nellis, and G. Shabbir Cheema. 1983. *Decentralization in Developing Countries: A Review of Recent Experience.* Washington, DC: World Bank. Available at http://documents.worldbank.org/curated/ en/868391468740679709/pdf/multi0page.pdf.

Rueschemeyer, Marilyn, ed. 1998. *Women in the Politics of Postcommunist Europe.* 2nd ed. Armonk, NY: M. E. Sharpe.

Rule, Wilma, and Joseph F. Zimmerman. 1992. *United States Electoral Systems: Their Impact on Women and Minorities.* New York: Praeger.

Saito, Fumihiko. 2000. "Decentralization for Participatory Development in Uganda: Limitations and Prospects." Available at http://www.world.ryukoku .ac.jp/~fumis96/docs/jic2000.pdf.

Sanbonmatsu, Kira. 2006. *Where Women Run: Gender and Party in the American States.* Ann Arbor: University of Michigan Press.

Sawer, Marian. 2003. "The Life and Times of Women's Policy Machinery in Australia." In *Mainstreaming Gender, Democratizing the State?* edited by Shirin M. Rai, 243–263. Manchester, UK: Manchester University Press.

Sawer, Marian, and Jill Vickers. 2010. "Introduction: Political Architecture and Its Gender Impact." In *Federalism, Feminism, and Multilevel Governance: Gender in a Global/Local World*, edited by Melissa Haussman, Marian Sawer, and Jill Vickers, 3–18. Surrey, UK: Ashgate.

Sayeed, Khalid Bin. 1997. "Some Reflections on the Democratization Process." In *State, Society, and Democratic Change in Pakistan*, edited by R. Rais, 1–21. Oxford: Oxford University Press.

Schedler, Andreas. 1998. "Measuring Democratic Consolidation." *Studies in Comparative International Development* 36 (1): 66–92.

Schneider, Aaron. 2003. "Decentralization: Conceptualization and Measurement." *Studies in Comparative International Development* 38 (3): 32–56.

Schwartz-Shea, Peregrine, and Dvora Yanow. 2012. *Interpretive Research Design: Methods and Processes.* New York: Routledge.

Schwindt-Bayer, Leslie A., and William Mishler. 2005. "An Integrated Model of Women's Representation." *Journal of Politics* 67 (2): 407–428.

Scott, Joan Wallach. 2010. *The Politics of the Veil.* Princeton, NJ: Princeton University Press.

Scottish Government. 2016. "Violence against Women." Available at http://www.gov .scot/Topics/People/Equality/violence-women.

Scottish Parliament Information Centre. 2016. "Scottish Parliament Fact Sheet: Female MSPs, Session 4." Available at http://www.parliament.scot/ResearchBrief ingsAndFactsheets/Female_MSPs_S4.pdf.

"Sexual Offences (Scotland) Act 2009." 2016. *Wikipedia*, November 27. Available at https://en.wikipedia.org/wiki/Sexual_Offences_(Scotland)_Act_2009.

Shafqat, Saeed. 1997. "Transition to Democracy: An Uncertain Path." In *State, Society, and Democratic Change in Pakistan*, edited by R. Rais, 235–254. Oxford: Oxford University Press.

Shah, A. 2002. "Democracy on Hold in Pakistan." *Journal of Democracy* (1): 67–75.

Siahaan, Asima Yanty. 2004. "Women and Decentralization in Indonesia: Bringing Local Government Closer to Women?" Available at http://www.policy.hu/siahaan/ Policypaper1.htm.

Siemieńska, Renata. 2003. "Women in the Polish Sejm: Political Culture and Party Politics versus Electoral Rules." In *Women's Access to Political Power in Post-communist Europe*, edited by Richard Matland and Kathleen A. Montgomery, 217–244. Oxford: Oxford University Press.

———. 2008. "Women's Representation in the Polish Parliament and Determinants of Their Effectiveness." Available at http://www.asdo-info.org/public/Siemienska 12marzo08.pdf.

Smith, Miriam. 2010. "Federalism and LGBT rights in the USA and Canada: A Comparative Policy Analysis." In *Federalism, Feminism, and Multilevel Governance*, edited by Melissa Haussman, Marian Sawer, and Jill Vickers, 97–100. Surrey, UK: Ashgate.

"Spending Review: The Winners and Losers by Government Department." 2010. *The Telegraph.* Available at http://www.telegraph.co.uk/news/newstopics/spending -review/8077222/Spending-Review-the-winners-and-losers-by-Government-de partment.html.

Squires, Judith. 2005. "The Implementation of Gender Quotas in Britain." Paper written for International IDEA Project on Electoral Quotas for Women. Available at http://www.quotaproject.org/CS/CS_Britain_Squires.pdf.

Stotsky, Janet G. 2016. "Gender Budgeting: Fiscal Context and Current Outcomes." International Monetary Fund Working Paper WP/16/149. Available at https://www.imf.org/external/pubs/ft/wp/2016/wp16149.pdf.

Szczerbiak, Aleks. 2001. "Party Structure and Organisation in Post-communist Poland." *Journal of Communist Studies and Transition Politics* 17 (2): 94–130.

Tavits, Margit, and Natalia Letki. 2009. "When Left Is Right: Party Ideology and Policy in Post-communist Europe. *American Political Science Review* 103 (4): 555–569.

Thomas, Susan. 1994. *How Women Legislate.* New York: Oxford University Press.

Thomas, Susan, and Clyde Wilcox, eds. 2005. *Women and Elective Office.* 2nd ed. Oxford: Oxford University Press.

Tiebout, Charles. 1956. "A Pure Theory of Local Expenditures." *Journal of Political Economy* 64 (5): 416–424.

"The Transfer of Functions (Equality) Order 2007." 2007. *Statutory Instruments* 2007 (2914). Available at http://www.legislation.gov.uk/uksi/2007/2914/pdfs/uksi_20072914_en.pdf.

Treisman, Daniel. 2002. "Defining and Measuring Decentralization: A Global Perspective." Available at http://www.sscnet.ucla.edu/polisci/faculty/treisman/Papers/defin.pdf.

———. 2007. *The Architecture of Government: Rethinking Political Decentralization.* New York: Cambridge University Press.

Trimble, Linda, Jane Arscott, and Manon Tremblay, eds. 2013. *Stalled: The Representation of Women in Canadian Governments.* Toronto: University of British Columbia Press.

Tripp, Aili Mari. 2006. "The Challenges of Gendering Comparative Politics." *Politics and Gender* 2 (2): 249–263.

True, Jacqui. 2003. "Mainstreaming Gender in Global Public Policy." *International Feminist Journal of Politics* 5 (3): 368–396.

Tunio, Hafeez. 2014. "Sindh Assembly Passes Bill Declaring Marriage below 18 Punishable by Law." *Express Tribune*, April 28. Available at http://tribune.com.pk/story/701321/sindh-assembly-passes-bill-declaring-marriage-below-18-punishable-by-law.

UK Political Info. n.d. "Women MPs and Parliamentary Candidates since 1945." Available at http://www.ukpolitical.info/FemaleMPs.htm (accessed December 21, 2016).

UK Visas and Immigration. 2014. "Guidance: Public Funds." Available at https://www.gov.uk/government/publications/public-funds--2/public-funds.

UNITE. n.d. "Human Rights Violation." Available at http://www.un.org/en/women/endviolence/situation.shtml (accessed November 22, 2016).

United Cities and Local Governments. 2013. "The Paris Agenda Asserts the Role of Women in Local Policy Decision-Making." April 2. Available at http://www.uclg.org/en/media/news/paris-agenda-asserts-role-women-local-policy-decision-making.

United Nations. n.d. "Goal 3: Promote Gender Equality and Empower Women." Available at http://www.un.org/millenniumgoals/gender.shtml (accessed November 22, 2016).

———. 1993. "Declaration on the Elimination of Violence against Women." Available at http://www.un.org/documents/ga/res/48/a48r104.htm.

————. 2010. "Guidelines on Women's Empowerment." Available at http://www
.un.org/popin/unfpa/taskforce/guide/iatfwemp.gdl.html.

————. 2014. "United Nations Regional Groups of Member States." Available at
http://www.un.org/depts/DGACM/RegionalGroups.shtml.

United Nations CEDAW (Committee on the Elimination of Discrimination against
Women). 1995. "Third Periodic Reports of States Parties: United Kingdom of
Great Britain and Northern Ireland." Available at https://documents-dds-ny
.un.org/doc/UNDOC/GEN/N95/316/26/IMG/N9531626.pdf.

————. 2007. "Sixth Periodic Reports of States Parties: United Kingdom of Great
Britain and Northern Ireland." Available at https://documents-dds-ny.un.org/doc/
UNDOC/GEN/N07/398/67/PDF/N0739867.pdf.

United Nations Development Fund for Women. n.d. "Gender Responsive Budgeting."
Available at http://www.un.org/en/ecosoc/julyhls/pdf10/2-pager_on_grb_portal.
pdf (accessed November 22, 2016).

United Nations Development Programme. n.d. "Gender Inequality Index (GII)."
Available at http://hdr.undp.org/en/content/gender-inequality-index-gii (accessed
November 23, 2016).

————. 2007. *Human Development Report 2007/2008: Fighting Climate Change* (New
York: UNDP), 330–333, table 29. Available at http://www.rrojasdatabank.info/
hdr20072008tab29.pdf.

————. 2010. "Women's Representation in Local Government in Asia-Pacific." Available at http://www.capwip.org/readingroom/TopotheShelf.Newsfeeds/2010/
Women's%20Particiipation%20in%20Local%20Government-Asia%20Pacific
%20(2010).pdf.

United Nations Division for the Advancement of Women. 2004. "The Role of National Mechanisms in Promoting Gender Equality and the Empowerment of
Women." Available at http://www.un.org/womenwatch/daw/egm/nationalm2004/
docs/EGM%20final%20report.26-jan-05.pdf.

United Nations Population Fund. 2005. "Frequently Asked Questions about Gender Equality." Available at http://www.unfpa.org/resources/frequently-asked-ques
tions-about-gender-equality.

United States Institute of Peace. n.d. "What Is U.N. Security Council Resolution 1325
and Why Is It So Critical Today?" Available at http://www.usip.org/gender_peace
building/about_UNSCR_1325 (accessed August 12, 2016).

UN Women. n.d. "Gender Responsive Budgeting." Available at http://asiapacific
.unwomen.org/en/focus-areas/women-poverty-economics/gender-responsive-bud
geting (accessed December 1, 2016).

————. 2006. "National Action Plan for Counteracting Domestic Violence." Available
at http://evaw-global-database.unwomen.org/-/media/files/un%20women/vaw/
full%20text/europe/poland%20-%20national%20action%20plan%20for%20
counteracting%20domestic%20violence.pdf.

————. 2013. "Directory of National Mechanisms for Gender Equality." Available
at http://www.un.org/womenwatch/daw/documents/National-Mechanisms-Web
.pdf.

U.S. Department of State. 2003. "Country Reports on Human Rights Practices 2002:
Pakistan." Available at http://www.state.gov/j/drl/rls/hrrpt/2002/18314.htm.

Vengroff, Richard, Zsolt Nyiri, and Melissa Fugiero. 2003. "Electoral System and Gender Representation in Sub-national Legislatures: Is There a National–Sub-national Gender Gap?" *Political Research Quarterly* 56 (2): 163–173.

Verloo, Mieke, ed. 2007. *Multiple Meanings of Gender Equality: A Critical Frame Analysis of Gender Policies in Europe.* New York: Central European University Press.

Vickers, Jill. 1991. "Why Should Women Care about Constitutional Reform?" In *Entre Amis: Conversations among Friends—Women and Constitutional Reform*, edited by David Schneiderman, 18–22. Edmonton, AB: Centre for Constitutional Studies.

———. 1994. "Why Should Women Care about Federalism?" In *Canada: The State of Federation*, edited by Douglas M. Brown and Janet Hiebert, 131–151. Kingston, ON: Queen's University and McGill-Queen's Press.

———. 2010. "A Two-Way Street: Federalism and Women's Politics in Canada and the United States." *Publius* 40:412–435.

———. 2011. "Gender and State Architectures: The Impact of Governance Structures on Women's Politics." *Politics and Gender* 7 (2): 254–262.

———. 2013. "Is Federalism Gendered? Incorporating Gender into Studies of Federalism." *Publius* 43 (1): 1–23.

Vickers, Jill, Louise Chappell, and Petra Meier, eds. 2013. "Gendering Federalism." Special issue, *Publius* 43 (1).

Violence against Women Watch Group. 2010. "Statistics of Violence against Women in Pakistan in 2009." Available at http://www.af.org.pk/PDF/Eng%20Ver%20 Report%202009.pdf.

Walsh, Declan. 2014. "Attack on Journalist Starts Battle in Pakistani Press." *New York Times*, April 26. Available at http://www.nytimes.com/2014/04/27/world/asia/ attack-on-journalist-starts-battle-in-pakistani-press.html.

Walsh, Declan, and Salman Masood. 2014. "Pakistan Is Asked to Shut Down News Channel." *New York Times*, April 22. Available at http://www.nytimes .com/2014/04/23/world/asia/attack-on-journalist-spurs-new-dispute-in-pakistan .html.

Walsh, Denise. 2010. *Women's Rights in Democratizing States: Just Debate and Gender Justice in the Public Sphere.* Cambridge: Cambridge University Press.

"The War on Pakistan's Aid Workers." 2013. *New York Times*, January 4. Available at http://www.nytimes.com/2013/01/05/opinion/the-war-on-pakistans-aid-workers .html.

Watson, Peggy. 1993. "The Rise of Masculinism in Eastern Europe." *New Left Review* 1 (198): 71–82.

Watts, Ronald L. 2008. *Comparing Federal Systems.* 3rd ed. Kingston, ON: McGill-Queen's University Press.

Waylen, Georgina. 2007. *Engendering Transitions: Women's Mobilization, Institutions and Gender Outcomes.* Oxford: Oxford University Press.

Weaver, K., 2007. "Women's Rights and Shari'a Law: A Workable Reality?" *Duke Journal of Comparative and International Law*, no. 17: 483–509.

Weiss, Anita. 2003. "Interpreting Islam and Women's Rights: Implementing CEDAW in Pakistan." *International Sociology* 18 (3): 581–601.

Weldon, S. Laurel. 2002a. "Beyond Bodies: Institutional Sources of Representation for Women in Democratic Policymaking." *Journal of Politics* 64 (4): 1153–1174.

————. 2002b. *Protest, Policy, and the Problem of Violence against Women: A Cross-National Comparison.* Pittsburgh: University of Pittsburgh Press.

————. 2006. "Inclusion, Solidarity and Social Movements: The Global Movement on Gender Violence." *Perspectives on Politics* 4 (1): 55–74.

Wieringa, Saskia Eleonora. 2006. "Islamization in Indonesia: Women Activists' Discourses." *Signs* 32 (1): 1–8.

Winetrobe, Barry K. 2011. "Enacting Scotland's 'Written Constitution': The Scotland Act of 1998." *Parliamentary History* 30 (1): 85–100.

"Women AMs 'Making a Difference.'" 2009. *BBC News,* January 30. Available at http://news.bbc.co.uk/2/hi/uk_news/wales/7859639.stm.

Women Development Department. n.d. "History." Available at http://www.sindh.gov.pk/dpt/WDD/index.html (accessed November 27, 2016).

"Women in the 40th Canadian Parliament." 2016. *Wikipedia,* February 10. Available at https://en.wikipedia.org/wiki/Women_in_the_40th_Canadian_Parliament.

Women's National Commission. n.d. "Weblinks." Available at http://wnc.equalities.gov.uk/web-links/131-links-to-partner-organisations.html (accessed August 17, 2016).

Women's Support Project. n.d. "Legislation." Available at http://www.womenssupportproject.co.uk/vawtraining/content/legislation/219,218 (accessed August 16, 2016).

World Bank. 1999. *Entering the 21st Century: World Development Report 1999/2000.* New York: Oxford University Press.

————. 2004. "Devolution in Pakistan: An Assessment and Recommendations for Action." Available at https://www.openknowledge.worldbank.org/handle/10986/14373.

————. 2009. *Local Government Discretion and Accountability: Application of a Local Governance Framework.* Washington, DC: World Bank. Available at http://documents.worldbank.org/curated/en/135671468162248429/pdf/490590ESE0Box30ion0for0Distribution.pdf.

————. 2012. "Indicators." Available at http://data.worldbank.org/indicator/.

World Economic Forum. 2013. *The Global Gender Gap Report.* Geneva: World Economic Forum.

Zahid, Ranaa. 2007. "Gender Reform Action Plan—a Breakthrough for Pakistani Women? A Policy Research Using Health Rights of Women Assessment Instrument (HeRWAI)." Master's thesis, University of Washington. Available at http://citeseerx.ist.psu.edu/viewdoc/download?doi=10.1.1.471.7584&rep=rep1&type=pdf.

Zia, Maliha. "2013 Elections: Women's Representation in Legislatures." *Legislative Watch,* March–November 2013, p. 1. Available at https://www.af.org.pk/newsl/1390295273.pdf.

Ziring, Lawrence. 1997. *Pakistan in the Twentieth Century: A Political History.* Oxford: Oxford University Press.

Index

ability to exit, 30–31
abortion, 47, 59–60, 64, 74, 189, 198
abuse, 71, 73, 95, 113, 197, 198. *See also* violence against women, as priority
administrative decentralization, 4–5, *27*, 48; gender inequality and, 37, *39*, 39–41; in Pakistan, 87; in Poland, 62. *See also* decentralization
aggregation, 9, 136, 146
Agha, Rahat, 102, 104
Ahmed, Leila, 85
Akhtar, Nasreen, 102
All Pakistan Women's Association, 102
all-women shortlists, 115–116, 119, 195, 196
ambition, 12–14
antiviolence organizations in Poland, 65
applied policy, 146
The Architecture of Government (Treisman), 6
Arscott, Jane, 16–17
Asian Development Bank, 31, 32, 34–35, 94
Australia, 17, *42*, 49
authoritarian states, 38
autocratic centralized states, 38
Awami National Party, 103
Ayub Khan, Mohammad, 86
Azad Jammu and Kashmir, Pakistan, 86, *89*, *91*, *103*, 136

Baldez, Lisa, 9, 15

Balochistan, Pakistan, 80, 83–84, *89*, *91*, 92, 95, 98, *103*, 104
Balochistan National Party, 84
Banaszak, Lee Ann, 44
Beckwith, Karen, 6, 44
behaviors, political, 10–11, 133
Bhutto, Benazir, 80, 83, 84, 99
Bhutto, Zulfikar Ali, 83, 84–85
black, Asian, or minority ethnic (BAME) rights, 117, 119, 122. *See also* intersectionality; race; women's interests
Bochniarz, Henryka, 56, *57*
Boehner, John, 21
bo zupa była za słona (because the soup was too salty) public awareness campaign, 69, 71, *71*
Brazil, *42*, 140
Brown, Alice, 106
Brown, Gordon, 117
budgeting. *See* gender-responsive budgeting
bureaucracies, 16–18. *See also* women's policy agencies (WPAs)
burka (full-length veil), 85
Bush, George W., 82
business leadership, 88

Cabinet Subcommittee for Women's Issues (United Kingdom), 117
Cameron, David, 107–108, 118, 119